The Management of the Matobo Hills in Zimbabwe

THE MANAGEMENT OF THE MATOBO HILLS IN ZIMBABWE

Perceptions of the Indigenous Communities on their Involvement and Use of Traditional Conservation Practices

Simon Makuvaza

Leiden University Press

Archaelogical Studies Leiden University is published by Leiden University Press, the Netherlands
Series editors: M. E. R. G. N. Jansen and H. Kamermans

Cover design: Joanne Porck
Coverpage image: Simon Makuvaza
Layout: Samira Damato
Illustrations: Joanne Porcke

ISBN 978 90 8728 264 6
e-ISBN 978 94 0060 264 9
NUR 682

This book is distributed in North America by the University of Chicago Press

Table of Contents

Abstract

Beginning in 1992 when the category of world heritage cultural landscapes was adopted by the World Heritage Committee, scholarly debates have ensued on how best they could be managed. One approach, which appears to have gained significance over the past two decades or so, is to consider the use of traditional conservation practices and the involvement of local indigenous communities in the management of world heritage cultural landscapes. To examine the efficacy of the approach, this thesis explores the concept of indigenous communities, the nature of the Matobo Hills in which the study was conducted, the indigenous communities of the area, and the management history as well as the traditional conservation practices of the Hills. Based on the perspectives of the Matobo Hills indigenous communities, this thesis examines the extent to which traditional conservation practices and the involvement of local indigenous communities can be germane in the management of the cultural landscape. Findings of this study shows that although some of the traditional conservation practices still survive in the Hills, some of them are declining as a result of the survival of local indigenous communities that is going through rapid change. The study also shows that a number of factors and management issues such as loss of value and meaning of traditional conservation practices, lack of support by the local indigenous communities as a result of their failure to benefit from the management of the Hills, politics and the breakdown of traditional leaders' authority, christianity which result in the breakdown of traditional conservation practices and power struggle between the main stakeholders to manage the area, make it difficult to use traditional conservation practices and to involve local indigenous communities in the management of the world heritage site. Based on the results, the thesis argues that the preservation of existing practices, incorporation of traditional conservation practices in legal heritage frameworks, harmonisation of heritage legislations with related state and international legislations and compliance with the legal frameworks are some of the challenges that affect the idea of using traditional conservation practices and of involving local indigenous communities in the management of world heritage cultural landscapes. In conclusion, the study contends that for the idea of using traditional conservation practices and of involving local indigenous communities in the management of world heritage cultural landscapes to work, there is need to understand the local indigenous communities themselves, existing traditional conservation practices of the area, politics of the cultural landscape, views of local indigenous communities and to address the issues which affect them.

Acknowledgements

The research for this thesis was conceived and carried out under the supervision of the late Professor Dr. Willem J.H. Willems, my original promotor. When Professor Willems unexpectedly passed away in december 2014, Professor Dr. Maarten Jansen and Dr Sada Mire took over this task from him. Without their inspirational guidance, encouragement, and unselfish help, I could never have finished my doctoral work at Leiden University. In the Matobo Hills, I am indebted to Pathisa Nyathi who not only offered me accommodation at Amagugu International Heritage Center free of charge but was also readily available for interviews and discussions regarding the traditional conservation practices of the cultural landscape. My sincere thanks also go to all the informants who agreed and were available to be interviewed while gathering data in the Matobo Hills. Of these, I wish to single out Misheck Dube, Fili Tshimba Ncube (now late), and Surrender Sibanda who were my key informants during the many fieldtrips in the Matobo Hills. At the University of Zimbabwe, I would like to extend my gratitude to Professor Gilbert Pwiti for agreeing, on very short notice, to review the draft of my thesis. His comments and suggestions as a specialist outside of my supervision team to review the draft thesis and to provide helpful feedback has enormously benefited this study. Dr. Terence Mashingaidze, a historian at the Midlands State University in Zimbabwe also commented on chapter 4 of the thesis. His knowledge on the history of south western Zimbabwe has enormously benefited this thesis. The external examiners namely Professors Peter Pels, Ian Lilley and Paul Lane constructively criticised the earlier draft of this thesis. The literature that they suggested and their comments helped me reshape and clarify large chunks of the text. I gratefully acknowledge their time and valuable feedback on the preliminary version of the thesis. The production of maps for this study was done by my friend, Albert Chirima. Chirima accurately drew the maps and ensured that my deadline for the maps was met. The help that Chirima offered during the difficult time of writing this thesis has showed me that a friend in need is a friend indeed. I would also like to include a special note of thanks to Jenny Hill who offered me, free of charge, her expert English language editing and proof-reading services. Using her editing knowledge, Jenny has ensured that my thesis is free of English grammar mistakes, syntax errors, typos, and spelling errors as well as punctuation errors. This has exceptionally improved the flow and meaning of this thesis. I am also very greatful for the opportunity to have my doctoral thesis published in the Archaeological Studies Leiden University (ASLU) book series. In this respect, I would like to recognise the work of Dr. Hans Kamermans and, especially Sara Damato and Joanne Porck who have taken the difficult task of putting together my thesis into a book. However, they and others acknowledged in this study do not share the responsibility of any errors that remain within it. Any remaining inaccuracies are entirely my own responsibility. Lastly, I would like to thank my family for love, support, and encouragement. Without the sacrifices of my family and especially my wife Violah, this thesis would never have been a success.

1. Introduction

BACKGROUND

In pre-colonial Africa and other parts of the globe, many local indigenous communities inhabited lands, established powerful states and, in some cases, constructed enormous settlements in areas which are now regarded as cultural landscapes. These cultural landscapes ranged from sacred forests, to dry-stone walls, and to historic settlements of symbolic and sacred values, some of which are now designated as National Parks, Transfrontier Conservation Areas, and World Heritage Cultural Landscapes.

In southern Africa, certain well-known cultural landscapes which are also World Heritage Sites include the Mapungubwe and uKhahlamba/Drakensberg Mountains in South Africa, Tsodilo Hills in Botswana, Chongoni Forest in Malawi, Twyfelfontein in Namibia and the Matobo Hills in Zimbabwe. These cultural landscapes bear evidence of the past and present, and it is the memories of the local indigenous communities and associated histories that define the significance of these areas. The local indigenous communities subsisting in the vicinity of these cultural landscapes regard them as their ancestral homes and are culturally and spiritually attached to them. They also consider them as traditional lands where they can practice farming and perform diverse cultural activities. These cultural landscapes are highly revered for their significance as rainmaking, fertility, and cleansing areas. They are also important as symbols of identity that bond many indigenous African communities together and with their past.

In many parts of Africa, traditional leaders such as clan heads, chiefs, and spirit mediums were the authority and managers of these cultural landscapes. These community leaders were selected through traditional procedures, and communities were involved in determining the authority that leaders were allowed to exercise over their subjects such as keeping peace, settling of disputes, performance of rituals, and protection of the land.

Land was owned and shared communally. Group communities possessed common property rights to the land; however, access rights to the same land were held by different individuals and were transferred from one generation to the next. Decisions about who owned a particular piece of land were made by family heads, and this was guided by traditional practices that considered the needs of various individuals within the community. Today, although land is still under the authority of traditional elders in some African countries, their roles have been, to some extent, redefined to that of the state system (Makuvaza and Makuvaza 2012).

Prior to colonialism, the protection of cultural landscapes were perhaps the result of the accumulation of indigenous knowledge systems that had been practiced by local indigenous communities within these landscapes. Each indigenous community may have formed its own legal system based on traditional customs and practices that were enforced by clan elders, chiefs, and spirit mediums who performed both community and spiritual duties (Musonda 2005; Makuvaza 2007; Mahachi and Kamuhangire 2008). All members of the community may also have possessed traditional knowledge about the conservation of their cultural landscapes, though this may have varied with gender and age as well as with social and economic status. Punishment and penalties for contravention of practices were sanctioned by the traditional courts based on cultural procedures (Chiwaura 2005).

Contrary to general assumptions by a number of Europeans that there was no conservation prior to their appearance in Africa, many cultural landscapes may have been therefore, protected by traditional conservation practices (cf. Joffroy 2005). According to Ndoro (2004, 2005), the fact that Europeans discovered several cultural landscapes intact indicates that a form of conservation could have been practiced, however, many of the traditional conservation practices were not recorded but only observed and practiced by the local indigenous communities.

THE CONSERVATION OF CULTURAL LANDSCAPES IN COLONIAL AFRICA

The arrival of Europeans on the African continent, and especially in southern Africa, profoundly influenced and transformed the manner in which local indigenous communities were managing and protecting their cultural landscapes. From the beginning of the 19th century, European missionaries and travellers extended their explorations and opened up much of the African continent to the outside world. According to Ellert (1993, 10), the crusading zeal to bring Christianity to the "heathen" was pursued just as vigorously in Africa as it was in Asia and the Americas. Missionaries began to execute active evangelical work, during which time they visited unfamiliar regions and peoples of the continent. They also began to develop mission stations and introduce formal western education to the local African indigenous communities that they visited.

The effects of this missionary work on Africans were such that traditional systems of managing cultural landscapes were condemned through unfamiliar ideas, religious values and morals. Consequently, the work of traditional elders, chiefs, and spirit mediums to protect cultural places began to be perceived as ungodly and associated with the practice of witchcraft. The introduction of Christianity and education, especially in southern Africa, led to the creation of new values which eventually led Africans to despise and abandon their past cultural values (Pwiti and Ndoro 1999). Additionally, in many instances, the missionaries also heralded trade and the building of empires by European states that later conquered much of the entire African continent.
European explorers of Africa not only added considerable geographical knowledge about the continent, they also obtained information about local traditional communities, languages, and cultural and natural histories of the countries in which they sojourned (Ellert 1993). In Europe, reported accounts about the success and fame of missionaries and voyagers assisted in the advancement of the obsession of the Europeans' geographical "discovery" and colonial penetration of the African continent. Consequently, scientific curiosity and missionary spirit were soon subordinated to mercantile considerations such as mining, trading, hunting, and concession seeking. In due course, this resulted in the colonisation of the entire continent during the second half of the 19th century.

In southern Africa, many cultural landscapes were first presented to Europeans as barriers to the movement of farming communities in the early migrations of people in the region. Cultural landscapes of this nature were thus perceived as not suitable for modern human habitation and, as a result, were appropriated and given a new status as national parks or game reserves for the conservation of wildlife and nature. The appropriation of these cultural landscapes was also driven by the notion that these lands were "terra nullius" (vacant lands) as many local indigenous communities were believed to be transitory migrants. These ideas were based on the Bantu migration, a millennia-long series of migrations of speakers of the original proto-Bantu language groups. The migrations were speculated to have begun from west Africa by about 1000 BC and reaching southern Africa in about 300 AD (see Phillipson 1985; Beach 1986; Vansina 1995). However, attempts to trace the exact routes of the Bantu expansion in order to correlate it with archaeological evidence and, more recently, with genetic evidence, have not been conclusive. Thus, many aspects of the expansion remain uncertain or are highly contested (Berniell-Lee et al. 2009). Although the exact routes of Bantu expansion remain contested, archaeological studies have now disproved the preconceived notion of "empty lands" prior to European settlement in southern Africa. It has now been firmly established that the region was occupied for more than 25, 000 years by the hunter-gatherer communities before the arrival of the Bantu people (see, for example, Mitchell 2002, 2013; van Doornum 2008; Lombard 2013).

In the context of Zimbabwe, the occupation of the country by Europeans was, in part, motivated by the economic greed that was based on reports of abundant goldfields in the country. When these reports failed to achieve fruition, the Europeans' dreams of economic opulence were crushed, and they shifted their interests to farming as a substitute for gold mining (Pwiti and Ndoro 1999). This resulted in the demarcation and appropriation of cultural landscapes that were inhabited by the local indigenous communities.

Europeans also began to initiate the enactment of various pieces of land legislations which subsequently empowered them to evict Africans from their ancestral lands. In Zimbabwe, the Land Apportionment Act of 1930 and the Land Husbandry Act of 1951 are the most well known land repressive legislations. The Land Apportionment Act, which implemented provisions in 1931, resulted in the division of land into European Areas, Native Reserves, Native Purchase Areas, and Forest Areas. There was also land that was appropriated as "Unassigned Land" (Ndlovu-Gatsheni 2009b). The Land Husbandry Act, on the other hand, was designed to enforce private ownership of land and improve the rural economy in the African reserves that had experienced the pressure of a growing population within these fixed areas. However, its provisions violated local traditional conservation practices. Rather than expanding the size of the reserves, the Act limited cattle grazing in specified areas and provided for the destocking of African herds; allowed officials to dictate patterns of cultivation and crop growing as well as fix dwelling sites on farm land; and also prohibited cultivating or grazing without a permit. Implementation of the Act signified the depletion of highly valued herds, reduction of land under cultivation, and the forced uprooting of families and entire traditional villages (Weitzer 1990; Wels 2003).

When many southern African countries were later colonised, cultural landscapes were subsequently sub-divided into European and African areas based largely on the agricultural potential of the colonised countries. As a result of this subdivision, substantial African populations were forcibly removed from their ancestral homes to make way for establishing European commercial farming areas, forest areas, and national parks. A number of evicted indigenous communities were relocated along the edges of protected areas while others were settled in marginal areas, some of which were a long distance from their original cultural landscapes. In Zimbabwe, as in South Africa (see Meskell 2012, 18), local indigenous communities were relocated to newly established native reserves. The native reserves formed the basis of ethnically-defined administrative units, known then in Zimbabwe as Tribal Trust Lands, and reclassified as Communal Lands after the independence of the country in 1980 (Pwiti and Ndoro 1999).

Government Commissions on natives, forestry and wildlife, monuments and relics, and nature reserves were subsequently established to institute new conservation programmes within southern African cultural landscapes. The eviction of local indigenous communities from their original settlements by the Europeans meant that culture and nature were separated. However, it has been generally agreed upon that these two entities should not have been separated since their interaction provided richness and depth to the narratives of cultural landscapes (see Bender 1999; Layton and Ucko 1999).

Even though Europeans had recognised that many African cultural landscapes had been previously inhabited by the hunter-gatherer communities, they did not recognise the presence and legitimacy of the modern African local indigenous communities that now primarily inhabit these landscapes. In fact, many Europeans had come to believe that Africans did not have any right to the use of these cultural landscapes and that the Africans had no objective views over them (see Ranger 1999; Meskell 2012). As the cultural landscapes were appropriated, European ideas of romantic and natural history traditions were prioritised over the traditional conservation practices of protecting these areas. McGregor (2003) argued that, during the appropriation of these landscapes, cultural meanings were overridden with local indigenous communities often featuring a generic exotic or servile other. Instead, new values such as research and tourism were inscribed on cultural landscapes which then benefited Europeans as they celebrated colonial science and modernity on the African continent (Ranger 1999; McGregor 2003).
Protective legislations based on European concepts of conservation were also introduced to manage cultural landscapes that were now designated as national parks, forests, game and nature reserves. In many cases, boundaries were then demarcated,

and these areas were subsequently fenced to effectively prevent local indigenous communities from entering their cultural landscapes. Between 1961 and 1962 in Tanzania for example, Neville Chittick a British archaeologist and founder of the Antiquities Department, fenced several rock art sites including the Mongomi wa Kolo site in the Kondoa World Heritage Cultural Landscape to prevent local indigenous communities from accessing the sites (Bwasiri 2008) while several cultural sites in the Matobo Hills were fenced as a means of protecting them from vandalism (Makuvaza 2008). Meskell (2012) noted that the fencing and enclosure of Kruger National Park in South Africa, which is now part of the Great Limpopo Transfrontier Park, was the defining cause for the desitution of indigenous communities as well as new designations of trespassing, poaching, and criminality that resulted from changes in colonial topographies.

The eviction of Africans from their original settlements meant that they were forced to leave their immovable cultural heritage in areas that were now designated as protected properties (Pwiti and Ndoro 1999). In many instances, these cultural heritage sites were later systematically inventoried and subsequently proclaimed as national monuments. These sites were then subjected to archaeological research programmes during which time local indigenous communities were neither consulted nor asked to participate. The archaeology of Africa, therefore, became a preserve of colonial, military, and missionary officials (Shephered 2006) as, throughout most of the colonial period until after independence, the archaeology of Africa was generally dominated by western ideology (Atalay 2006b). During the colonial period, the management of cultural landscapes was dominated by foreign people. It was only after independence when certain African people began being trained in archaeology that western ideas of managing cultural landscapes began to be challenged.

As a result of the introduction of European conservation and management practices, local indigenous communities realised that they were no longer able to access and use cultural sites as they had before Europeans had settled into these areas. Thus, many local indigenous communities were detached from an important element of their culture as they were moved to new areas with cultural heritage they were not associated with and could not relate to (Pwiti and Ndoro 1999). The combination of an increasing African population along with the allocation of only minimal sections of land in the native reserves created an increasingly acrimonious point of contention in the appropriation of cultural landscapes. In some cases, local indigenous communities contested removal from their traditional cultural landscapes which eventually resulted in warfare in many African countries. As argued by Silverman and Ruggles (2007), these contestations, when unresolved, can lead to resistance, violence and war, and the colonial legacy of evicting Africans from their cultural landscapes is still affecting some local indigenous communities even now.

The introduction of European ideas of conservation approaches for cultural landscapes and sites in Africa have been heavily criticised by many scholars (see, for example, Mumma 2003, 2004; Munjeri 2005). These scholars have described European management approaches as instruments of oppression rather than protection, and they are considered to have suppressed the long established African traditional conservation practices of managing cultural landscapes. In many parts of southern Africa, formal heritage management systems are, therefore, perceived as having failed to protect cultural heritage sites (see, for example, Jopela 2011; Ndlovu 2005).

THE CONSERVATION OF CULTURAL LANDSCAPES IN INDEPENDENT AFRICA

Since gaining independence, many local indigenous communities expected to be resettled in previously appropriated cultural landscapes. They also anticipated that colonial management systems of cultural landscapes would be abolished while traditional conservation practices were to be reintroduced (Makuvaza and Makuvaza 2012). In many parts of southern Africa, local indigenous communities began to demand that their opinions be addressed regarding their history and management of cultural landscapes as these communities had other perspectives of their past and also attached different values to their cultural landscapes and sites (Creamer 1990).

Disappointingly, many African communities were not permitted to return to their ancestral homes. The new, autonomous African governments, like their colonial predecessors, began to embrace the modernist doctrines of international conservation which, according to Ranger (1996), in the interest of the "whole community", does not allow local indigenous communities to collect firewood and plants, hunt, or visit holy places within the protected areas. Instead, state laws were consolidated which weakened local traditional management systems, and the powers of traditional authorities were shifted to the state (cf. Kayambazinthu et al. 2003). In fact, many government departments that address cultural heritage continued to implement state conservation practices while several protective legislations have largely remained unrevised to accommodate the rights and interests of local indigenous communities. Those that have been revised appear to be dilatorily accommodating the rights and interests of the local indigenous communities.

Despite these challenges, a number of local indigenous communities continue to regard the cultural landscapes from which they were evicted as their own and persist that the management of the landscapes should involve the communities. They continue to desire access to resources such as timber, thatching grass, water, firewood, charcoal, wild fruits, and medicinal plants. In addition, they would also like to continue farming and grazing their domestic animals in areas they had previously inhabited. In South Africa, for example, local indigenous communities living along the frontier of the Kruger National Park have been exerting new claims of restitution for their loss of this cultural landscape (Meskell 2012).

Given these hopes and claims, disputes have persevered in many parts of southern Africa between local indigenous communities and the state administrators who are managing world heritage cultural landscapes, some even to the extent that the conservation of the landscapes is threatened. Where these disputes occur, state administrators treat local indigenous communities not as legitimate beneficiaries of these areas but, instead, as poachers and criminals. The administrators accuse them of encroaching and threatening the integrity and authenticity of these cultural landscapes and also often regard local indigenous communities as intruders rather than the "original" people who had inhabited and traditionally used these cultural landscapes (Meskell 2012, 21). Consequently, the local indigenous communities perceive state administrators as perpetuating the colonial management styles that prohibit them to access and associate themselves with their lost cultural heritage (Makuvaza and Makuvaza 2012).

Upon attainment of independence, some African governments, especially Zimbabwe, embarked on resettlement programs that were based on a land policy of willing-seller/willing-buyer. However, this policy continued to allow private ownership of previously appropriated cultural landscapes since many Europeans were not willing to sell their land for resettlement programs (Katsamudanga 2003). This has generally failed to address the concerns of many local indigenous communities who had hoped to be reconnected with their ancestral homes. The ongoing land reform program in Zimbabwe that was enacted to address the historical land imbalances between black and white Zimbabweans, however, did not improve the situation as black Zimbabweans were not necessarily resettled back into their original cultural landscapes. This has resulted in the continued alienation of local indigenous communities from their cultural landscapes even several decades following independence (Ndoro and Pwiti 1999; Segobye 2005).

Today, many local indigenous communities also continue to be embroiled in struggles with governments and business corporations in areas where mineral wealth has been discovered in cultural landscapes as this cast the value of cultural landscapes in a different light. Where cultural landscapes had previously been valued for cultural and natural reasons, they have now become vital as mining landscapes and perceived as propelling the development of modern African states. The Kalahari

Game Reserve in Botswana, for example, is now considered more important in terms of economic benefits and development of the country as a result of the mining of kimberlite from that land (Segobye 2006). In a mining venture of uranium in the Kakadu World Heritage Cultural Landscape in Australia, Banergee (2000) has argued that, while the benefits of mining could be quantified in terms of jobs, dollars from export income, percentage of royalty payments, etc., the socio-cultural impacts such as the breakdown of traditional relations, the destruction of sacred sites, and the displacements and disruptions in patterns of local indigenous communities cannot be quantified and measured in economic terms. As further argued by Banergee, the destruction of traditional hunting land, depletion and contamination of freshwater resources, siltation and pollution of rivers, and widespread deforestation also irreversibly affect local indigenous communities. The major concern is that local indigenous communities have no power to stop the mining ventures that are considered to be of "national interest" and, in many instances, are authorised against the desires of the local indigenous communities.

VALUES AND NEW MANAGEMENT APPROACHES

In 1992, the category of World Heritage Cultural Landscapes was adopted by the World Heritage Committee. One of the major considerations by expert groups and the committee was to link nature and culture in the implementation of the 1972 Convention Concerning the Protection of the World Cultural and Natural Heritage. This afforded innovative thinking about human beings and their environment and to link culture and nature with a vision of sustainable development (Rössler 2003).
Following this development, there have been arguments and advocacy to consider and recognise local indigenous communities and their traditional conservation practices of managing cultural landscapes when proclaiming the places as World Heritage Sites (see, for example, Sullivan 2004; Ndoro 2005, 2004; Jopela 2011). Sullivan (2004) noted that the world heritage management documents had ignored other social and contemporary values that may be contained within these sites. As she further asserted, even though these values may not be universal in terms of the World Heritage Convention, they may still be of immense importance to the local indigenous communities. Ndoro (2004) also contended that, the moment a place is declared as a World Heritage Site, the interests of the local and traditional communities become irrelevant to its management ethos. He further contended that the international interests expressed by international conventions become paramount. Considering these arguments, it is now generally agreed that local indigenous communities living around world heritage cultural landscapes must be involved in their management, and specified traditional conservation practices must also be regarded in the management systems of these landscapes.

New approaches to proclaim and manage cultural landscapes have subsequently been incorporated into the Operational Guidelines for the Implementation of the World Heritage Convention. States parties to the Convention are now required to ensure the involvement of a wide variety of stakeholders including local indigenous communities in the identification, nomination, and protection of World Heritage Sites. It is also required to have long-term legislative, regulatory, institutional, and traditional protection as well as management to ensure the safeguarding of these World Heritage Sites. In addition to this, states parties are obligated to adequately demarcate delineated boundaries for the protection of the sites. For properties nominated under the cultural criteria, states parties are further expected to draw boundaries that include all those areas and attributes that are a direct tangible expression of the outstanding universal value of the property (see, for example, UNESCO 2008, Operational Guidelines, Paras. 12, 97 and 100).

As a result of the establishment of the cultural landscapes category by the World Heritage Committee and review of the Operational Guidelines, certain cultural landscapes were successfully proclaimed as world heritage cultural landscapes. The first such properties to be inscribed were Tongariro National Park (1993) in New Zealand and Uluru Kata Tjuta (1994) in Australia. In southern

Africa, a number of these sites include Tsodilo Hills (2001), Mapungubwe (2003), and the Matobo Hills (2003). The proclamation of these and other similar landscapes across the globe as World Heritage Sites signifies that they now embrace outstanding universal values and conditions of integrity and authenticity which must be protected and maintained for future generations. Their proclamation was also in accordance with the Global Strategy for a Representative, Balanced, and Credible World Heritage List (WHL) that was initiated in 1994 by the World Heritage Committee. The list inadequately balances and continues to be deficient in the types of inscribed properties and in the geographical areas of the world that are represented. The vast majority of these sites are located in developed regions of the world, notably in Europe. Generally, developing countries are, therefore, less well represented on the List (see Breen 2007; Willems and Comer 2011). The move to establish these World Heritage Sites also demonstrated a deviation from previous management approaches where state departments responsible for cultural heritage autonomously administered these sites without contribution from local indigenous communities for their effective management and protection.

The new process of proclaiming and managing World Heritage Sites enforced the necessity of involvement of local indigenous communities because, as noted by Bandarin (2009), it is the daily work of the local indigenous people and the manner in which they live that maintain these sites, often through their own protection measures and not by official legal provisions. Involvement in such endeavours would increase their sense of pride and their understanding of the need for the continued survival of cultural heritage sites (Ndoro 2004; Joffroy 2005). The stipulation for local indigenous communities to be involved in the management of world heritage cultural landscapes has raised hopes that, after decades of alienation from their cultural landscapes, they would eventually be reconnected with their ancestral homes.

Although some communities may have welcomed the chance to participate in the management of these landscapes, the operationalisation of the approach appears to be fraught with dilemmas and uncertainties. In fact, local indigenous communities are now regarded as stakeholders of the world heritage cultural landscapes that they had long regarded as their own. Their interests in the management of these landscapes are now encased within the rubric of stakeholder management and international laws in which issues of ownership and benefits are ambiguous. In southern Africa, as many local indigenous communities may now be discovering, the clarion call to become involved in the management of these landscapes in no way signifies that they now control and benefit from them. Many local indigenous communities are still not able to perform their cultural rituals and traditional practices of management despite encouragement to have their interests considered and represented when managing these world heritage cultural landscapes. However, to the disappointment of several local indigenous communities, they continue to observe powerful government departments and private players including tour operators, research institutions, farmers, and hoteliers benefiting from these cultural landscapes and, especially, from tourism ventures. This has created resentment and has resulted in many southern African world heritage cultural landscapes becoming contested areas (see Segobye 2006; Meskell 2012).

AIM AND OBJECTIVES OF THE STUDY

The underlying issue with the many attempts to consider the use of traditional conservation practices in the management of world heritage cultural landscapes seems to stem from a lack of understanding of the individual practices and the local indigenous communities that should be involved in the management of these landscapes. It appears that the opinions of the local indigenous communities regarding the suggestion to consider traditional conservation practices when managing world heritage cultural landscapes and the need to involve local indigenous people in the management of these areas is also not adequately understood. As a result of this insufficient knowledge, there are wide-ranging assumptions that regard local indigenous communities as homogeneous and consider traditional conservation practices as having

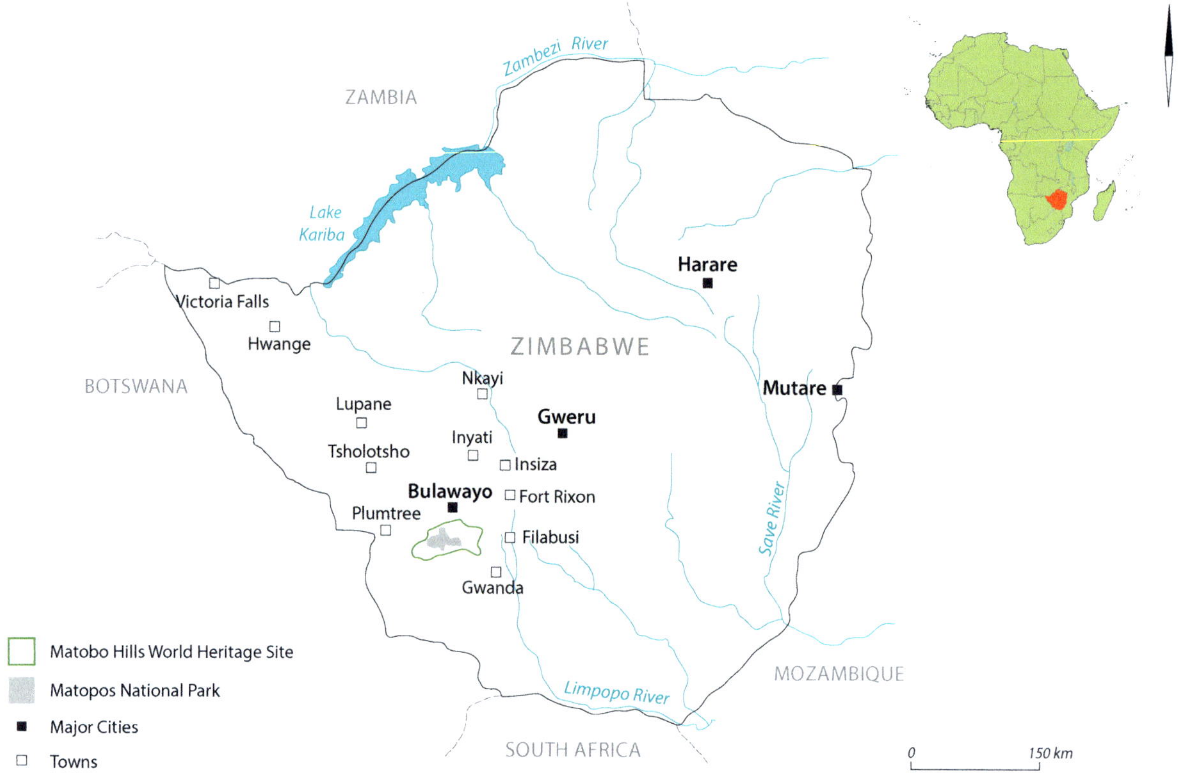

Fig. 1.1 Map of Africa and Zimbabwe showing the location of the Matobo Hills World Heritage Cultural Landscape in Zimbabwe and some of the places mentioned in the study.

always existed and which, if they are considered, can solve some of the management issues with world heritage cultural landscapes. These assumptions, however, do not take into consideration the fact that there are other factors which may deter attempts to incorporate traditional conservation practices into the management ethos of world heritage cultural landscapes. Further, these assumptions do not take into account the fact that, other than the local indigenous communities, there are other interest groups such as the local government, private investors, and individuals who also play diverse roles in the management of these cultural landscapes. As a result of the above assumptions, the extent to which the traditional conservation practices and the involvement of local indigenous communities can play a role in the management of world heritage cultural landscapes in southern Africa has always remained a problematic area.

The main focus of this thesis, therefore, is to examine the existence and use of traditional conservation practices in the Matobo Hills World Heritage Cultural Landscape and explore the extent to which the local indigenous communities can be involved in the management of the area (Fig. 1.1). The Matobo Hills are located approximately 35 kilometres south of the modern city of Bulawayo in the Matabeleland South Province of Zimbabwe. They encompass an area of almost 3100 km² that includes the buffer zone extending between 20° 25′ and 20° 45′ South and 28° 14′ and from 20° 45′ East. The area, which is an extensive granite landscape, extends nearly to the Botswana border in the west while it merges with the Mbalabala granite pluton to the east. Isolated granite outcrops also occur further in the southeast, south, and southwest.

While the aim of this research is broad and provides the study with thematic and theoretical direction, there are three specific objectives that emerge. Although the concept of local indigenous communities is not the individual primary focus of this research, it is, nevertheless, extremely important to examine it as understanding this issue would assist in understanding the local indigenous peoples and establish how they have become associated with the practice of archaeology and, in particular, the management of cultural landscapes. In this aspect, the first objective of this study is to examine the local indigenous communities that currently exist in the Matobo Hills. During this exploration, the studied local indigenous communities would be useful as informants during data collection to examine if traditional conservation practices really exist and work in the Matobo Hills, which is the second objective of this thesis. Kigongo and Reid (2007) have argued that, although the suggestion that the consideration of traditional conservation practices when managing cultural landscapes might be working elsewhere, this can be misleading and result in flawed management approaches that are guided by nostalgic and stereotyped perceptions about their ability to manage world heritage cultural sites. The argument that traditional conservation practices should be considered for the effective management of world heritage cultural landscapes and that the local indigenous communities should be involved in their management has rarely been, in my opinion, examined from the point of view of the local indigenous communities themselves. Instead, these suggestions have thus far remained very much academic and theoretical. This is quite paradoxical given that it is the initiatives of the local indigenous communities and not of the academics to protect cultural landscapes using traditional conservation practices, yet their views are not well understood. Rather, it is the local context, according to Pikirayi (2014), that should inform the global context and not vice versa. Pikirayi further argued that we should, in the practice of archaeology, consider voices from the periphery or we risk being irrelevant in the communities where we conduct our research. The third objective, therefore, is to determine from the local indigenous communities themselves if suggestions by academics regarding the use of traditional conservation practices and their involvement would help in the effective conservation of world heritage cultural landscapes.

APPROACHES TO THE STUDY

To aggregate the data for this study, I used qualitative research approaches as these have become the key methods in cultural heritage studies in recent years (see Sørensen and Carman 2009). Qualitative research is a method of study employed in many different academic disciplines, traditionally in the social sciences such as anthropology, sociology, and psychology. It seeks to understand a specified research problem or topic from the perspective of the local population that is involved. Therefore, the most common sources of data collection are reviewing manuscripts, interviews, observations, and group discussions (Flick 2009; Bhattacherjee 2012).

In accordance with the qualitative approach, I began this research by conducting a desktop survey of literature in the following libraries in Bulawayo: the Natural History Museum Library, Bulawayo City Council Library, the National Free Library, and Dambari Wildlife Trust Library. The Dambari Wildlife Trust is based near Bulawayo and is a non-profit conservation and research organisation that has been active since 1997. Its focus is on the Matobo Hills, the national park, private wildlife and tourism areas, commercial livestock farms, and subsistence agro-pastoralist areas. In the above libraries, I read and utilised a wide variety of secondary sources such as books, journals, newspapers, letters, government reports, legislations, and internet websites. The idea was to establish a theoretical basis for the research and to also provide insight into the history of proclamation of the Matobo Hills as a national park. The idea was to also gain insight into the history of land use and past management approaches of the Matobo Hills area.

In addition to reviewing literature in various Bulawayo libraries, I also conducted field work in the Matobo Hills between March and October 2014. In order to reach out to as many areas of the Matobo Hills as possible, I divided the fieldwork into two phases. During the first phase of the fieldwork, which began in April and ended in June, I stayed at the Amagugu International Heritage Center established by Pathisa Nyathi in 2012 (Fig. 1.2).

Fig. 1. 2 The Amagugu International Heritage Centre in the Matobo Hills (Photo by Author).

Fig. 1.3 The Cecil John Rhodes Campfire Community Cultural Village Project and Craft Center in the Lushumbe area (Photo by Author).

According to Nyathi, he established the Amagugu International Heritage Center to "revive" and "restore" the cultural heritage practices which he contended had once existed in the cultural landscape prior to the arrival of the Europeans in the area. Nyathi also affirmed that he is fighting the legacy of colonialism through his project which, he argued, is perpetuating the colonial approaches of management in the Matobo Hills (P. Nyathi., pers. comm., March 10, 2014). The Center is located approximately 60 kilometers at Tshapo Business Center near Whitewaters School along the Bulawayo-Maphisa road. My stay at Amagugu, however, afforded me a perfect opportunity to reach a broader area of the central, southern, and western parts of the Matobo Hills to interview ordinary members of the local indigenous communities, traditional chiefs, and traditional religious leaders. The stay also presented me with an opportunity to interview the staff members that Nyathi recruited to help him manage the project. Among the staff members at Amagugu was Misheck Dube who became one of my key informants during my numerous excursions into the various parts of the Hills. Dube was selected to represent the local indigenous communities in the Rhodes Matobo Committee until it was dissolved in 2009. The Rhodes Matobo Committee was established on the instruction of the Cecil John Rhodes' Will of 1902 which directed that his estates in the Matobo Hills and in Nyanga in north eastern Zimbabwe be left to the "People of Rhodesia" (now Zimbabwe) for recreational purposes (Stead 1902). In the Matobo Hills, the Committee plays a supervisory role in the administration of the Matobo National Park. Given his wealth of experience and intimate knowledge of the research area, Dube was a very useful informant during data collection for this research in the Matobo Hills.

While at Amagugu, I also had an opportunity to visit the Cecil John Rhodes Campfire Community Cultural Village Project and Craft Center in Lushumbe, an area which is in the south-central part of the Matobo Hills (Fig. 1.3). According to the members, the aim of the project, which I found to be similar to Nyathi's, is to revive and promote traditional cultural practices in the Matobo Hills. This is because, as the villagers argued, they have observed for a very long time that many cultural practices are disappearing at an extremely rapid rate in the Matobo Hills. The project, which was initially funded by the United States Agency for International Development (USAID) was part of helping rural communities around Lushumbe to manage their resources through the Communal Areas Management Programme for Indigenous Resources (CAMPFIRE) programme. The programme, which is administered by the Zimbabwe Parks and Wildlife Management Authority (ZPWMA), was aimed at alleviating rural poverty by giving rural communities self-government over resources management, especially wildlife (Logan and Moseley 2002). CAMPFIRE was developed primarily around the concept of managing wildlife and wildlife habitat in the communal lands of Zimbabwe for the benefit of the people living in these areas (Frost and Bond 2007). Revenue generated from safari hunting or from selling wildlife is endowed to the CAMPFIRE programme. The theory behind CAMPFIRE is that communities will positively contribute to environmental conservation if they can exploit these resources on a sustainable basis for their own benefit. The programme is based on creating appropriate institutions under which resources can be legitimately managed and utilised by the resident communities. Profits from the enterprise may be used for communal benefits or distributed to individual households at the discretion of the community (Murindagomo 1990). The cultural village project was to be developed as a popular tourist attraction in the Matobo Hills from which the villagers would survive from tourism without being dependent on the resources of the area. My visit to the Rhodes Campfire Community Cultural Village, however, provided insight into several traditional conservation practices of the Hills through the interviews and in depth discussions with some villagers in Lushumbe.

The second part of the fieldwork, which occurred between August and October 2014, was designed to conduct additional interviews and discussions in the south eastern and the eastern locations of the Matobo Hills. I managed to secure accommodation at Camp Dwala, a safari lodge located in the valley of an escarpment in the Matobo Hills. With the help of Surrender Sibanda, who became my key informant, I was able to conduct interviews and discussions in areas around the Matopo Mission, Ntunjambili Township, Silobi, Dula, and in Gulati communal area. During the entire fieldwork, I also interviewed archaeologists, historians, souvenir sellers, and ecologists working or who have previously worked in the Matobo National Park and business entrepreneurs operating within the world heritage landscape. This facilitated obtaining various perspectives of local indigenous communities and professionals with an interest in the management of the Matobo Hills. The use of the qualitative approach enabled me to obtain data on the knowledge, beliefs, opinions, emotions, behaviours, and experiences of the local indigenous communities in the Matobo Hills particularly concerning traditional conservation practices and the management of the cultural landscape in general. These approaches were also effective in clarifying intangible issues such as their beliefs, norms, politics, and religion whereby these aspects of the study may not have been readily apparent if other research approaches were applied.

SCOPE AND ORGANISATION OF THE STUDY

In this chapter, I have discussed that, before colonialism in Africa, local indigenous communities may have used traditional conservation practices to manage their cultural landscapes. I have also discussed that, with the arrival of Europeans, many cultural landscapes were appropriated and given a new status as protected areas for wildlife and nature which resulted in the local indigenous communities and their traditional conservation practices being relegated with the introduction of new management systems. However, with the attainment of independence, many local indigenous communities had hoped to return to their original cultural landscapes. Unfortunately, the new independent African states failed to change the management practices that were established during the colonial era. Thus, the idea to involve local indigenous communities in the management of world heritage cultural landscapes and reintroducing traditional conservation practices has raised new hopes for their involvement, but there are challenges to the full implementation of these objectives.

In the following chapter, I explore the idea of local indigenous communities and attempt to explain why the concept is now associated with the study of indigenous archaeology and, specifically, the management of cultural landscapes. I also demonstrate and argue that, in cultural landscapes, local indigenous communities are not homogenous and have different values and cultural beliefs which they attach to their cultural landscapes. Lastly, I examine the types and nature of indigenous communities that are associated with cultural landscapes.

In chapter 3, I describe the Matobo Hills where this study was specifically carried out. In this chapter, I present the Hills as a unique and distinctly granite area that is interspersed with thickets of vegetation and inhabited by several local indigenous communities. I also describe the different economic pursuits that are practiced in the Matobo Hills and that it is the nature of the Hills which has attracted both humans and animals into the cultural landscape.

In the fourth chapter, I explore the settlement history of the Hills by various indigenous communities. It is illustrated in this chapter that the San people, who had occupied the Hills approximately 12 000 years ago and left behind a succession of rock art and settlement sites were displaced by the farming communities, the Bantu, in the first millennium AD (Walker 1995, 1996). The chapter also explains that the Hills are currently populated by various indigenous communities who now attach diverse values to the cultural landscape.

In chapter 5, I argue that the Matobo Hills appear to have been initially managed by traditional conservation practices before the arrival of the Europeans to the area. I then show how the traditional conservation practices were replaced by the European management approaches which resulted in the establishment of the Matobo National Park, the eviction of the local indigenous communities from various sections of the Hills, and the protection of cultural heritage sites in the area. I argue in this chapter that cultural heritage sites, which were later subjected to archaeological research, created a tourist attraction which emphasised the Matobo Hills as a home of past hunter-gatherer communities and not of the descendant local indigenous communities that had recently been coerced out of the area. I further contend in this chapter that the eviction process resulted in the separation of culture and nature which ultimately created rivalry between the colonial authorities and the local indigenous communities.

In chapter 6, I make an effort to explain the idea of traditional conservation practices. This explanation is closely followed by an investigation of the traditional conservation practices that previously existed or that still survive in the Matobo Hills. I then describe how the local indigenous communities have used or are currently using the traditional conservation practices to manage the world heritage cultural landscape.

The opinion that the traditional conservation practices of the local indigenous communities should be reintroduced or revived in the Matobo Hills and that they should be involved in their management for the effective protection of the World Heritage area is discussed in chapter 7. The discussion is based on the articulation of the local indigenous communities whose voices have usually remained on the periphery when their ancestral lands are proclaimed as World Heritage Sites and when addressing management issues affecting world heritage cultural landscapes such as the Matobo Hills.

Chapter 8 discusses factors that deter the consideration of traditional conservation practices and the involvement of local indigenous communities in the management of the Matobo Hills World Heritage Cultural Landscape. The chapter concludes and discusses what I consider to be important considerations if local indigenous communities and their traditional conservation practices are to be successfully involved in the management of world heritage cultural landscapes.

2. Indigenous Communities, Archaeology and World Heritage Landscapes

INTRODUCTION

As demonstrated in the previous chapter, the recognition of local indigenous communities and the use of traditional conservation practices to manage world heritage cultural landscapes have increasingly gained enhanced support from many archaeologists and cultural heritage managers. Even though this is the case, the concept of indigenous people, as I will demonstrate in this chapter, has been debated within academic circles, and there is no agreement on the meaning of the term or even the process by which its meaning might be established. The absence of a precise definition for the term presents challenges to scholarly analysis, especially in its use in archaeological studies, and to the conservation and management of world heritage cultural landscapes.

In this chapter, I will attempt to briefly trace an element of the history of the concept of indigenous communities. I then examine a number of the definitions while also attempting to explain how this term has been used to describe indigenous people in Africa and especially in southern Africa where this study is situated. The increasing recognition of the concept by international organisations has led to a situation where it has become inevitable that the concept be applied to the study of archaeology and the protection of world heritage cultural landscapes. As a result of this development, I also examine how the concept has, to a certain extent, led to the development of a method of archaeology now referred to as indigenous archaeology and how its practise has influenced the idea that indigenous communities and traditional conservation practices be considered in the protection and management of cultural heritage sites.

Lastly, I examine the types and nature of indigenous communities, and I contend that it is the local indigenous communities that are regarded as still possessing traditional conservation practices that must be recognised and employed to protect and manage world heritage cultural landscapes. In presenting this chapter, I do not claim to have exhaustively and properly explained the meaning of indigenous communities which, in my opinion, is an exceptionally protracted and controversial subject.

BRIEF HISTORY AND EXPLANATION OF INDIGENOUS COMMUNITIES

Considering the multiplicity and nature of people that can be considered as indigenous in the world, there is no single definition of the term indigenous communities that can be universally agreed upon (Kiene 2011; Sawyer and Gomez 2012). Such a definition is difficult to derive, in part, as a result of the increasing association of the term over recent decades with new indigenous rights, benefits and demands, and people who may be claiming indigenous status (Niezen 2003). The definition of the term appears, therefore, to change from time to time to reflect on the shifting perceptions of people and organisations that are concerned with indigenous people and their issues (Ndahinda 2011). Consequently, there are several approaches for understanding the term indigenous communities, and each approach has its own origins and implications. In the following paragraphs, I explore several definitions and perceptions about indigenous people.

The term indigenous communities appears to have emerged from the colonial practices that were experienced by the "first" or "original" inhabitants of America, Australia, and Asia during their different colonial periods (Smith 1999). A number of well known examples of indigenous people in these regions of the world are the Pueblos and the Amerindians of North and South America, the Aborigines and Torres Strait Islanders of Australia, and the Māori of New Zealand (Lane 2014). These and many other indigenous communities have retained distinct characteristics which are clearly different from those of other segments of their national populations. During the colonial period, these communities were overpowered and began to be marginalised by their colonial masters, many of whom subsequently became dominant over the indigenous people (Anaya 1996).

The status of the indigenous communities in the conquered relationship was characterised, in most instances, by marginalisation, isolation, and non participation, especially when compared with the mainstream and influential groups within the country. Their ability to influence and participate in the external policies that exercised jurisdiction over their traditional lands and conservation practices was very frequently limited. The suppression of the original inhabitants of America, Australia, New Zealand, and other countries in the Pacific region resulted in the formation of several movements for indigenous communities, especially during the 1960s and the 1970s (cf. Saugestad 2004; Blaser, Feit and McRae 2004; Sawyer and Gomez 2012). During these periods, the development of these movements was extensively impelled by the decolonisation of formerly colonised countries and by the recognition of the rights of indigenous communities by international bodies such as the United Nations (UN) and certain non-governmental organisations (NGOs). The issues that stimulated the formation of the movements were broken land treaties (many of which were dubious) that had resulted in the loss of traditional lands as well as conflict and gross violations of the rights of indigenous people including, in some cases, massacres (see United Nations 2009). These movements were primarily established to demand the return of pilfered lands and property as well as compensation for centuries of cultural heritage destruction and marginalisation from the former colonial powers (Night 2003).

It is against this colonial background that, from the dawn of colonial rule until decolonisation, the concept of indigenous communities was born and associated with all of the "original" or "first" people living on territories that were conquered by colonial countries (see Anaya 1996; Ndahinda 2011). Thus, according to Anaya (1996, 3), the term indigenous broadly refers to living descendants of pre-invasion inhabitants of lands that are now dominated by others. As further explained by Anaya, these communities are considered indigenous in the sense that their ancestral roots are embedded in the lands in which they live and that they are distinct communities with a continuity of existence and identity that connects them with the people, ethnic groups, or nations of their ancestral pasts. Eldredge (2002) views the term indigenous communities as generally being understood to refer to tribes, nations, or ethnic groups that have historically inhabited lands prior to the advent of colonialism. However, Eldredge further elaborated that indigenous communities are usually minorities within larger societies which are discriminated against in socioeconomic life, disadvantaged in terms of power and opportunity in their respective states, and are also linguistically or culturally distinct from the mainstream population (Eldredge 2002, 436).

The definition of indigenous people has also been a subject of intense discussion in various UN specialised agencies such as the International Labour Organisation (ILO), the World Bank, and the Food and Agriculture Organisation. Nevertheless, since its establishment in 1945, the UN has addressed several situations which affect indigenous people as part of its overall human rights work. The concerns of indigenous people began to be recognised in a number of instruments and studies prepared over the years and in the activities of human rights organisations dealing with, for example, minorities, slavery, servitude, and forced labour. However, although there is no general agreement within the UN on what are and what are not indigenous people, there are several definitions that have been developed and have gained broad recognition as guiding principles for the description and identification of indigenous communities. In this study, I focus only on the UN ILO Convention No. 107 of 1957 and 169 of 1989 as well as José R. Martínez Cobo's Study on the Problem of Discrimination against Indigenous Populations which, in my opinion, are the primary guiding standards and statements of coverage on indigenous people and, therefore, pertinent to this research.

The ILO was the first UN agency to address indigenous issues by establishing the Indigenous and Tribal Populations Convention No. 107 in 1957. In this Convention, a distinction was made between tribal and semi-tribal populations, on one hand, and indigenous tribal populations on the other. The former were then described as members of tribal or semi-tribal populations in independent countries whose social and economic conditions are at a less advanced stage than the stage achieved by the other sections of the national community and whose status is regulated wholly or partially by their own customs or traditions or by special laws or regulations. The latter, however, were defined as members of tribal or semi-tribal populations in independent countries which are regarded as indigenous because of their descent from the populations which inhabited the country or a geographical region to which the country belongs at the time of conquest or colonisation and which, irrespective of their legal status, live more in conformity with the social, economic, and cultural institutions of that time than with the institutions of the nation to which they belong (see ILO 1957, Article 1).

This definition of indigenous people was later criticised by several scholars who argued that the definition denoted a condescending attitude towards indigenous and tribal people as they were perceived as "backward" and "temporary" societies. The belief at the time the definition was coined was that, for them to survive, indigenous communities had to be brought into the mainstream populations which should be achieved through integration and assimilation (see, for example, United Nations 2009). However, in the years following its adoption, the limitations of this Convention became evident, and demands were made to re-examine it. This was largely due to an increasing consciousness and increasing numbers of indigenous people participating in the international fora such as the UN Working Group on Indigenous Populations. This prompted the ILO to begin revising the Convention so that it became more relevant to indigenous communities. After its revision, the Convention was renamed Indigenous and Tribal Peoples Convention No. 169 and was adopted by member states in 1989 (see ILO 2003).

With Convention 107 revised, Convention 169 marked a change in the initial ILO's approach to the definition of indigenous people. Based on Cobo's definition of indigenous people, which I explain below, the new Convention now defines indigenous people as people in independent countries who, on account of their descent from populations which inhabited the country or a geographical region to which the country belongs at the time of conquest or colonisation or the establishment of present states boundaries and who, irrespective of their legal status, retain some or all of their own social, economic, cultural, and political institutions. During the review of Convention 107, however, protection was, and still is, the primary objective and must be based on respect for indigenous and tribal people's cultures, their distinct ways of life, and their traditions and customs. It is also based on the belief that indigenous and tribal people have the right to continue to exist with their own identities and the right to determine their own way and pace of development (ILO 2003). However, prior to the adoption of ILO Convention No. 169, there were also extensive debates within the UN Sub-Commission on Prevention of Discrimination and Protection of Minorities regarding indigenous people. As a result of this debate, a decision was made in 1970 by the Sub-Commission which recommended that a comprehensive study be conducted on the issue of discrimination against indigenous populations. In the following year of 1971, José R. Martínez Cobo from Ecuador was appointed as a Special Rapporteur for the study which was to suggest national and international measures for eliminating such discrimination (see Cobo 1986). The range of issues covered in Cobo's study included a definition of the term indigenous people, the role of inter-governmental and NGOs, the elimination of discrimination, and basic human rights principles as well as special areas of action in fields such as language, culture, social and legal institutions, land, political rights, religious rights and practices, and equality in the administration of justice. His conclusions, proposals, and recommendations became a significant landmark in the UNs' definition and considerations on human rights and problems that are currently faced by indigenous communities. After an extensive discussion of the issues involved, Cobo offered a working, but long, definition of indigenous communities, people, and nations whereby he articulated a number of basic ideas which included the rights of indigenous communities to define themselves. Cobo's working definition of indigenous communities reads as follows:

Indigenous communities, peoples and nations are those which, having a historical continuity with pre-invasion and pre-colonial societies that developed on their territories, consider themselves distinct from other sectors of the societies now prevailing on those territories, or parts of them. They form at present non-dominant sectors of society and are determined to preserve, develop and transmit to future generations their ancestral territories, and their ethnic identity, as the basis of their continued existence as peoples, in accordance with their own cultural patterns, social institutions and legal system. This historical continuity may consist of the continuation, for an extended period reaching into the present of one or more of the following factors:

a) Occupation of ancestral lands, or at least part of them;
b) Common ancestry with the original occupants of these lands;
c) Culture in general, or in specific manifestations (such as religion, living under a tribal system, membership of an indigenous community, dress, means of livelihood, lifestyle, etc.);
d) Language (whether used as the only language, as mother-tongue, as the habitual means of communication at home or in the family, or as the main, preferred, habitual, general or normal language);
e) Residence on certain parts of the country, or in certain regions of the world;
f) Other relevant factors.

According to Cobo, on an individual basis, an indigenous person is one who belongs to these indigenous populations through self-identification as indigenous (group consciousness) and is recognised and accepted by these populations as one of its members (acceptance by the group). This preserves for these communities the sovereign right and power to decide who belongs to them, without external interference (Cobo 1986).

Examining Cobo's definition, it should be noted that it emphasises the important common attributes that many diverse indigenous people may share such as being original residents of lands that were later colonised by other people and forming distinct, non-dominant sectors of society with distinctive ethnic identities and cultural structures. Other commonalities implied in the definition include a strong intimacy with the land and territory; experiences or threats of dispossession from their ancestral lands; the experience of living under foreign control and institutional structures; and the threat of assimilation into dominant sectors of society and loss of distinctive identity. McNeish and Eversole (2005) also observed that each category of Cobo's definition contains substantial diversity, comprises many groups and sub-groups of indigenous communities, and is distinguished by language, lineage, or geographical area which becomes an overall great complexity of ethnic identities.

Cobo's definition gained wide recognition, however, it was criticised by several researchers as applying primarily only to the "conquered" lands of the American continent and some parts of the Oceania and cannot be practically applied in other parts of the globe such as Asia and Africa (see Kiene 2011; McNeish and Eversole 2005). According to McNeish and Eversole (2005), Cobo's definition was designed to encompass the experiences of the Americas, Australia, and New Zealand with their comparatively recent overseas colonisation and then adapted to other parts of the world that also have culturally distinct and marginalised ethnic groups. As further noted by McNeish and Eversole, the second problem with this definition is that it implies a minority population living within a numerically and politically dominant "mainstream" culture. Yet, according to these researchers, in countries such as Bolivia, indigenous communities may be the majority but can still be marginalised. Additionally, a majority ethnic group may define itself as indigenous and exploit this position to deny rights to smaller groups as is sometimes the case in South-East Asia (see McCaskill and Rutherford 2005). The other difficulty with Cobo's definition is that, in countries that have not experienced overseas colonisation such as Japan, Thailand, and Nepal or that were never effectively colonised such as Liberia and Ethiopia in Africa, definitions of indigenous communities are less unambiguous given that the historical continuity of pre-invasion or pre-colonial communities is more difficult to trace or demonstrate. The term indigenous communities itself and its assumptions cannot, therefore, adequately address the circumstances of some ethnic groups in the world and those that live near to or in world heritage cultural landscapes.

However, whilst this is the case, the idea of indigenous communities can also be understood in many ways that are quite contrary to the definitions and ideas explained previously but which are a justifiable meaning of the word itself. In Africa, the expanded definitions were to account for the experiences of communities who lived in places where descent could not clearly confer indigenous status (Igoe 2006). For instance, the expanded versions could be co-opted politically by the descendants of colonial settlers who may lay claim to an indigenous identity through their occupation and settlement of land over several generations or simply by being born in that territory (Smith 1999). Also, as argued by Anaya (1996, 5), the dominant settler populations that were born in colonial patterns have created communities that could possibly now be described as indigenous to the place of settlement. The difficult position of these perspectives is that this indigeneity would have been founded on a colonial history (see also Fisher 2010, 126), and this can be considered as not truly indigenous. However, although the meaning of indigenous communities can be understood in this context, there is always a distinction between an indigenous person and an outsider as it is considerably difficult for the foreigner to understand or practise certain nuances of a culture or a people.

THE CONCEPT OF INDIGENOUS COMMUNITIES IN AFRICA

Indigenous movements in Africa and Asia are a recent phenomenon that were introduced in the continents roughly in the early 1980s and gained international acknowledgment in the late 1980s and early 1990s (Niezen 2003; Pelican and Maruyana 2015). From the 1990s onwards, the concept of indigenous people in Africa began to have a wider recognition. During the early 1990s in east Africa for instance, a broader network of culturally based NGOs, which made up the Tanzanian indigenous peoples' movement, was established. This movement included NGOs representing the Barabaig, Maasai and the Hadzabe hunter-gatherer communities. These organisations worked together through a forum called Pastoralist and Indigenous NGOs (PINGOs) that was established in 1994 (Igoe 2003). In southern Africa, the San people in Botswana were involved in the indigenous rights movement from the late 1980s while in west Africa, the Mbororo of Cameroon, a pastoralist group gained international recognition as an indigenous people in 2005. An association for the promotion of ethnic interests called Mbororo Social and Cultural Development Association of Cameroon (MBOSCUDA) was founded by the Mbororo people in 1992 (see Pelican 2008; Mouiche 2011).

One common feature about the establishment and development of the indigenous rights movement in Africa is that, they all drew motivation from the definition of "indigenous peoples" adopted by the UN as a legal category, and have connected with the global indigenous rights movements, several of which are NGOs. Nonetheless, unlike in the Americas and the Pacific, the indigenous movements in Africa did not develop as a critique of European colonialism and imperialism; they were instead established as a way of responding to the policies adopted by their post-colonial African states which made their traditional ways of living untenable (Pelican and Maruyana 2015). In east Africa for example, movements that were formed by the Masaai, Hadzabe and the Barabaig were aimed at resisting dislodgement from their traditional grazing areas that had been turned into national parks and large scale commercial farms when the government of Tanzania liberalised its economy during the 1990s (Igoe 2003). In Botswana, the First People of the Kalahari, representing the Basarwa (San) communities was formed in 1991 as a way of opposing their eviction from the Central Kalahari Game Reserve to pave way for the mining of kimberlite in the cultural landscape (Marobela 2010). What is clear with these cases is that that the discrimination and marginalisation experienced by the indigenous people throughout the world matches the experiences of the indigenous people in Africa under the administration of their post-colonial indipendent governments.

Under the adiministration of their African governments, the formation of African indigenous rights movements are aimed at reviving their cultural practices, claiming their traditional lands, improving their socio-economic practices and promoting their education. These movements are also aimed at seeking political representation in government. A number of the programmes outlined above however, began to be supported by the local indigenous communities, national and international NGOs. This has led many athropologists to conclude that claims of authochtony and indigeneity in Africa have not been completely and genuinely aimed at returning to the traditional practices that have to be safeguarded, but at gaining access to resources that come along with the national and international support of the movements (see Igore 2003; Pelican 2008). The problem of supporting indigenous rights movements in Africa has been that, it categorise Africans into two camps; those that are considered indigenous and those that are considered not. Meskell (2010) correctly observed that, as a result of interventions by outside agancies, such approaches have created landscapes of exclusion, rather than inclusion among the indigenous communities in the continent.

Given the above background, it can be argued that the establishment of indigenous rights groups in Africa, many of which were influenced by foreign indigenous rights movements and by the internal policies of their governments [most of which remained unchanged at indipendence], has fashioned new ways of explaining indigeneity in Africa. Following the establishment of indigenous rights movements in Africa, there are now several communities that can be described as indigenous people such as the San of southern Africa, the Pygmies of the Great Lakes Region, the Hadzabe and Ogiek of Tanzania, and the Sengwer and Yakuu of Kenya in east Africa. Although these people were traditionally hunter-gatherers, many of their descendants have now modernised their lives as a result of African government-mandated modernisation programmes and, in many cases, they no longer inhabit their ancestral or original lands as will be described in chapter 4. However, apart from these communities, the pastoralists and farming communities such as the Pokot in Kenya and Uganda, the Barabaig in Tanzania, the Maasai in Kenya and Tanzania, the Samburu, Turkana, Rendille, Endorois and Borana in Kenya, the Karamojong of Uganda, the Himba in Namibia and the Tuareg, Fulani and Toubou in Mali, Burkina Faso and Niger can also be considered as some of the indigenous people of the continent (Lee and Hitchcock 2001; ACHPR 2006). As indigenous people, they have different cultures and social institutions and also practise different religious systems (ACHPR 2006).

The major problem with regarding the above Africans as the only indigenous people in Africa is that, other African people are technically denied the same status, even though they are known to have originated from the same continent. If the definition of indigenous people is based on the idea of "original" or "first" people, then it cannot be applied in Africa as all Africans are considered to have originated from the same continent (see Sylvain 2002; Saugestad 2004; Kiene 2011).

However, definitions of indigenous people in Africa began to worry many African governments that the restricted application of the term indigenous to certain sections of their people is likely to cause tension and conflict among various ethnic groups surviving in their territories. The African governments began to also argue that the absence of defined parameters of the groups to whom the concept "indigenous" applies is likely to cause juridical problems of implementation, especially when the view that all Africans are indigenous to the continent is considered. The rights and demands of the indigenous people in Africa however, began to be viewed as retrogressive and an impediment to the development of their national governments (Laher 2014).

The above arguments by the African governments appears to have been founded on the observations that indigenous people were now seeking a seperate and distinct identity from that of the state (ACHPR 2007). These concerns by the African governments were however, dismissed as the struggle by the indigenous peoples for recognition was considered as not constituting a demand for special treatment or seperate legal regime but was considered as a way of guranteeing the equal rights and freedoms of groups that have been historically marginalised (Wachira 2012). For African States, a definition for indigenous people was considered to be not essential or useful as there is no universally agreed definition of the term and no single definition can capture the characteristics of indigenous populations (ACHPR 2007).

Although African States argue that the definition of indigenous people is not necessary in Africa, there is a general view among archaeologists in southern Africa that the Late Stone Age or the Later Stone Age hunter-gatherer communities were the first or original communities to inhabit the region prior to the arrival of the Bantu people (see, for example, Klein 1983, 1984; Huffman 2005; Segobye 2006; Pikirayi 2011, Lane 2014). These communities were the San people whose current descendants are mostly found in the distant parts of Botswana, Namibia, South Africa, Zambia, and Zimbabwe (Hall 1993; Sadr 2005; Denbow 2009). Evidence of their genesis from the region has been confirmed by the remains of the Late Stone Age archaeological material and rock art, which has been discovered in many cultural landscapes in the region. For approximately the past two millennia, these hunter-gatherer communities were in contact with herders and farmers and, more recently, with people of European descent (Hausman 1984; Klein, 1983, 1984; Mitchell 2002; Sadr 2005). Some researchers have argued that these hunter-gatherer communities were displaced or assimilated into the expanding and dominant Bantu communities and, during the process, were forced to abandon some of their cultural traditions such as painting on rocks (see, for example, Klein 1983, 1984; Brooks, Gelburd and Yellen 1984). However, the impact of the contact, especially with the pastoralist and farming communities, has been a subject of intense research and debate. This is because, as argued by Lee and Hitchcock (2001), there has been minimal archaeological evidence that points to the nature of the contact. Thus, according to Mitchell (2002), it has not been certain if the arrival of the Bantu people in southern Africa inevitably led to the subordination of the hunter-gatherer communities. Hausman (1984) had, in fact, speculated that the existence of distinct populations of the descendants of hunter-gatherer communities in southern Africa today indicates that there may not have been a complete assimilation of these communities by the Bantu communities. Archaeological research in the Kalahari desert by Karim Sadr, however, now indicates that assmilation of hunter-gatherer communities indeed took place but this happened at different times and under varying circumstances as they turned to herding, farming and trading following their contact with farmers and herders (Sadr 2005). Archaeological research in the Kalahari desert further suggests that while some hunter-gatherer communities were assimilated, others may have continued to maintain their traditional lifeways in the face of change while at the same time slowly adapting to herders and farmers as well as to traders (Denbow 2009).

Given the extensive and complicated history of human migration and settlement in many parts of Africa including southern Africa, being the "first peoples in the land", therefore, has been disregarded as being a necessary precondition for describing indigenous communities on the continent (see ACHPR 2006, 2007; Gilbert and Couillard 2011). The dismissal of this opinion was based on the argument that domination and displacement was not exclusively practised by European settlers and colonialists in many parts of Africa and Asia, but dominant groups have also suppressed marginalised groups well before the arrival of European settlers in the continent as in the case of the San people that were dominated by the farming communities in southern Africa. To address this issue, it was suggested that the most constructive approach is that indigenous identity should relate more to a set of characteristics and practices than the priority of arrival or of domination (see Saugestad 2004; ACHPR 2006, 2007). This is because, while formal definitions are problematic, the term indigenous communities recognises clear commonalities of experience amongst diverse people and the characteristics that they share (McNeish and Eversole 2005; Smith 1999). In general, indigenous people should identify the characteristics that demonstrate that their cultures could be under threat, to the point of extinction in some cases, and that the survival of their particular way of life depends on access and rights to their traditional lands and the natural resources that are found on those lands. As indigenous communities, they are discriminated against and regarded as less developed and less advanced than other more dominant sectors of society. They often live in geographical areas that are isolated and experience various forms of marginalisation, both politically and socially. They are also subjected to domination and exploitation within national political and economic structures that are commonly designed to reflect the interests and activities of the national majority. This discrimination, domination, and marginalisation violates their rights as indigenous communities; threatens the continuation of their cultures and ways of life; and prevents them from being able to fully participate in decisions about their own future and development. These attributes are important for the indigenous communities to identify themselves, and self identification has, in fact, become a key criterion for describing and identifying indigenous people (see ILO 2003; ACHPR 2006, 10, 2007). This identification can be made or acknowledged by the other surrounding indigenous communities and nation-states, although there are some instances where the identity claim can be a subject of some dispute, especially with regard to recognising assertions made over traditional land rights and claims.

INDIGENOUS ARCHAEOLOGY AND THE COMPLICITY OF INDIGENOUS COMMUNITIES

As has been demonstrated in chapter 1, the involvement of local indigenous communities in the management of world heritage cultural landscapes is a persistent concern in cultural heritage management, which is one of the sub-disciplines of archaeology. This has, to some extent, influenced the development of a type of archaeology which is now known as indigenous archaeology where indigenous people are involved in the excavation, analysis, interpretation, and management of the cultural remains of their ancestors (Moser et al. 2002; Watkins 2000; Nicholas 2008). Indigenous archaeology was, therefore, primarily developed as a sub-discipline of archaeology in the late 20th century in order to rectify some of the historical discrepancies that had resulted from the "traditional" academic practice of the discipline. Non-indigenous archaeologists had been responsible for the excavation and management of archaeological remains during which time they frequently ignored the desires and sensibilities of the indigenous descendants (see McNiven and Russel 2005; Nicholas 2008; McGhee 2008). The indigenous rights movement previously discussed, and the rise of cultural heritage management have been, according to Allen and Phillips (2010), two major factors which led to the development of indigenous archaeology. Thus, the growing consciousness of archaeologists regarding indigenous issues and the complicity of indigenous people in research, interpretation, and management of cultural heritage landscapes and sites have been perceived as a process of decolonising the subject of archaeology (see Atalay 2006a, 2006b; McNiven and Russel 2005). This reflected broader anti-colonial changes in the attitudes of indigenous communities about who has a right to control their lives and manage their cultural heritage sites.

In the present day, it has become vital to integrate aboriginal rights considerations at the early stages of World Heritage identification and nomination. The human rights issues when managing World Heritage Sites, now requires that the indigenous communities participate in decision making, contribute to management through their traditional knowledge of conservation and also benefit from the management of the sites. In addition, as part of human rights in World Heritage Sites, the indigenous people should be allowed access to resources and to their sacred sites. Furthermore, modern World Heritage management now requires that there should be no oppressive enforcement of conservation measures and that indigenous communities should be informed before any decisions are taken when managing the sites. Logan (2014), views the endorsing of the rights of local and indigenous communities in World Heitage Sites as an effort by UNESCO to restore the credibility of the WHL, which as has been discussed in the previous chapter, as heavily biased towards the western world.

Based on the above arguments, the involvement of indigenous communities in the management of world heritage cultural landscapes is increasingly becoming considered as a democratic right and is now being supported by archaeologists, as seen in the previous chapter, and is also now imbedded in UN documents, as we have seen in this chapter. McGhee (2008) asserted that these adjustments were not initiated by archaeologists, however, they were developed by several archaeologists who were reacting to demands of the socially and economically marginalised indigenous communities to afford those communities greater control of their cultural heritage remains (see, for example, Meskell 2010). Given this development, there is now a general agreement among many archaeologists that indigenous peoples must be involved in the research, interpretation, and management of their cultural heritage sites (see, for example, Moser et al. 2002; Colwell-Chanthaphonh et al. 2010; Pikirayi 2011) although, according to Lane (2014), the idea of "indigenous archaeology" still has a more restricted narrower range in Africa. Not only does the involvement of indigenous people in research provide specific information about the traditional management of these cultural landscapes, it also provides access to different perspectives and interpretations (George and Hollowell 2007). The involvement of indigenous communities in the management of these cultural landscapes provides them with an opportunity to create a counter-discourse that challenges the power relations that are involved in existing approaches of managing the past (Moser et al. 2002). It also has the potential to recast the roles and responsibilities of archaeologists and researchers from other disciplines to the communities in and with which they work (Pikirayi 2011).

NATURE OF INDIGENOUS COMMUNITIES IN WORLD HERITAGE CULTURAL LANDSCAPES

Applying the concept of indigenous communities in the management of world heritage cultural landscapes is exceptionally cumbersome. This is because, according to Marshall (2002, 215) "communities are aggregations of people that are seldom, if ever, monocultural and are never of one mind". In areas near or in world heritage cultural landscapes, as has been previously discussed, the term indigenous communities can refer to a diverse range of ethnic people who have different traditions, religions, cultures, and beliefs. In general, the relations and connections of the communities do not stop at designated boundaries but typically transcend the administrative boundaries of world heritage cultural landscapes and even of nation states, and it is often difficult to establish where each community begins or ends. Consequently, communities and cultures constitute a much wider and more common phenomenon close to or in world heritage cultural landscapes than is usually believed. Considering this situation, it is often difficult to identify those communities that have the greatest stake in any given management issue in a world heritage cultural landscape. At this juncture, I explore the types of communities that may or may not be indigenous to world heritage cultural landscapes.

Four broad but overlapping types of communities can be determined in areas bordering or in world heritage cultural landscapes. These are local descent communities, non-local descent communities, non-descent local communities, and the "stakeholder" communities (Singleton and Orser 2003; Marshall 2002, 2009; Pikirayi 2011). According to Singleton and Orser (2003) and to Pikirayi (2011), descent communities are those communities that are local and ancestrally attached to a particular archaeological site or a specific cultural landscape. In this study, I consider descent communities as local indigenous communities as they live near or in the world heritage cultural landscapes that they are ancestrally attached to. These communities include those that were evicted during the colonial period and resettled in adjacent territories to facilitate the establishment of national parks and conservation areas in Africa, some of which have now acquired world heritage or transfrontier conservation area status as discussed in chapter 1. In my opinion, it is the local descent communities that are believed to possess the traditional conservation practices or knowledge that must be recognised and considered when managing world heritage cultural landscapes. However, other than descent communities, there are also other communities that may claim indigenous status to an archaeological site or cultural heritage landscape but may no longer necessarily be living in or near the cultural landscape. Singleton and Orser (2003) regard these communities as non-local descent communities who are ancestrally linked to a specific archaeological site or a cultural landscape but are now living in a different geographical location, potentially hundreds or even thousands of kilometres away. It has already been indicated in the preceding chapter that a number of these communities are those that were resettled in distant areas when some of the cultural landscapes were proclaimed as national parks or conservation areas. However, even though they may be physically separated from their original cultural landscapes, many of the non-local descent communities may still be spiritually attached to them. Given that these communities are no longer physically attached to their original lands, they cannot be expected to have traditional conservation practices of managing the cultural landscapes that they had previously populated. The third category is that of non-descent local communities which are communities that either live close to or in cultural landscapes but are not culturally or ancestrally connected to such places (Marshall 2002). In southern Africa, as observed by Pikirayi (2011), non-local descent communities are perhaps in the majority given the complicated histories of the pre-European migrations and later of European land possessions which led to the removal of local descent communities from their ancestral lands. Although these communities may be indigenous in the sense that the majority may have been born and bred in and around the cultural landscape, their knowledge of the management of world heritage cultural landscapes using traditional conservation practices can be very much limited or even nonexistent. The last category is that of "stakeholder" communities who may not be local in terms of residence or even descent, however, these communities have vested interests in the management of world heritage cultural landscapes (Pikirayi 2011). This category includes tour operators, hoteliers, local administrative organisations, mining companies, church organisations, and many others (Makuvaza and Makuvaza 2012). This class of communities is not, therefore, indigenous to world heritage cultural landscapes and cannot be expected to possess knowledge of traditional conservation practices of such cultural landscapes.

SUMMARY

It has been demonstrated in this chapter that the term indigenous communities can signify different things to different people, organisations, and even to national governments. Considering this fact, there cannot be an agreement on the accurate meaning of the term. However, what appears to be generally agreed is that, within a particular geographical location, there are some groups that can be identified as indigenous communities while others may not. The decisive factors used for these considerations, however, are also usually ambiguous and often very controversial. In this study, I regard local indigenous communities as those people who lived in the Matobo Hills prior to the arrival of the Europeans or other non-African ethnicities, and before the process of colonisation had begun.

While it is clear that there can be a multiplicity of indigenous communities subsisting close to or in world heritage cultural landscapes, it must also be stated that these communities and the existing traditional conservation practices are susceptible to various transformations. Both indigenous communities and their traditional conservation practices are also dynamic, and they adapt to external as well as internal and local experiences and pressures, many of which may not be directly related to the management of world heritage cultural landscapes. Present-day indigenous communities are experiencing a dramatic change and remain threatened in many parts of the world. The transformation of many indigenous communities includes the permanent loss of native language, loss of traditional lands, and disruption of traditional ways of life. As is discussed in chapter 7, existing traditional conservation practices in world heritage cultural landscapes also survive under the threat of environmental, urbanisation, social, developmental, educational, political, demographic, and external management policies that are often different from those of the past. These factors usually result in the demise or cause major changes to traditional conservation practices as they are engulfed by the general progression of modernism (Taylor 2007). As the local indigenous communities transform, their traditional conservation practices and management approaches will change as well. In view of that, the values that local indigenous communities attach to world heritage cultural landscapes also frequently changes. This means that the extent to which local indigenous communities' issues and traditional conservation practices can be recognised and implemented in world heritage cultural landscapes, can be a mammoth task depending on the objectives that have to be achieved.

3. The Matobo Hills: Nature of the World Heritage Cultural Landscape

INTRODUCTION

This chapter describes and examines the nature of the Matobo Hills World Heritage Cultural Landscape where this research was specifically conducted. The study of the physical aspects of the Hills facilitates understanding the complex and intimate relationship that exists between the local indigenous communities and the natural environment they inhabit. This chapter, in part, will demonstrate and argue that human and animal settlement into the area was greatly influenced by the physical features of the Matobo Hills and that this inextricable interlink has added richness and depth to the archaeological and historical narratives of this world heritage cultural landscape.

THE MATOBO HILLS

When the Hills were proclaimed as a world heritage cultural landscape, both the natural and man-made features such as drainage, roads, and administrative boundaries were utilised to demarcate the boundary. The Tshatshani River marks the western boundary of the research area while its eastern boundary is marked by the Matobo, Nswazi, and Umzingwane communal areas. Their southern boundary is demarcated by the Khumalo communal area and parts of the Matobo communal area. In the north, the boundary is marked by large commercial farming areas and extends just north of Lake Matopos. The boundary extends further east of the lake through large commercial farming areas which border the city of Bulawayo and joins the Mzinyathini communal area in the east (Fig. 3.1). Although the area west of the Tshatshani River is an extension of the Matobo granite and falls under Bulilima and Mangwe Districts, it was not included as part of the World Heritage Site in order to curtail administrative problems. Also, even though they play a very important role as administrative centres of the entire world heritage cultural landscape, the Matobo and Umzingwane Rural District Councils are outside the designated boundary of this World Heritage Site (Technical Committee 2004). The Matobo Hills form part of the southwest periphery of the granitic shield of Zimbabwe, with an impressive relief of inselbergs and a wide-range of landforms. These hills comprise well-exposed and elevated granite blocks that were sliced up by deep drainage systems carved into joints and faults. The name Matobo is derived from the word "Matombo" in the local Kalanga language and means rocks. Legend states that the name of the Hills was corrupted by the early European settlers and, over time, the name Matopo or Matopos became more acceptable than Matobo. Many of the individual hills and locations have local names and historical narratives that are attached to them indicating the long established intimacy that exists between the local indigenous communities and their natural environment (Tredgold 1956).

GEOLOGY

In Zimbabwe, many granitic landscapes are characterised by the presence of roughly defined residual hills called inselbergs that rise abruptly from monotonously flat, endless, adjacent plains untrammelled by forests (Twidale 1981, 1982; King 1948). Most granitic inselbergs are an expression of compartments of rock that are massive and resistant to weathering and erosion (Twidale 1986). These hills formed tens of millions of years ago when overlying rocks gradually eroded away, exposing the granite rocks underneath. Inselbergs are typically found in the semi-arid or in savanna regions and especially in the southern and central parts of Africa. The granitic shield in Matobo is more deeply embedded to the south and east of the Hills (Walker 1996). The inselbergs of Matobo are steep sided, and their erosion and weathering have generated a distinct range of landforms which rises from the surrounding plains.

The most distinctive landforms of the Matobo inselbergs are the whalebacks or turtlebacks and the castellated hills, which are also known as castle kopjes. These hills are also collectively known

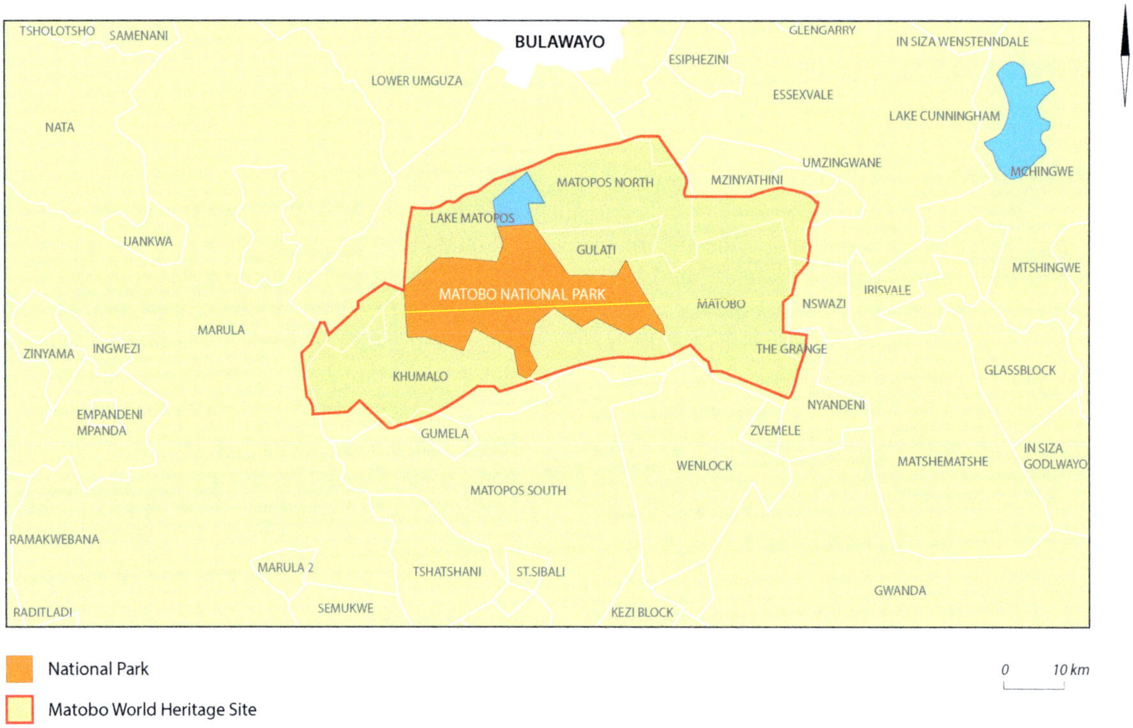

Fig. 3.1 Map of the Matobo Hills area showing the boundary of the World Heritage Site and, inside it, the boundary of the Matobo National Park. The World Heritage Site is bounded by communal lands, large scale commercial farming areas, resettlement areas, and small scale farming areas.

Fig. 3.2 Shumbashaba, a whaleback hill located in the south central part of the Matobo Hills (Photo by Author).

as bornhardits, and they are steep sided, bald, and dome shaped (Twidale 1981). In whatever terrain they appear, bornhardts are known to display a homogeneity of form that is conspicuous. These rocks are also intrinsically hard and moderately resistant to weathering so that their faces are usually steep (King 1948). Whalebacks or turtlebacks elongate along one axis, and they can be hemispherical, rounded, or dome shaped (Fig. 3.2). In the Matobo Hills, whalebacks have been formed through a weathering process referred to as spheroidal exfoliation or "onion skin peeling" in which curved layers split away to produce dome shaped hills, also known as amadwala in Ndebele, one of the local languages widely spoken in the area (Nobbs 1924; Tredgold 1956; Cooke 1965, 1986; Walker 1995, 1996). Some of the well known whalebacks in the Matobo Hills are Pomongwe, Bambata, Njelele, Shumbashaba, and Malindadzimu which is also now known as World's View Hill. These whalebacks or turtlebacks stand in marked contrast with the angular castle kopjes formed by natural fractures along the lines of weakness called joints (Cooke 1965, 1986). Castle kopjes, which are also called tors by the British or kopjes by the Dutch, are steep sided and are usually bound by essentially vertical cliffs comprising large blocks in their original form and in arrangements that reflect the pattern of the orthogonal joint sets (Twidale 1981; Walker 1995). Their constituent blocks are typically angular and essentially unmodified by weathering (Twidale 1981) (Fig. 3.3). The Matobo Hills are thus typified by rugged, hilly terrain divided by moderately narrow but plain sandy valleys. These valleys lay between enormous fracture zones which were formed along the NNW-SSE axes during the cooling of the granite (Walker 1996). The splitting, tumbling, and the natural hanging of huge granite boulders has resulted in the formation of numerous shelters and caves that are found in the Hills today (Fig. 3.4).

Fig. 3.3 A typical castle kopje in the Matobo Hills viewed from the south in Dewe village, Khumalo West (Photo by Author).

Fig. 3.4 Gulubahwe Cave is one of the several rock art sites found in the Matobo Hills (Photo by Author).

As indicated in the next chapter, it is in these shelters and caves where the hunter-gatherer indigenous communities lived and painted the surfaces of granite rocks, transforming this natural landscape into one of the rock art galleries of the world (Walker 1995, 1996; Garlake 1987; Walker and Thorp 1997). The descendants of the contemporary local indigenous communities also later settled and established permanent homes and sacred shrines in some of the shelters and caves of the Hills. One of the prominent shrines, Njelele, is located just outside the south-western fringes of the Matobo National Park in the Khumalo communal area. This shrine is a part of the Matobo Hills which was discovered in a granite kopje and is similar to several others in the same area. Mwari (God), as he is known among the Shona/Kalanga-speaking people and as Mlimo or Ngwali among the Ndebele, is believed to have lived at Njelele. The personal presence of Mwari at Njelele was indicated by his voice that was believed to be heard from the rocks. The local indigenous communities in the Matobo Hills believed that Mwari/Mlimo was the highest and final authority behind their ancestors known as Vadzimu in Kalanga/Shona or Amadlozi in Ndebele (Nobbs 1924). After the establishment of Njelele in the Matobo Hills, several other cult centres such as Dula, Zhilo and Khozi were also established in the same locality thereby spreading their influence far and wide (Makuvaza 2008).

Like much of the country, soils in the Matobo Hills are derived from granite boulders and are characteristically sandy. Approximately 70% of Zimbabwe's soils are comprised of granite and have limited inherent agricultural potential. These soils are light textured, generally infertile, and deficient in nitrogen, phosphorous, and sulphur. In Zimbabwe, sandy soils are also found in most communal areas and are highly leached and thus depleted of bases and contain very low reserves of minerals that would have the potential to weather and release elements necessary for plant growth (Nyamapfene 1989).

In Matobo, the soils tend to reflect variations in relief, vegetation, and water in different parts of the Hills. The surface weathering, which runs to unspecified depths, has resulted in intense bedrock decomposition, and this has produced the coarse grained sands common to the area. As a consequence, soils are primarily sandy to sandy loam derived from granite rocks. These soils are immature due to the short distance from their site of formation to the site of removal (nearest stream), and they contain a high proportion of incompletely weathered rock minerals (Lightfoot 1980a). Profiles are rapidly leached of clay and fertility during the short, but intense, rainy seasons and by runoff from upper slopes. Due to their nature and low clay content, these sandy soils also possess low water-holding capacity (Nyamapfene 1989). However, rich humic soils can still be found in the piles of leaf mounds behind natural barriers such as rock boulders (Walker 1995). In valleys, soils consist of siallitic and fersiallitic sands. In depressions, they are alkaline and sodic to varying degrees while minor areas where the soils are derived from basic schists range from red brown siallitic soils to dark grey vertisols. The infertile and erodible sands on steep hill slopes are held in place by a beneficial vegetation cover and the resultant organic matter (National Parks and Wildlife Management Authority 2000). Outside the national park and private commercial farms, soils are light textured and, especially in the communal areas of Matobo, Gulati, Mzinyathini, Khumalo and Nswazi, they are generally unproductive due to long-established and continuous farming practices by the local indigenous communities who mainly practice agriculture in small patches of sandy eluvia and alluvial soils between peaks and along river valleys.

CLIMATE: PAST AND PRESENT

The reconstruction of past climates in the Matobo Hills is exceptionally complex because studies of this nature in the research area are scarce and may not be available at all. Past climates can only be inferred and reconstructed from a plethora of studies that have been largely carried out in South Africa and elsewhere in southern Africa (see, for example, Tyson and Lindsay 1992; Tyson et al. 2000). However, these studies have been criticised for being contradictory, especially when they are applied to elucidate past climatic occurrences in the region. Walker (1995) advises that it is necessary to treat these data with caution while Pwiti (1996) asserts that, if climatic changes have occurred in the past, a generalised picture may be agreed upon as a sub-continental guide although it must also be accepted that parts of southern Africa may not have necessarily experienced the same climatic changes on the same scale.

There are three major climatic periods that are generally agreed to have occurred in the past including the Medieval Warm Epoch (AD 900-1300), the Little Ice Age (1300-1850), and the Post Little Ice Age (1850 to the present) (see Tyson and Lindsay 1992; Tyson et al. 2000). During the Medieval Warm Epoch, the climate is believed to have been warmer and highly variable with warm periods being punctuated by short cool periods (see Tyson and Lindsay 1992; Ekblom et al. 2012) while, during the Little Ice Age (1300-1850), climatic conditions are thought to have changed and were cooler, widespread, and experienced globally. The early period of the Little Ice Age is deemed to have been dry and severe and is argued by Huffman (1996a, 2008) to have been the reason for abandonement of settlements in the Shashe-Limpopo basin. This period was also

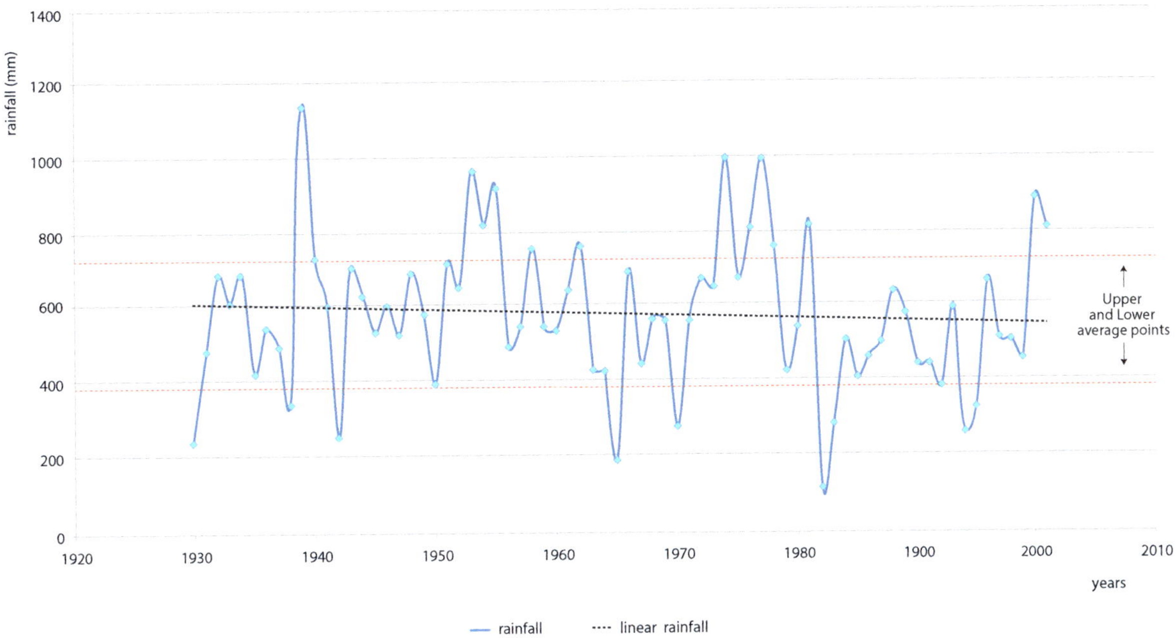

Fig. 3.5 Rainfall statistics of the Matobo Hills from 1920 to 2000 (Courtesy of the Department of the Meteorological Services, Harare).

characterised by alternating arid periods and warm wet periods with two wet periods extending from 1300 to 1500 and from 1675 to 1850. Between 1500 and 1675, the climate appears to have been warm and encapsulating the entire area of southern Africa. Wetter conditions are thus speculated to have returned during the Little Ice Age (Tyson and Lindsay 1992; Huffman 1996a; Pwiti 1996; Manyanga 2007). The Post Little Ice Age (1850 to the present) is considered to have been generally warm and wet while cooler and drier conditions were experienced in the first half of the 20th century (Tyson et al. 2000; Manyanga 2007). From this period forward, climate and rainfall patterns in southern Africa have been highly variable, leading to droughts of varying severity. The region is considered to have experienced regular wet and dry spells, i.e., several years of abundant rain followed by periods of scarcity (Chenje and Johnson 1996; Ekblom et al. 2012).

A study of the rainfall statistics for the Matobo Hills between 1920 and 2010 (Fig. 3.5) demonstrates that rainfall varied with extreme conditions of droughts and floods in the area. Between 1920 and 2000, nineteen severe droughts have been experienced in the Matobo Hills, which is an occurrence of one in every four years. The most severe droughts were in 1930-31, 1938-39, 1942-43, 1950-51, 1964-65, 1970-71, 1982-83, 1992-93 and 1994-95 when below 400-200 mm of rainfall was recorded in the area. The latter two periods have been described as the most severe, and they also encompassed the entire country and the whole of southern Africa. These periods were also major El Niño years, a weather condition which begins with the warming of waters in the western Pacific Ocean. These natural warming events alter the weather pattern throughout the world, and they are believed to possibly induce droughts in southern Africa or contribute to their severity (Chenje and Johnson 1996). In contrast, twelve incidences of extreme rainfall were recorded in the Matobo Hills, which is an occurrence of one in every six years. From these recordings, the most extreme rainfall was in 1940-42, 1952-53, 1956-57, 1974-75, 1978-79 and 2000-01 when more than 800 mm of rainfall was recorded in the Hills. This was

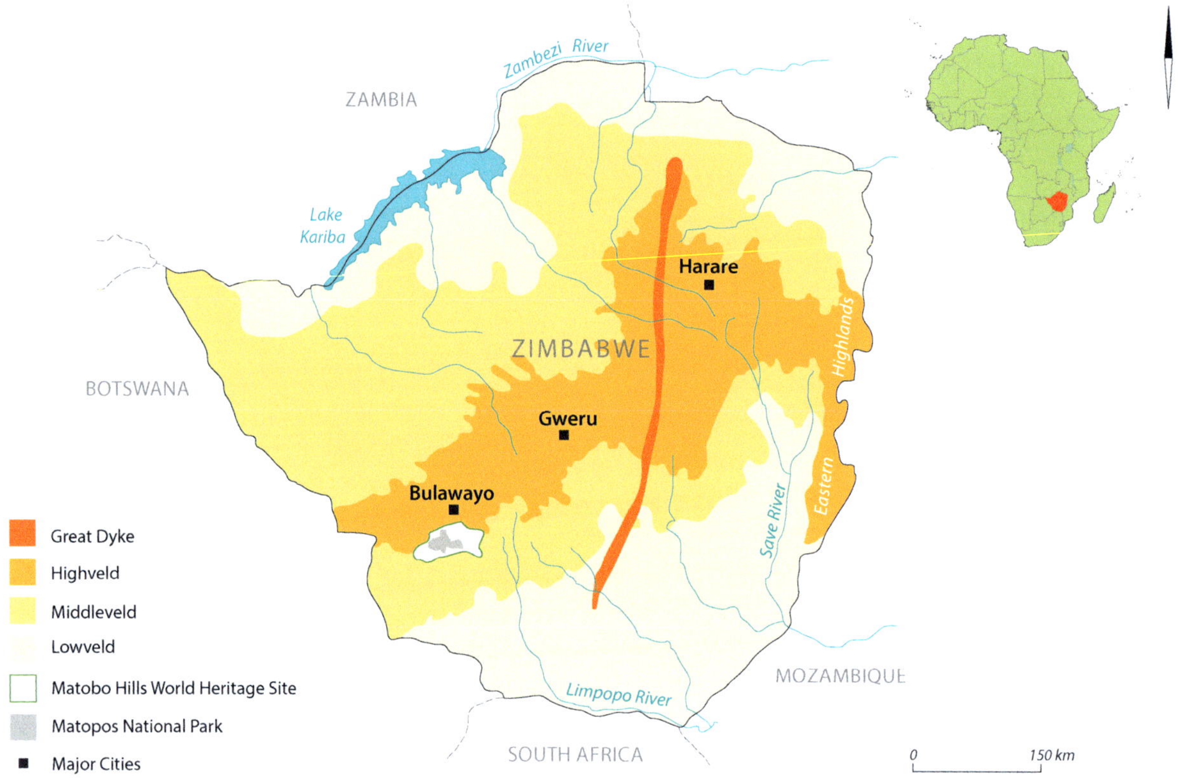

Fig. 3.6 Map of Zimbabwe showing relief of the country (after Moyo, O'Keefe and Sill 1993).

possibly as a result of La Niña which is the opposite of El Niño. La Niña occurs when the Pacific is cooler than the Indian Ocean, and the wind system moves from the Indian Ocean towards the Pacific. This brings unusually heavy rain in southern Africa (Chenje and Johnson 1996). The rest of the years received an average rainfall of 583 mm per annum.

The current climate of the Matobo Hills is strongly influenced by the country's distance from the equator. Rainfall in Zimbabwe is influenced by the interplay of ocean and continental air masses in southern Africa converging in the area during the summer periods (McCartney et al. 1998; Ngara et al. 1998). These air masses form the Inter-Tropical Convergence Zone (ITCZ) which is responsible for most of the rain in the country. The ITCZ is an area of intense rain-cloud development created from a collision of the Southeast Trade Winds (from the southern section of the region), the North East Monsoons (winds from the north), and the moist Congo air masses (Ngara et al. 1998). The presence of the ITCZ in Zimbabwe marks the beginning of the major rains in the country. In Zimbabwe, rainfall and temperature is also substantially influenced by the relief and altitude of the country which is: (1) the highveld at more than 1 200 m above sea level and traverses the country in a north easterly direction until it meets the eastern highlands; (2) the middleveld, which is the largest region and has elevations ranging between 900 m and 1200 m above sea level; and (3) the lowveld, which lies below 600-900 m above sea level and consists of the Zambezi and the Limpopo river basins. These low lying areas are generally dry and hot (Fig. 3.6). The influence of the rainfall weakens south of the watershed which causes the dryer conditions in the lowveld, and this also affects the Matobo Hills (Walker 1995). Rainfall occurs predominantly during the summer period which is from November to March. However, the rainfall is characterised by considerable spatial and temporal variation and unpredictability throughout the country (McCartney et al. 1998). This period is followed by a transitional season during which both temperature and rainfall decrease. The cool dry season follows, usually lasting from April to mid-August. Finally, there is a warm, dry season which lasts until the onset of the summer rains. Occasionally, the ITCZ and other main rain bearing systems are inadequate and not effective in producing rainfall in the country and are usually caused by an atmospheric system called the Botswana Upper High (Moyo, O'Keefe and Sill 1993; Ngara et al. 1998). The Botswana Upper High is a high-pressure cell that is generally centred over Botswana between three to six kilometres above sea level. This anticyclone tends to push the ITCZ and active cloud bands out of southern Africa and over the Indian Ocean. During the winter and dry periods, the Botswana Upper High along with the eastern mountain belt stretching from the Drakensberg mountains in South Africa all the way to Tanzania blocks the moist air from entering the region (Chenje and Johnson 1996; Chiuta, Johnson and Hirji 2002). This usually causes uneven rainfall distribution and dry spells in Zimbabwe. Considering the proximity of the research area to Botswana, rainfall in the Matobo Hills differs significantly both geographically and annually while storms can be isolated. As a consequence of the Botswana Upper High, rainfall in the Matobo area can be erratic and highly variable both spatially and temporarily. In the Matobo Hills, the rain season normally begins in November and ends in April. Rainfall variations also include delayed on-set and premature end of the season. In Matobo, rainfall can also occur as highly intense, short duration convective storms which result in severe soil erosion. The mean annual rainfall ranges from 650 mm north of Matobo to 450 mm, although precipitation is usually higher in the actual Hills than in the surrounding plains, especially in the southern and the eastern sections of the area. However, non-seasonal drizzle called guti in Kalanga/Shona is caused by an influx of cool, moist air from the south that often occurs in winter. This light drizzle usually counterbalances the high summer runoff in such a way that several natural and manmade reservoirs in the Matobo Hills generally always have plentiful water throughout the year (Walker 1995, 1996; Chiweshe 2007).

Daily mean temperatures tend to be moderately high while the mean night daily range can be as low as 8.6 degrees Celsius, making the nights relatively cool. High temperatures are recorded during the months of September to November, with October being the hottest and having a mean monthly temperature of between 32.8 degrees Celsius and 21.9 degrees Celsius and a daily range of 11 degrees Celsius. Temperatures tend to decrease during the months of December to March due to overcast days. The period of May to mid-August experiences temperatures between 20.4 and 14.6 degrees Celsius. This period is also characterised by cloudless days and cold nights with frequent frost (Technical Committee 2004).

DRAINAGE AND HYDROLOGY

The majority of the rivers that rise from the Matobo Hills are ephemeral with a declining annual unit runoff but are artificially semi perennial, especially those which are dammed downstream. Many of these rivers are closely flanked by cliffs, rock pillars, and steep, boulder-strewn wooded hilltops with an occasional open grassland backdropped by granite domes. The flow of these rivers is generally restricted to the months when the rain occurs which is usually from November to March with most of the flow recorded between December and January (Chibi, Kandori and Makone 2005; Love et al. 2005). During years of drought, these rivers are reduced to a few stagnant pools, and the water level in the nine dams constructed in the Matobo Hills between 1942 and 1956 decrease or dry out completely (Gargett 1990). To the east, the Matobo Hills are flanked by the Umzingwane River and by the Shashani River to the west. The Umzingwane River is a major left bank tributary to the Limpopo River. It emerges near Fort Usher in the Matobo communal area and flows into the Limpopo River near Beitbridge, downstream of the mouth of the Shashe River and upstream of the mouth of the Bubye River (Love et al. 2005). Major tributaries of the Umzingwane River include the Insiza, Inyankuni, Ncema, Mtshabezi, and Mtetengwe. The Shashani River arises from near Figtree and marks the western end of the Matobo Hills and is also a tributary of the Shashi River in the south. The Shashi River begins near Francistown in Botswana and forms part of the international

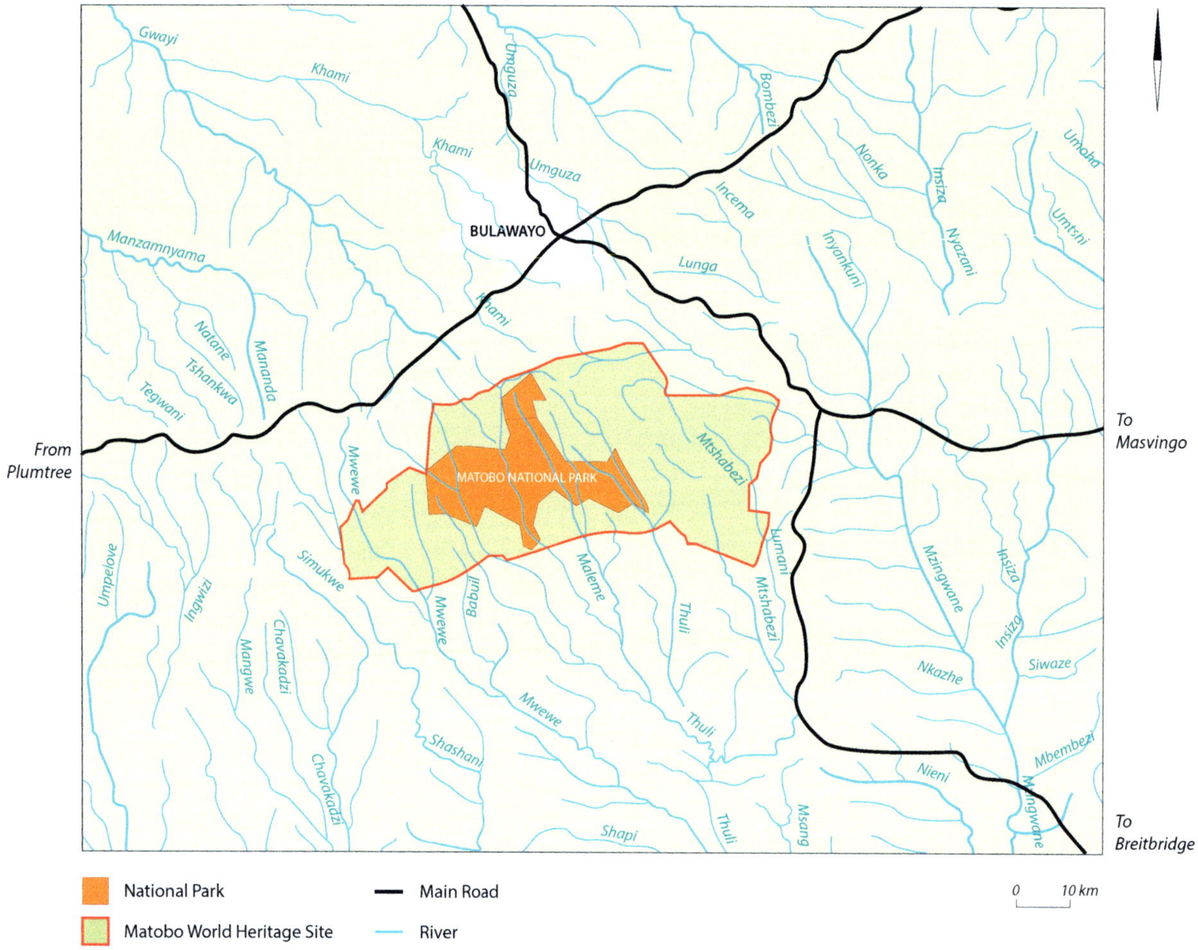

Fig. 3.7 Map depicting the drainage system of the Matobo Hills.

boundary between Botswana and Zimbabwe. The Shashe is a major left bank tributary to the Limpopo River on the Zimbabwean side.

The Matobo Hills are also dissected by several rivers which emerge from the Hills and are tributaries of the Thuli River. The Thuli River develops near Matobo Mission and flows southwards through various communal lands to its confluence with the Shashe River. Thuli River is also sub-perennial in its upper reaches (above Thuli-Makwe) and ephemeral in its lower reaches. The major tributaries of Thuli River are the Mtshabezi, Maleme, Mtshelele, Whovi, and Mwewe Rivers which all develop in the Matobo Hills (Fig. 3.7). A series of dams on the Whovi River and its tributaries in the upper part of the Thuli basin supply water to the Matobo National Park for recreational and domestic use while the Mtshabezi Dam on the Mtshabezi River augments the water supply for the city of Bulawayo. The outcropping of the granite frequently creates barriers to water movement such that certain valleys are marshy or contain permanent water pools. Therefore, within the Hills, ground water is usually available within one square kilometre even during the drier months of the year. Also, during the rainy season, increased runoff from the Hills transform some grasslands into marshy vleis or swampy areas, and they can remain as such late into the dry season (Walker 1995; Chiweshe 2007).

FLORA AND FAUNA

In the Matobo Hills, vegetation and wildlife is primarily concentrated in the national park and in private commercial properties where there is protection and management, therefore, the park has become a sanctuary for wildlife. Outside these areas, vegetation is less dense, however, even though this is the case, a diversity of vegetation and wildlife still thrives in much of the research area. Both the vegetation and wildlife have economic and social significance for the local indigenous communities living in the Matobo Hills. The Matobo Hills area has a variety of vegetation much of which grows on soils derived from granite rocks. The variety of this vegetation is also largely determined by the topography of the area, the nature of climatic conditions as described previously, and human factors. Soil texture, depth, and moisture content also determine the vegetation pattern within this geological unit.

The Matobo vegetation is typical of vegetation found in the higher rainfall areas of the country (Grobler and Wilson 1972; Chiweshe 2007; Walker 1996). The vegetation is primarily located on hills, slopes and bases, along river banks, and in open valleys. Outside these areas in much of the Matobo, Khumalo, Gulati, and other surrounding communal areas, vegetation is generally restricted to areas such as river valleys and hill slopes where local indigenous communities are unable to cultivate crops. In the open flat valleys which are traditional settlements and agricultural lands, vegetation is generally less dense. However, much of the vegetation in the Matobo Hills thrives as an effect of ideal climatic conditions.

Vegetation has major ecological, economic, and social importance among the local indigenous communities of the Matobo Hills. Apart from its contribution to the natural balance of the Hills, there are also a wide range of products that the vegetation provides to the local indigenous communities and their livestock. There are many vegetation species that have nutritional value and can be utilised as plant foods and herbs, browse for both livestock and wildlife, and as timber and wood (Palgrave 1977; Hedberg and Staugård 1989; Timberlake, Fagg and Barnes 1999). A comprehensive study of plant foods in the Matobo National Park by Walker (1995) indicated that there are appromxately 42 edible fruits within the park as well as almost 35 outside its boundaries. Underground foods such as tubers, bulbs, corms, and rhizomes as well as cereals and other plant foods are also elements of the vegetation that is found in the Matobo Hills although these may no longer be part of the diet for contemporary communities. Most of these plant foods are found in the kopje areas and in woodlands and a few in grasslands and on watersheds of the park. Some of these plants may have been exploited by the hunter-gatherer communities and by the farming communities who later settled in the Matobo Hills (Walker 1995). Currently, however, the availability of alternative modern foods and medicines and the lack of knowledge about plant use make vegetation less relied upon by the contemporary local indigenous communities of the Matobo Hills.
Apart from vegetation and regardless of their location in the dry semi-arid savannah, the Matobo Hills represent a western extension of the ranges of many fauna species characteristic of the higher rainfall areas in eastern Zimbabwe and parts of Mozambique (Grobler and Wilson 1972). The combination of physical and climatic factors has, in fact, resulted in the establishment of unique habitats for diverse wild animals in the Hills.

However, much of the wildlife that is found in the Matobo Hills is confined only to the national park, and this includes rhinoceros species (Diceros bicornis and Ceratotherum sinum), rock dassie (Procovia capensis), and the yellow spotted hyrax (Heterohyrax brucei). The Hyrax population density in the Matobo Hills is considered to be one of the highest in southern Africa (Barry and Mundy 1998; Chiweshe 2007). Other herbivores such as the klipsringer (Oreotragus oreotragus), the common duiker (Sylvicapra grmmia), and the steenbok (Raphicerus campestri) also habitate in the Matobo Hills (Smith 1977). In total, there are approximately 13 species of antelope and 25 different rodents found in the Matobo Hills. The diversity of herbivores provides major prey for vertebrate predators such as the leopard, baboon, raptors, and humans. The leopard (Panthera pardus) is considered to be the biggest predator residing in the Matobo Hills,

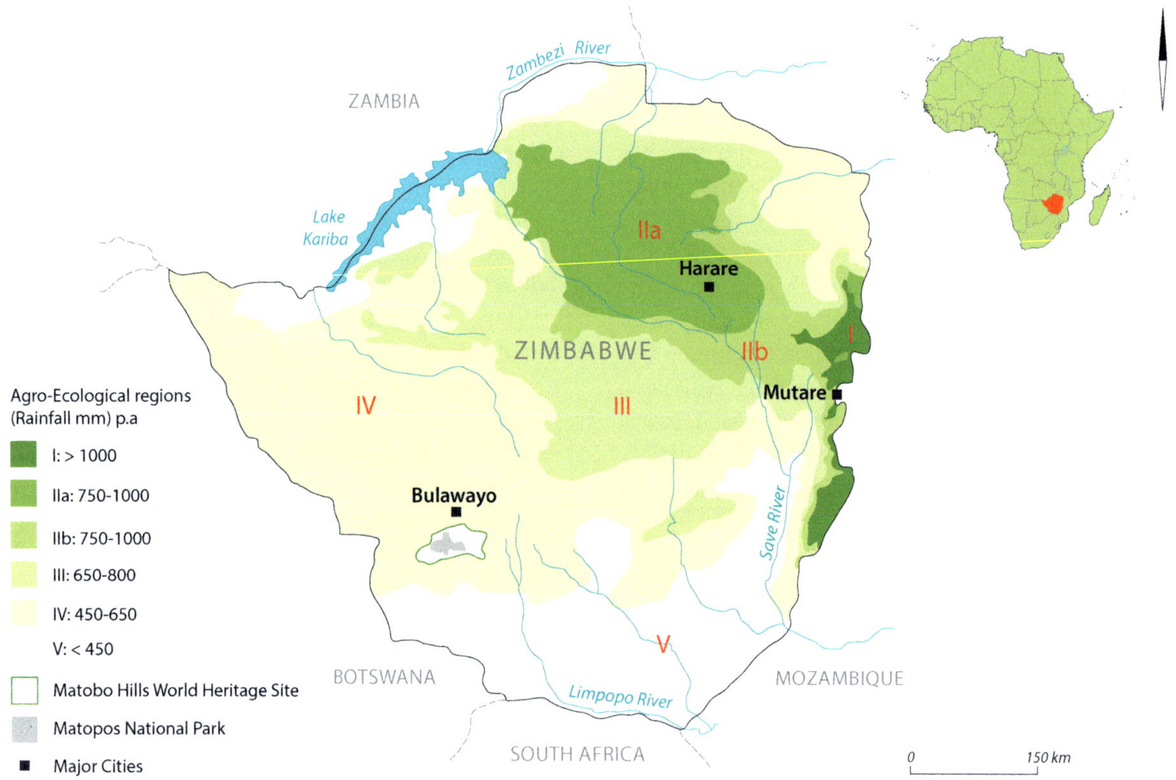

Fig. 3.8 A map of Zimbabwe showing the agro-ecological regions of the country (modified after Vincent and Thomas 1961).

however, is also almost exclusively confined to the national park. In Matobo, leopards prey on small mammals which comprise about 69% of their diet (Grobler and Wilson 1972; Smith 1977).

The Matobo Hills are also known for their importance as a sanctuary for birds of prey such as the black eagle (Aquila verreauxii) (Garget 1990). The eagles are known to defend extensive territories and, in Matobo, nest in very close proximity with more than seventy other pairs also nesting in the area. This has been attributed to the abundance of the dassie populations which comprise almost 98% of the eagles' prey (Barry and Mundy 1998). The enormous concentration of raptors in the Hills is closely associated with the availability of a high range and density of niches and suitable nest sites as well as the unusual substantial population of prey species, especially small mammals, birds, and reptiles.

PRESENT LAND USE

This section will explain the present land use in the Matobo Hills in regard to the agro-ecological regions of the country. The use of the agro-ecological regions helps to understand a range of human contemporary economic activities in the Matobo Hills based on the research area's land use. Vincent and Thomas classified the country into five agro-ecological regions based on the natural potential of the different parts of the country for various agricultural activities (Fig. 3.8). In Region I, annual rainfall is the highest and encapsulates approximately 2% of the land area. It is a specialised and diversified farming region with plantation, forestry, fruit, and intensive livestock production. Region II, which covers 15% of the land area, receives less rainfall than Region I. It is suitable for intensive farming based on crops or livestock production while Region III is a semi-intensive farming region and encompasses 19% of Zimbabwe.

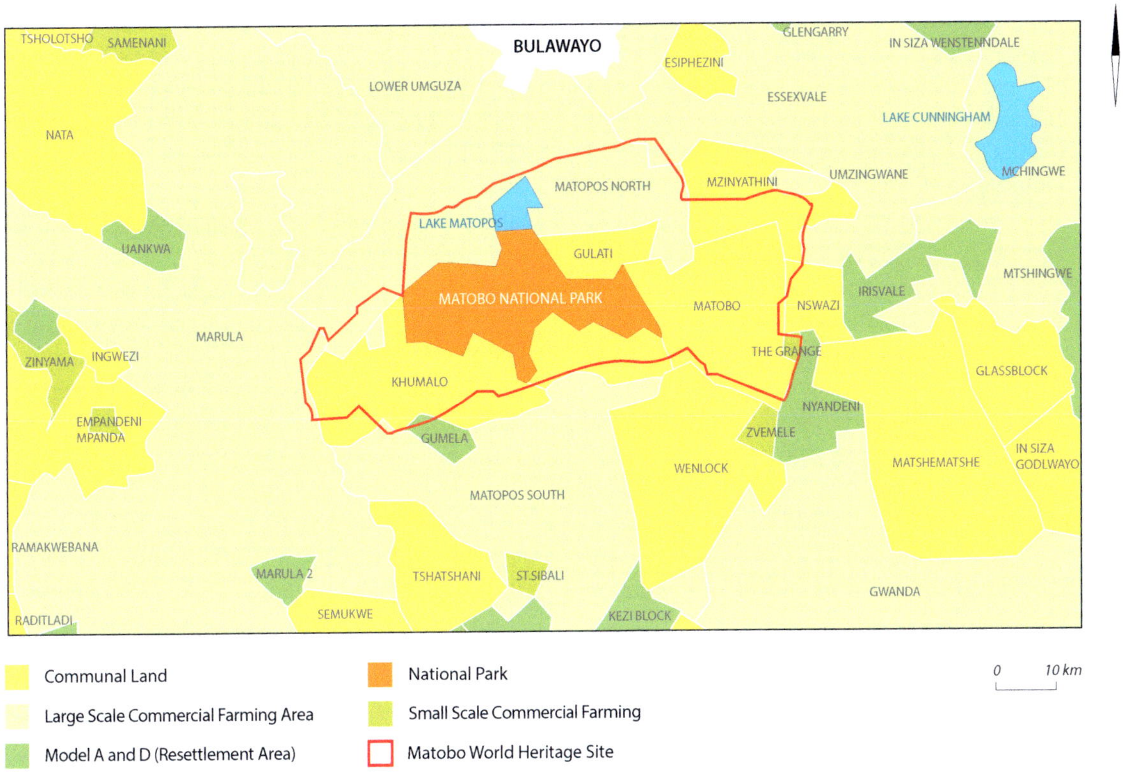

Fig. 3.9 Land use in the Matobo Hills.

Although rainfall in this region is moderate, severe mid season dry spells make it marginal for maize, tobacco, and cotton or for enterprises only based on crop production. The farming systems are, therefore, based on both livestock and cash crops. Region IV is a semi-extensive farming region covering about 38% of Zimbabwe. Rainfall is minimal, and periodic seasonal droughts and severe dry spells are common during the rainy season. Crop production, therefore, is risky except in certain favourable localities where limited drought resistant fodder crops are grown and livestock is kept. Region V, which is the last, is an extensive farming area covering about 27% of the country. Rainfall is too low and erratic for the reliable production of even drought resistant fodder and grain crops, and farming includes only grazing natural pasture. Extensive cattle or game ranching is the only stable farming system for this region (Vincent and Thomas 1961). Based on the above classification, the Matobo Hills is categorised under Region IV, which is a semi-extensive farming region of the country. The existing climatic conditions and infertile sandy soils, as discussed above, make the Matobo Hills less viable for serious agricultural pursuits. Although this is the case, mixed farming is practised involving growing a variety of crops and keeping livestock, especially in Khumalo, Matobo, Gulati, and other communal areas. Cattle, goats, sheep, and donkeys are kept while subsistence farming of drought resistant crops such as millet and sorghum is practiced. Maize is also grown, especially in flat valleys and in several marshy swamps and sponges, although on a very small scale. Local indigenous communities living near these areas also engage in market gardening and selling their produce at small shopping centres such as at Whitewaters, Silozwe, Ntunjambili, Natisa, and even as far as Kezi and Maphisa in the south or at Esigodini, Esibomvu, and Mawabeni in the east, and in Bulawayo.

The continued farming in the communal areas that has resulted in the exhaustion of the soil means that there is demand for more arable and grazing land. This has caused encroachment into fragile areas such as marshy swamps and on the outer edges of the Hills. This has also caused additional pressure on the national park and on private commercial farms which ultimately threatens the conservation of resources (Fig. 3.9). As a result of too many livestock and inadequate pastures in the communal areas, cattle are often illegally driven into the national park for grazing. Considering that land is communally owned, there is always competition for resource extraction, particularly firewood, timber for construction and fencing of homesteads, and farming fields. As will be shown in the next chapter, the areas that are currently the Matobo National Park and private commercial farms were historically communal lands, and the local descent communities subsisting near or in these lands believe that they still have a right to utilise them. This has often incited disagreements with government administrative departments in the national park. Apart from subsistence farming and livestock rearing, there are also a number of commercial activities performed in the communal areas including the selling of wood carvings, pottery, and other artefacts to tourists who visit the park. However, the primary issue relates to over exploitation of some vegetation species, especially the grey mukwa (kirkia accuminata), which is used for carving wood crafts.

In large commercial areas, some farmers engage in crop farming while others keep livestock, especially cattle for beef and dairy products. These products are sold in the city of Bulawayo and in the rest of the Matabeleland region. In addition to cattle rearing, tourism has become an important economic pursuit on some private commercial areas, which offer accommodation for tourists who utilise the park for scenery and game viewing, close to the national park. Some of the lodges that are found in the Hills offering accommodation are Amalinda, Ingwe, Shumbashaba, Big Cave, and Touch the Wild, which is also known as the Matobo Lodge. Within the national park, the main land use is the conservation of nature and wildlife. As such, the park is an invaluable game sanctuary used to breed and reintroduce endangered faunal species such as the rhinoceroses. The national park, which is state land, is primarily managed by the ZPWMA. There are also site museums in the park, which have been constructed at archaeological and historical sites. The site museums and the archaeological and historical sites are under the jurisdiction of the department of the NMMZ, and it charges entrance fees to tourists who visit these places. In an area just north of the Matobo Hills in the Sauerdale farm, which borders the city of Bulawayo, there are several formal and informal gold mining activities. This section is part of the Rhodes Matopos estate which is currently being administered by the ZPWMA on behalf of the Rhodes Matobo Committee (Makuvaza and Burret 2011).

Historically, prospecting and mining of gold in the north-western parts of the Hills and the entire region of Matabeleland began in the late 19th century when Europeans penetrated the south western part of the country. This was motivated by the false belief that a second Witwatersrand was found north of the Limpopo River after the "discovery" of the first in South Africa in 1886 (Oliver and Atmore 2005, 127). An archaeological survey conducted in the northern parts of this farm around the site of Old Bulawayo, a 19th century Ndebele settlement, revealed numerous ancient gold mines spread all over the cultural landscape. Old Bulawayo was a royal capital of the Ndebele state established by King Lobengula in 1870 but abandoned in 1881. The survey was performed as a component of the reconstruction and development of the site by the NMMZ as a theme Park between 1993 and 2006 with staff reliving the 19th century Ndebele life (Hughes 1995, 2000; Hughes and Muringaniza 2003; Makuvaza and Burret 2011; Makuvaza and Hubbard 2012). Currently, panning for gold is rampant in the eastern part of the Matobo Hills, especially along the Umzingwane River near Esibomvu and along the rivers that feed the lower and upper Ncema, Inyankuni, and Insiza Rivers. Panning in these areas and other parts of the country is being carried out by small scale miners largely in response to the ever deteriorating economy of the country. It is now one form of economic survival and a way of livelihood for local indigenous communities who live along the banks of rivers that generally originate from the Hills.

SUMMARY

In this chapter, a summary of the physical background of the Matobo Hills has been presented. It has been demonstrated that much of the research area is a broad granite landscape. These Hills have been settled from the prehistoric times to the present, and the present traditional communities in Matobo have long been associated with them. These granite rocks produce sandy soils which are shallow and not suitable for serious agricultural activities. This is exacerbated by the low and erratic rainfall frequently experienced in the entire area, thus droughts are quite common in the Matobo Hills. Keeping of livestock has become a major economic activity of a number of private commercial farmers while, for others particularly in the north of the national park, gold mining is the main economic pursuit. The traditional communities also keep livestock and grow crops along river basins and in marshy areas where water is usually available. In the national park, the primary economic activities are mainly viewing of archaeological sites, scenery and the offering of accommodation by tour operators and hoteliers.

There are several vegetation communities in the Matobo Hills. There are, however, no major differences between the vegetation communities found in the national park and private commercial farms from those which are found in the neighbouring communal areas. This vegetation is utilised more in the communal areas than in the national park and in private commercial farms where it is safeguarded. Some plant species are edible while others are therapeutic and generally used by the local indigenous communities as traditional medicines. Wildlife is also abundant in the Matobo Hills but is more confined in the national park and in private commercial areas where it is protected. The physical environment of the Matobo Hills appears to have been the main attraction of the area for both human beings and wildlife.

4. Profile of the Matobo Hills Local Indigenous Communities and the History of Settlement

INTRODUCTION

Although there is an abundance of literature that discusses the settlement history in the Matobo Hills by different local descent communities, the amount of detail that is available is sometimes conflicting as it converges and diverges in several ways. The cultural identity of the area, therefore, is difficult to simplify as it has been inhabited by mixed populations, some of which are closely related to each other though they are intimately attached to the Hills in many different ways. This chapter discusses the original inhabitants of the Matobo Hills who were the Late Stone Age hunter-gatherer communities and whose existence in this cultural landscape is evidenced by rock art and other cultural material. This chapter will also demonstrate and contend that, while the successors of these hunter-gatherer communities can no longer be ascertained, the Matobo Hills were also inhabited by several farming communities and later by Europeans, some of whose descendants are still surviving in parts of this world heritage cultural landscape today. In exploring the history of settlement in Matobo, it will be shown that the arrivals and departures as well as contacts of different communities has, in many ways, influenced and contributed to the shaping of cultural traditions and management practices that may be currently surviving in the Hills.

THE LATE STONE AGE HUNTER-GATHERER INDIGENOUS COMMUNITIES IN THE MATOBO HILLS

Existing archaeological evidence in southern Africa indicates that much of the region was originally inhabited by the Stone Age communities and later by several farming communities (Klein 1983). As will be demonstrated below, many descendants of the farming communities are still found in the Matobo Hills today.

The Stone Age is a broad prehistoric period during which stone was used extensively to produce a range of basic stone tools. Archaeologists have divided the Stone Age into the Early Stone Age, Middle Stone Age, and Late Stone Age based on the anatomical development of humans and the degree of complexity in the styling and use of tools as well as other considerations (Summers 1955; Cooke, Summers and Robinson 1966). The identity of the hominids associated with the Early and Middle Stone Age in southern Africa, however, has become more clearer as there has been extensive research on this topic (see, for example, Phillipson 2005; Wadley 1993, 2015). As elaborated in chapter 2, the Late Stone Age has been identified with modern humans who, in this case, were the hunter-gatherer indigenous communities. These hunter-gatherers had gradually evolved from the early members of the genus homo who employed simpler stone tools during the Early and Middle Stone Ages. Although this is now known to have been the case, the chronology of the Stone Age lacks accuracy in all the regions of the world. In southern Africa, the Early Stone Age is estimated to have existed from 2 500 000 to 150 000 years ago; the Middle Stone Age from 150 000 to 30 000 years ago; and the Late Stone Age from 30 000 to 2000 years ago (Bousman 1998; Wadley 2015).

This thesis, however, will not delve deeper into archaeological time depths of the Stone Age period in the Matobo Hills or in southern Africa. In Zimbabwe, this work has already been completed by a number of researchers beginning at the turn of the last century when archaeological studies were initiated (see, for example, Armstrong 1931; Robinson and Cooke 1950; Cooke 1963; Walker 1980, 1983, 1995). The results of their research have contributed to the basic outline of the cultural sequence of the Stone Age in the country and in much of southern Africa. Instead, this chapter will concentrate on examining the settlement history of the Matobo Hills commencing from the beginning of the Late Stone Age when the hunter-gatherer communities are evidenced as

Fig. 4.1 Rock art painted by the hunter gatherer communities in the Silozwane Cave (Photo by Author).

having been the first indigenous people to inhabit this world heritage cultural landscape (see Walker 1980, 1995, 1996). In this aspect, it is certainly during the Late Stone Age that the hunter-gatherer communities began to develop complex social structures and cultural practices which perhaps established the foundation of traditional conservation practises in the Matobo Hills.

The hunter-gatherer communities lived in bands and were skilled in the making and use of stone and bone tools. By means of these tools, they exploited wild animals through hunting and also gathered wild fruits and plants as components of their diet (Schrire 1980; Ndagala and Zengu 1989). They were also responsible for rock art paintings that are found in many cultural landscapes in southern Africa and in the Matobo Hills (Woodhouse 1969; Cooke 1963) (Fig. 4.1). However, the subsistence lifestyle of the hunter-gatherer communities ended approximately 2000 years ago when farming communities appeared in southern Africa from further north (Mitchell 1997; Phillipson 2005). Archaeological studies have now established that, on their arrival, the farming communities did not immediately displace the hunter-gatherer communities but began to live and share the cultural landscapes which they both populated (Klein 1984; Walker 1996; Killick 2009). Although many studies have been conducted on the Stone Age of the Matobo Hills, the dates when the hunter-gatherer communities began to arrive in this world heritage cultural landscape are not quite clear. According to Walker (1995, 1996), the hunter-gatherer communities began to seasonally visit the Matobo Hills from about 13 000 years ago as a result of increased food resources and improved climate at the end of the last glacial period. Unlike their ancestors, the hunter-gatherer communities of the Matobo Hills used rock shelters and caves as their homes and lived in groups of around 40 people. According to Walker, these hunter-gatherer communities left the Matobo Hills every year in about May perhaps following large herds of wild animals which, it is believed, migrated south to the lowveld in winter before migrating into the watershed in spring and summer to take advantage of the seasonal changes in grazing and the availability of water (Walker 1996).

From about 9000 years ago, the hunter-gatherer communities began to permanently live in the Matobo Hills during which time they extensively exploited the local resources such as wild animals and fruits (Walker 1991, 1996). The rampant exploitation of resources was probably a result of the excessive amount of people that were now living in the Hills. Walker estimates that there were, at this time, several hundreds living in the Matobo Hills in fairly large groups of approximately 25 people (Walker 1995, 1996). The extensive exploitation of local resources by the hunter-gatherer communities in the Matobo Hills may have been based on their profound and accurate knowledge of the faunal and floral species of the area and on the close observation of their cyclical behaviour and activity (Hubbard and Mguni 2007). It is during this period that the hunter-gatherer communities began to paint rock shelters and caves which was, at times, a way of mastering nature rather than being subjected to it. Walker further observed that, about 4800 years ago, the social organisation appears to have changed again and the hunter-gatherer communities were then living in larger bands that more regularly required larger animals for food. The size of the group was probably determined by the need to balance social, security, political, and economic needs against environmental constraints and stress in the Matobo Hills (Walker 1995, 1996). The traditional life of the hunter-gatherer communities was most likely disrupted when the farming communities arrived in the Matobo Hills around 1800 or 1700 years ago. Upon arrival, however, the farming communities did not quickly displace the hunter-gatherer communities but, instead, began to trade with them. The diverse nature of hunter-gatherer and farming communities' material culture at shelter and cave sites such as Bambata, Nswatugi, Tshangula, Kalanyoni, Shashabugwa, Cave of Bees, and Pomongwe in the Matobo Hills indicated that there were varying degrees of hunter-gatherer interaction with the agriculturalists over the last 2000 years (see Robinson 1966; Walker 1980, 1993, 1995). By the sixth century AD, however, the hunter-gatherer communities may have gradually departed the Matobo Hills, and there is no archaeological trace of their survival in this world heritage cultural landscape within the last 1500 years (Walker 1996). The reasons for the disappearance of the hunter-gatherer communities from Matobo are not clear, and the area in which they settled after they left the Hills is also not evident. The disruption of their traditional settlement pattern by the farmers and probably conflict could be some of the reasons why the Later Stone Age communities left the Matobo Hills. Walker (1980, 1996) speculates that part of the population may have settled in the southern lowveld of the country while Simons (1968) suggested that they may have been pushed west into the Kalahari Desert, which is a large semi-arid sandy savannah covering much of Botswana as well as parts of Namibia and South Africa. Some of the hunter-gatherers may also have been assimilated by the farming communities who had permanently settled in the Matobo Hills (Mitchell 1997).

THE INDIGENOUS FARMING COMMUNITIES OF THE MATOBO HILLS

As has been shown above, in southern Africa, the farming communities period extends over the last 2000 years and, as a cultural term, it refers to groups of people known in archaeology as farming communities who used iron for various functions, made clay pots, practised agriculture, and reared domesticated animals (Huffman 1982; Klein 1984; Pwiti 1991; Pikirayi 2001). It is a term that is, in fact, used to describe and delimit a period during which the farming communities are presumed to have been distinctively different from those of the Late Stone Age communities (Sinclair, Thurstan and Bassey 1993).

The farming communities were basically composed of subsistence farmers who cultivated crops such as sorghum and millet and also domesticated animals such as sheep, goats, and cattle (Phillipson 2005). Hunting was also important and contributed to their diet although it subsequently declined (Pwiti 1991). Mining activities were limited to the production of

Fig. 4.2 Fumugwe Mountain, which was renamed Mount Francis (Photo by Author).

iron ore for the manufacturing of agricultural and hunting implements as well as jewellery (Killick 2009).

As previously indicated, it is not precisely evident when the first farming communities settled in the Matobo Hills. This is mainly because there has been no research conducted concerning the farming communities of this world heritage cultural landscape. Although the farmers may possibly have arrived in the Matobo Hills approximately 1800 or 1700 years ago, the research by Walker and others has not been able to establish which farming communities in particular were the first to inhabit the area.

Available historical manuscripts depict that the first farmers to settle in the Hills were probably the Kalanga people followed by the abeNyubi or Nyubi communities. Nobbs (1924, 32) believes that the Late Stone Age hunter-gatherer communities were probably succeeded by the Kalanga people whose descendants are still existing in some parts of the Hills today. This view is also maintained by Walker (1995) and by Ranger (1999). According to Ndzimu-unami (2012), the origins of the Kalanga people can be traced back to a people that originated in north-east Africa and settled in the Zimbabwean plateau at the turn of the Christian era. However, according to Walker, it is only after about 1600 AD that the Nyubi people began living in the Matobo Hills (Walker 1995, 19). To authenticate this chronology, Terence Ranger, who has extensively researched the history of the Matobo Hills, has contended that some of the hills were simultaneously identified with their original Kalanga names and later Ndebele and European ascribed names. According to Ranger, Igambinga Hill, for example, was renamed Ingwena while Fumugwe became Ntabakayikhonjwa (Fig. 4.2). Fumugwe was later renamed Mt. Francis by the

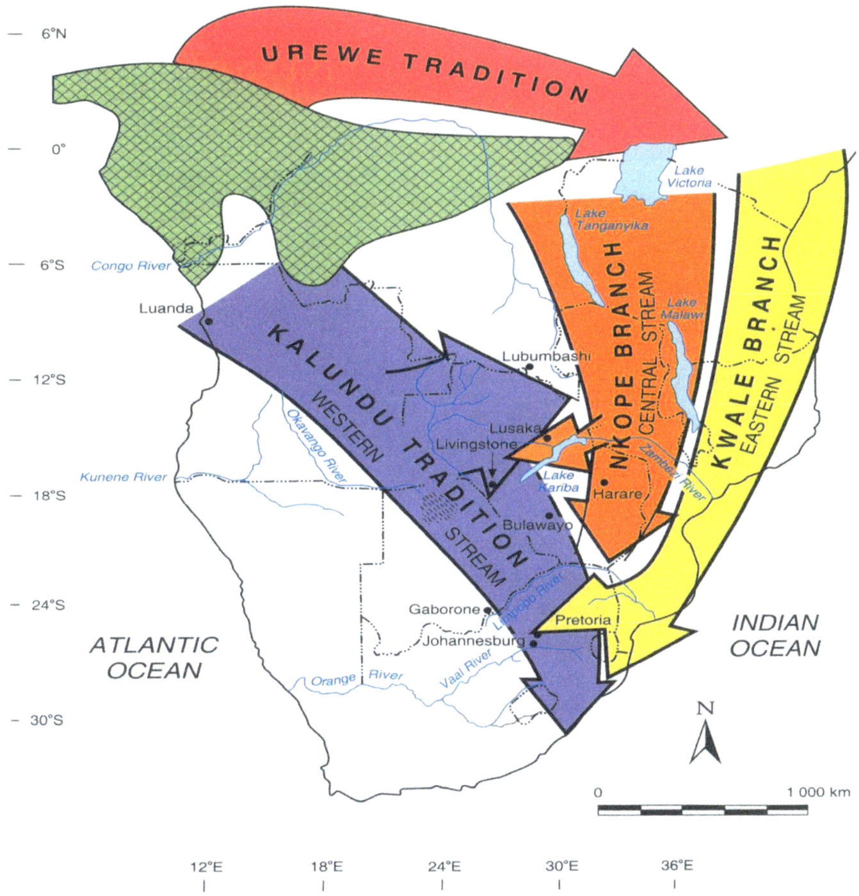

Fig. 4.3 Migration streams illustrating how farming communities moved into southern Africa (after Huffman 2007).

Europeans (Ranger 1999, 18). As a result of renaming the Hills, many of the original names may have lost any meaning that they may have had (Cooke 1963). Indeed, as already stated in the previous chapter, the name Matobo itself is Kalanga. In my opinion, however, the Nyubi were probably a minor farming community group whose presence in the Matobo Hills has largely remained unclear. However, if this chronology is correct, then the farming communities of the Matobo Hills were probably part of the western stream of the three separate farming community migrants into southern Africa from the north (Fig. 4.3). The eastern stream was from Kenya, Tanzania through Mozambique into eastern South Africa; the central stream was from the southern part of Kenya, Tanzania, Malawi, Zambia, and into Zimbabwe and the western stream was from Angola, the western parts of Botswana, and western Zimbabwe and eventually congregated in eastern South Africa (see Huffman 2007). The major problem with these streams is that they do not explain how some of the farming communities arrived in Namibia, the eastern half of Botswana, and South Africa as Huffman does not indicate how the groups may have migrated into these areas. Nevertheless, the early farming community period gradually ended around the 12th century AD when large scale political states began to emerge in much of southern Africa (Huffman 1974; Pwiti 1991).

In the middle Shashe-Limpopo valley, Mapungubwe (AD 1050-1200) developed into a political and cultural center founded by communities identified with the archaeological sites of Zhizo and Leopard's

Kopje. The growth of Mapungubwe was partly based on agriculture, cattle rearing and long distance trade with the east African coast (Huffman 2000). The Mapungubwe state collapsed during the early part of the 13th century. There are suggestions by archaeologists that the collapse of Mapungubwe could have been caused by various factors that includes climate change and the shift of long distance trade to Great Zimbabwe which had developed in the north from about AD 1250 to 1450 (Huffman 1996a; Pikirayi 2006). When Mapungubwe was eventually abandoned, the centre of regional power shifted from the Shashe-Limpopo valley to Great Zimbabwe in south central Zimbabwe. Like at Mapungubwe, the control of long distance trade and the accumulation of wealth in the form of cattle and grain contributed to the rise of Great Zimbabwe (Matenga 2011). Several centuries of intensive cropping and cattle herding would have eventually put pressure on the agricultural resources of Great Zimbabwe. Great Zimbabwe could also have been affected by the gradual shift of long distance trade to the north (Pikirayi 2001; Pwiti and Ndoro 2014). By the middle of the 15th century, Great Zimbabwe had declined in both political and economic importance. The collapse of Great Zimbabwe is suggested to have resulted in the rise of the Mutapa state (AD 1450-1900) in the north and the Torwa state (AD 1450-1830) in the south west (Pikirayi 1993, 2006). More than 350 archaeological remains of similar sites are now known to exist in Zimbabwe and in the lowveld areas of northern South Africa, eastern Botswana and central Mozambique. Archaeologists now refer to these archaeological remains as the Zimbabwe culture or the Zimbabwe tradition sites. The chronological development of the Zimbabwe tradition sites is however, now being challenged. A recent research at Mapela Hill by Chirikure et al. (2014), suggest that the Zimbabwe culture may have started at this site as it possesses massive prestige-stone walled terraces whose early construction date is 11th century CE, almost two hundred years earlier than Mapungubwe. The site lies two kilometres due east of the confluence of the Shashe and Shashani rivers in the south-western Zimbabwe lowveld. More research is however, needed before a concrete position is reached.

STATE FORMATION IN WESTERN ZIMBABWE AND LOCAL INDIGENOUS COMMUNITIES IN THE MATOBO HILLS

From the late 15th to the early 19th centuries, three powerful successive states emerged in south western Zimbabwe comprising the Torwa, Rozvi, and the Ndebele states. Much of the information for these states is derived from historical sources as their establishment somewhat coincides with the historical period in Zimbabwe. The historical period refers to the period following the introduction of education in Zimbabwe by the Europeans in around the 19th century. For this era, prehistoric archaeology now intermingles with historical archaeology, oral history, historical documents, ethnography, and cultural anthropology as sources to understand the African past (Pwiti and Ndoro 2014).

Immediately north of the Matobo Hills, the Torwa state emerged in the Guruuswa area in the south western edge of the country following the decline of Great Zimbabwe at the turn of the 15th century (Robinson 1959; Beach 1980, 1983; Huffman 1996b; Pikirayi 1997, 2001). According to Ellert (1993, 143), the Portuguese referred to this region as Abatua or Butua, which means “Mother of Gold” as they had inadvertently believed that the region was rich in gold and cattle. This expanse is characterised by grassland and a small number of acacia trees, and it stretches from the Gweru area to Bulawayo in Zimbabwe and merges with the Kalahari Desert margins, which was once dominated by the Toutswemogala chiefdom in north eastern Botswana (Pikirayi 1997; 2001).

The capital of the Torwa state was centred at Khami, which is located about 22 kilometres west of the modern city of Bulawayo. The stone building architecture at Khami represents an expansion of the culture that was once based at Great Zimbabwe. The distinct development of the Khami state was a modified style of the dry-stone wall architecture inherited from the free-standing walls at Great Zimbabwe. The Khami structures are terrace or retaining walls that are constructed around and over granite hill tops. The top surfaces of the hill tops were levelled to create platforms on which residential round clay houses were built. The platforms are also characterised by passages usually dividing the retaining walls towards the hill summit (Makuvaza and Makuvaza 2013). Southern African archaeologists have now named the dry stone sites that have a similar style of walls and construction as Khami type-sites or Khami-phase sites. The Torwa state was later conquered in approximately 1680 by Changamire Dombo of the Rozvi dynasty, who is thought to have emerged from the northeast and migrated to the southwest of the country. By about the middle of the 17th century, Khami was completely abandoned following a civil war in which the Portuguese were involved. From about the 1560s, the Portuguese from Mozambique had established themselves in the Mutapa state in the north eastern part of Zimbabwe with the aim of controlling gold trade in the interior of southern Africa (Newitt 1995). By helping overthrow the Torwa state at Khami, the Portuguse had wanted to seize an opportunity to monopolise gold trade in the Abatua region which they believed had a lot of gold. A new state was established at Dhlodhlo, which is also known as Danang'ombe, located about 100 kilometres to the east where the overpowered Torwa and triumphant Rozvi jointly continued to rule (Huffman 1996b; Pikirayi 2001). However, the authority of Khami is now also known to have spread into eastern Botswana and into northern South Africa.

It appears, however, that the supremacy of the Rozvi state had also spread into the Matobo Hills and beyond into the Venda and Tswana region in the south and southwest (see Manyanga 2007; Pikirayi 2011). In the Matobo Hills, the Nyubi and the Kalanga were also subjugated by the Rozvi people although this seems to have been short lived. It is also thought that it was during the reign of the Rozvi when Njelele and other shrines such as Dula, Manyenyegweni, and Wirirani were established in the Matobo Hills (Daneel 1970; Beach 1986; Makuvaza 2008). According to Beach, the Rozvi remained in control in the Matobo Hills until about the 1830s, however, some of them were linguistically absorbed by the Kalanga people over time (Beach 1986).

Rozvi hegemony in north-western Zimbabwe was eventually weakened during the Mfecane instabilities of 1815 to 1840 which triggered the various Nguni splinter groups from KwaZulu Natal in South Africa to many parts north of the country and to central Africa (see Omer-Cooper 1966; Eldredge 1992). Mfecane was a revolution initiated by the northern Nguni people and was popularised by the military and socio-political activities of Tshaka who was the Zulu king. Although it began in South Africa, the Mfecane had social and political ramifications as far afield as modern Mozambique, Zimbabwe, Malawi, and Zambia and as far north as southern Tanzania in east Africa (Ajayi 1998). These militarily powerful Nguni émigrés conquered and subdued many states and communities that they encountered as they migrated into many parts of south and central Africa (see Omer-Cooper 1966; Eldredge 1992).

After the supremacy of the Rozvi was weakened by the Nguni people, they began to disperse across the entire country. In the northeast, they settled at Mafungabutsi plateau under the Chireya dynasty and became part of the Shangwe people while others settled in the northwest among the Nambya and the Tonga people. Some settled in the southeast and became part of the Ndau and Hera people while others settled among the Venda and identified themselves as the Singo people (Beach 1980; see also Manyanga 2007). The Rozvi were thus probably a mixed and dynamic group of people with different cultures, totems, and traditional practices (Machiridza 2008). In the Matobo Hills, the Kalanga, Nyubi, and the remnants of the Rozvi people were also briefly subdued by the Nguni communities that were migrating north away from Tshaka's rule (Bhebe 1979). Though the Mfecane caused social transformation and upheaval among many ethnic indigenous groups, there was no complete dislodgment of the local indigenous communities in the Matobo Hills (Bhebe 1979; Beach 1986). This is undoubtedly evidenced by the continued presence of the Nyubi and the Kalanga people who are currently primarily settled in the western part of this world heritage cultural landscape. These indigenous communities, therefore, must have continued to practice and venerate their traditional religion while perhaps managing the Matobo Hills through traditional conservation practices until the Ndebele people arrived in the region.

It was during the Mfecane period that one of Tshaka's trusted lieutenants King Mzilikazi deserted him and later founded the Ndebele state in Zimbabwe. Subsequent to a series of protracted wars with Europeans and several indigenous communities on his way to the north, King Mzilikazi and his retinue eventually arrived in western Zimbabwe in about 1838 or 1840 (Ransford 1968; Rasmussen 1978). Having overpowered many indigenous groups such as the Birwa, Kalanga, Nyubi, Venda, Rozvi (or Lozwi), Suthu, and the Tonga, King Mzilikazi reorganised the new Ndebele order and first settled at Inyathi, and then Mahlokohloko, and later at Mhlahlandlela, which is located in the northern fringes of the Matobo Hills in the Sauersdale Farm (Omer-Cooper 1966; Lindgren 2002). As can be determined, the Ndebele did not begin by populating the Matobo Hills when they arrived in this part of the country (see also Ranger 1999). They only first settled in the Hills when they fled the European invasion of their state in 1893. More Ndebele people also entered and settled in the Matobo Hills and used them for hiding during the 1896-7 war when they fought against the Europeans' administration of the area (Beach 1986; Ranger 1999). As is indicated later in the next chapter, it was the war of conquest of 1896-7 which saw the dominance of the European perspective over the management of the Matobo Hills and which established the foundations of the non-indigineous control of this world heritage cultural landscape. The cultures and traditional conservation practices of protecting the Hills which had earlier been established by the Kalanga, Nyubi, and perhaps by the Rozvi, were probably not disregarded much by the Mfecane disturbances, the arrival of the Ndebele under King Mzilikazi, or the 1893 and 1896-7 wars. Later, when King Mzilikazi died in 1868, his son Lobengula who assumed authority and established a new capital in 1870 at Old Bulawayo is believed to have valued and consulted the traditional shrines in the Matobo Hills to obtain guidance on how to govern his state (Bhebe 1979; Ranger 1999). After they settled in western Zimbabwe, the Ndebele began to spread their influence among the other ethnic groups that had already populated the Matobo Hills and beyond (Becker 1962; Hachipola 1998).

CONTEMPORARY AFRICAN LOCAL INDIGENOUS COMMUNITIES IN THE MATOBO HILLS

The Matobo Hills are currently populated by various cultural groups, the dominant ones being the Kalanga and the Ndebele. Culturally, these two groups appear to have wielded significant influence on other ethnic groups as their languages are widely spoken within the Matobo Hills and beyond. Further south of the Hills, other ethnic groups that may be spiritually attached to the cultural landscape include the Venda who populate the low lying valleys of the Limpopo and Shashe Rivers. In the 19th century, traditional priests for Njelele and other shrines were drawn from Venda and Kalanga families who were said to have been deeply entrenched in the Mwari/Mwali cult (Nobbs 1924; Ranger 1999; Makuvaza 2008). It is also indicated that similar traditional institutions may have also existed in the south beyond the Matobo Hills amongst the Venda and Tswana people (Nobbs 1924; Cockcroft 1972).

South of the Hills among the Venda are also the Sotho, Hlengwe (Changani/Shangane), and the Remba/Lemba or Rembetu (Ruwitah 1997; Manyanga 2007). The Ndebele appeared to have also exerted their influence on many of these groups (Omer-Cooper 1966; Rasmussen 1978), and their authority also extended as far as the Zambezi River in the north (Beach 1980; McGregor 2003). To the southwest and west of the Hills, the authority of the Ndebele stretched as far as the Botswana-Zimbabwe frontier areas where the Kalanga, Sotho, Tsonga, and Tswana occupied the low lying areas of the Shashe River. To the east, their supremacy also seemed to have extended almost as far as the Mozambique frontier area (Omer-Cooper, 1966).

As will be disccussed in the next chapter, the dispersal of several of these indigenous communities within this large geographical expanse was also due to their later removal from the Matobo Hills when the Europeans began to settle and appropriate land around this world heritage cultural landscape and also when part of the area was turned into a national park. The Ndebele people were so dominant over other indigenous communities that it was decided that the western part of the country was to be officially named Matabeleland and was annexed with Mashonaland in 1901 with the latter being mainly dominated by the Shona speaking people (Northolt 2008). The territory, largely inhabited by the Ndebele and Shona peoples, was named Rhodesia after Cecil John Rhodes.

EUROPEAN LOCAL INDIGENOUS COMMUNITIES IN THE MATOBO HILLS

Before migrating to the north, the Ndebele had made contacts with Europeans who were establishing themselves in South Africa and the rest of southern Africa. As discussed in chapter 1, many of these Europeans were exploring the interior of southern and central Africa from the middle of the 19th century onwards. The Europeans who first settled in areas around the Matobo Hills were missionaries, miners, travellers, traders, and hunters. These Europeans were visiting the Ndebele state as far back as the early 19th century in South Africa, however, the existing European indigenous communities in the Matobo Hills are only indigenous because of being born there after their ancestors had settled in the area over several generations. Today, some families of these Europeans still own farms and mines around the Matobo Hills while others maintain their attachment to the cultural landscape through pilgrimages to monuments and memorials connected with European colonial settlement of the area. As will be discussed in the next chapter, the interest of Europeans in the Matobo Hills was primarily economic and recreational, and they did not value the African traditional conservation being practiced in the cultural landscape (see Ranger 1999).

Missionaries began to open up mission stations in areas near the Matobo Hills and initiated evangelical and educational work among the local indigenous African communities (Gelfand 1968; Lloyd 1979). The pioneers of missionary work in Matabeleland were the London Missionary Society. They established a mission station at Inyathi in 1859 close to King Mzilikazi's first capital (King 1959). The London Missionary Society was further granted additional land in 1870 to establish a mission station at Hope Fountain when King Lobengula founded a new state at Old Bulawayo while the Jesuits of the Sacred Heart were also allowed to open up a new mission station at Old Bulawayo (Makuvaza and Burret 2011). In 1881 when King Lobengula abandoned Old Bulawayo, the Jesuits were permitted to start a new mission station at Empandeni in 1887, which is located in the peripheral end of the Matobo Hills in the southwest (Gelfand 1968; Lloyd 1979; Zvobgo 1996). While searching for souls, missionaries began to proscribe traditional religion and management practices for protecting the Matobo Hills as they believed that the practices were the major hindrance to their evangelical work (Ranger 1999; Makuvaza 2008) because missionary work in Matabeleland and particularly in the Matobo Hills was proving to be a complete failure between 1859 and 1892 (Child 1968; Clarke 2010). Later, when Cecil John Rhodes took control of the country, additional grants were provided to the London Missionary Society to open up more mission stations at Dombodema near Plumtree town, west of the Matobo Hills. Rhodes also gave grants to the Brethren in Christ Church to open up the Matopo and Mtshabezi mission stations in 1898 in the Matobo Hills and Wanezi in 1924 in the Filabusi-Insiza area (King 1959). The granting of land to missionaries to establish their settlements in areas around the Matobo Hills and in other parts of the country have been perceived as Rhodes' plan to garner moral support in order to head off humanitarian and philanthropic suspicion and criticism of his plans to take over the country (Zvobgo 1996). It appeared that, in turn, missionaries also required the support of secular influence as the evangelisation of African indigenous communities in the Matobo Hills and in much of the western part of the country was proving to be a failure (cf. Bhebe 1979).

Inextricably linked to the establishment of mission stations was the pursuit of gold and ivory which also resulted in the establishment of European settlements in lands close to or bordering the Matobo Hills. As indicated in this and in the previous chapters, the pursuit of gold, however, was based on speculation and fabulous stories of mineral wealth north of the Limpopo River. This, as discussed in the last chapter, partially contributed to the mini-gold rush at the beginning of the 20th century when hordes of European fortune seekers streamed north from South Africa in search of the second Witwatersrand. Claims were pegged and mines opened at all known gold fields of Zimbabwe but primarily around the Matobo Hills, Bulawayo, Gwanda, Shurugwi, Kwekwe, and other parts of the country (Ellert 1993).

Elephant hunters and traders were also part of the European incursion that settled around the Matobo Hills trading in oxwagons, glass beads, cloth, guns, and ammunition in exchange for gold and elephant tusks believed to have been abundant in Matabeleland. During archaeological excavations at Old Bulawayo between 1995 and 2000, thousands of glass beads, hundreds of rounds of ammunition, and other exotic goods were recovered which had been traded or given to the Ndebele state by the Europeans as gifts (Hughes 1995, 2000; Gaffney, Hughes and Gater 2000).

The influx of Europeans in Matabeleland soon created rivalry and clash of interests amongst themselves. This resulted in the signing of a series of dubious treaties between the Ndebele state and different European agents including the British South Africa Company (BSACo), which was chartered in Britain in 1889. The infamous treaty, which led to the invasion of the Ndebele state, was the concession that was negotiated and signed in 1888 by Charles Rudd who was Rhodes' envoy. The signing of the concession was an element of Rhodes' pursuit of the exclusive mining rights in Matabeleland, Mashonaland, and the rest of the country, and it was also motivated by his wish to annex these lands into the British empire as part of his imperial ambition for a Cape to Cairo railway and a telegraph line (Fripp and Hiller 1949; Stocker 1979). A detailed discussion of the Rudd Concession, however, is beyond the scope of this study; it suffices to say that its signing paved the way for Europeans to occupy the country. However, it was after Mashonaland was initially conquered by a European volunteer force known as the Pioneer Column organised by Rhodes in South Africa when the dominant Ndebele state was fought and defeated in 1893 that the colonisation of the country was completed (Ransford 1968; Child 1968; Ndlovu-Gatsheni 2009a, 2009b). For the services rendered, each pioneer was promised 3 000 acres (12 km^2) of land and 15 mining claims. Empowered by the Rudd Concession, which gave Rhodes rights to mining and administration, the Europeans began to parcel out land to each other around the Matobo Hills and the rest of the country. The appropriation of land in the Matobo Hills was partially based on the power of the promises made to the Pioneers by Rhodes and also on dubious concessions signed between the Ndebele state and the Europeans (Fisher 2010). By 1900, most of the land around the Matobo Hills had been allocated, although some of it was never occupied (Ranger 1996). The narrative in the next chapter will show how the Europeans then enjoyed unfettered rights to introduce new management practices in the Matobo Hills which were based on western concepts of administration and conservation of landscapes.

SUMMARY

In this chapter, it is clear that the reconstruction of the cultural identity of the Matobo Hills is not an easy task. This is because the Hills have been continuously inhabited by various indigenous communities beginning in the Late Stone Age right to the present. This is further complicated by the fact that the relations of the indigenous communities that are linked to the Matobo Hills go beyond the World Heritage Site, the state, and other administrative boundaries. As a result of the intricate and long history of settlement, movement, and influx of different communities in the Matobo Hills and the region in which they are located, it is difficult to differentiate between indigenous and non-indigenous communities that may or may not be associated with this world heritage cultural landscape. This means that the traditional conservation practices that may have existed or that still survive in the Matobo Hills may not have been created by a single indigenous community but were a product of the different communities that have inhabited the cultural landscape at different times in the past.

As shown in this chapter, the communities of Matobo are all indigenous to the area despite their different dates of arrival to or inhabitation of the Hills. Except for the hunter-gatherer communities whose departure from the Matobo Hills has remained a mystery, all of the existing indigenous communities have the right to claim indigeneity and ownership of the cultural landscape. However, the main reasons for the absence of ownership claims of the Matobo Hills by the hunter-gatherer communities is that there are currently no known existing descendants that are historically associated with the Matobo Hills. In addition, the contemporary groups who are believed to have been the descendants of the Late Stone Age hunter-gatherers are a very marginal ethno-social group in Zimbabwe and in other southern African countries. They cannot effectively articulate claims and entitlements to the Matobo area either as a cultural heritagescape and a homeland. Although this is the case, the beliefs and practices of all of the indigenous communities that are associated with the Matobo Hills are likely to have changed over the millennia following the contact of the communities in the area. Given the existence of various local indigenous communities that have an attachment with the Hills, the management of this world heritage cultural landscape, therefore, must be understood through multiple voices, meanings, and practices.

5. European Approaches to the Management of the Matobo Hills

INTRODUCTION

This chapter begins by presenting European perceptions about the Matobo Hills when they first arrived in the area during the late 19th century. It is argued in this section that, before the appropriation of the Hills by the Europeans, the local descent communities could have managed the cultural landscape with traditional conservation practices. However, the omission of discussion regarding the traditional conservation practices of the Matobo Hills until the next chapter is intentional so that the practices can be better understood through the interviews and discussions with the local indigenous communities during fieldwork in the Hills. The following section of this chapter will demonstrate that the traditional conservation practices in the Matobo Hills were subsequently replaced with the European approaches of management which resulted in the establishment of a national park, eviction of the local indigenous communities from a number of locations within the cultural landscape, and the introduction of a formal legislation to manage the cultural heritage sites. Additionally, this chapter delves deeper to substantiate that the imperial conquest of the Matobo Hills has resulted in the demarcation of boundaries and altered the way the cultural landscape may have been traditionally managed by the local indigenous communities of the area. This chapter concludes with the assertion that, although the local indigenous communities had hoped that the European concepts of managing the Matobo Hills would be discontinued upon the country's independence, this was not realised as the new Zimbabwean government decided to continue with the dictates of international conservation which retained the European values that those managing the cultural landscape had acquired during the colonial era.

EUROPEAN VIEWS OF THE MATOBO HILLS

According to Ranger (1999), when the Europeans began to enter the Matobo Hills during the late 19th century, they regarded them as pre-eminently "scenery" and representing "nature". As Ranger further argued, the Hills became a European place of mediation and communion with nature and, more than anywhere else in the country, they later symbolised their special relationship with the landscape. However, even though the Europeans had recognised that the Matobo Hills had already been occupied in the distant past by the hunter-gatherer and Iron Age communities, they did not recognise the legitimacy of the descendant local indigenous communities who were now living and farming in the area (Adams 2004). Initially, the Europeans had believed that the local indigenous communities had no use for the Hills and that they did not have an objective opinion of the cultural landscape (Ranger 1999). Based on these beliefs and assumptions, they further thought that the local descent communities had no respect of the Matobo Hills and did not have the means of protecting the cultural landscape. The Europeans had, in fact, not realised that the "rocks, stones and trees" on which they looked indifferently were all incorporated into the local indigenous communities' historical oral geography (Ranger 1997). Contrary to their perceptions, however, the local indigenous communities had long developed a special bond with the cultural landscape. As a result of this cohesiveness, the setting of the Matobo Hills had taken on a sacred nature with numerous taboos relating to the use of the environment. Narratives about the Matobo Hills suggests that the the cultural landscape was always managed with traditional means prior to the arrival of the Europeans (see Nobbs 1924; Ranger 1996, 1999; Technical Committee 2004; Nyathi and Ndiweni 2005). As discussed in the next chapter, the respect that was accorded to the Hills and their environs lies partially in a series of traditional conservation practices and customary usage of the area.

THE MANAGEMENT OF THE MATOBO HILLS

When the Europeans arrived in the Matobo Hills, they began to perceive the traditional conservation practices as primitive and uncivilised even though the practices appear to have been organised and institutionalised (Makuvaza and Makuvaza 2012). Consequently, they began to introduce unfamiliar ideas of management which did not respect the traditional conservation practices that were already established by the local indigenous peoples in the area (Ranger 1997). The new concepts of management, however, were based primarily on science, education, and Christianity and sharply contradicted with the way the Hills could have been managed prior to their colonial appropriation by the Europeans. Colonisation, however, brought new ideologies that contradicted those espoused by the traditional conservation practices in the Matobo Hills (Nyathi and Ndiweni 2005). The following information will show that the new values that were introduced in the cultural landscape by the Europeans began to eclipse the core values that were enshrined in the traditional management systems. The result was that the existing traditional conservation practices of managing the Matobo Hills were threatened as they were involuntarily consumed by the conflicting demands from the two dominant but contrasting ideologies (Lightfoot n.d; Nyathi and Ndiweni 2005).

FOUNDING OF THE NATIONAL PARK IN THE MATOBO HILLS

From as early as 1900, Europeans began to consider it their individual responsibility to manage the Matobo Hills which they believed were being misused by the local indigenous communities who were surviving in the cultural landscape. The non-indigineous people began to proclaim stewardship of significant natural and cultural areas and established naturalistic theories for the development of the entire cultural landscape and of the national park, which they argued was going to be the first of its kind in the country. As discussed later, an assortment of arguments were soon presented by the Europeans in their efforts to justify the establishment of a national park and to evict the local indigenous communities from some sections of the Hills where the park was to be established.

Although attempts by the Europeans to manage the Matobo Hills began as far back as 1916, it was at the end of 1919 that the idea to establish a national park was formulated when the Duke of Abercorn and chairman of the BSACo visited the country from London to attend the burial of Leander Starr Jameson at World's View Hill. Jameson, who had become the Administrator of Matabeleland in 1894, was also a personal representative and a close associate of Rhodes. Previously in 1902, Rhodes had been buried at the World's View Hill while the remains of the Allan Wilson patrol members were also interred at the same precincts in 1904. The patrol members were all killed on the 4th of December 1893 during a fierce battle against the Ndebele warriors on the banks of Shangani River as they were pursuing King Lobengula who was fleeing away from European aggression and hegemony. When Charles Coghlan, who was the first Prime Minister of Southern Rhodesia, died on 28 August 1927, he was also buried at the World's View Hill on 14 August 1930. As a result of these burials, Ranger (1999, 2012) has, as a point of fact, concluded that the Hill that the local indigenous communities believed to have been sacred had become the Rhodesians' Valhalla or their heroes' acre.

It was during the burial of Jameson at World's View that the Duke became impressed by the surrounding landscape such that, upon returning to London, he recommended the reservation of "a considerable tract of land in the neighbourhood of the Hill to preserve its unique and unspoilt beauty" (Ashton 1981, 6). The person who played an important role in establishing the national park was Eric Nobbs who, at that time, was the director of agriculture and was also responsible for the administration of Rhodes' estates in the Matobo Hills and in Nyanga in the north eastern part of the country. Although the Duke had referred to the reservation of land immediately surrounding the World's View, Nobbs had assumed that he had proposed something much more grand than just the vicinity of the World's View Hill. Working from this assumption, Nobbs

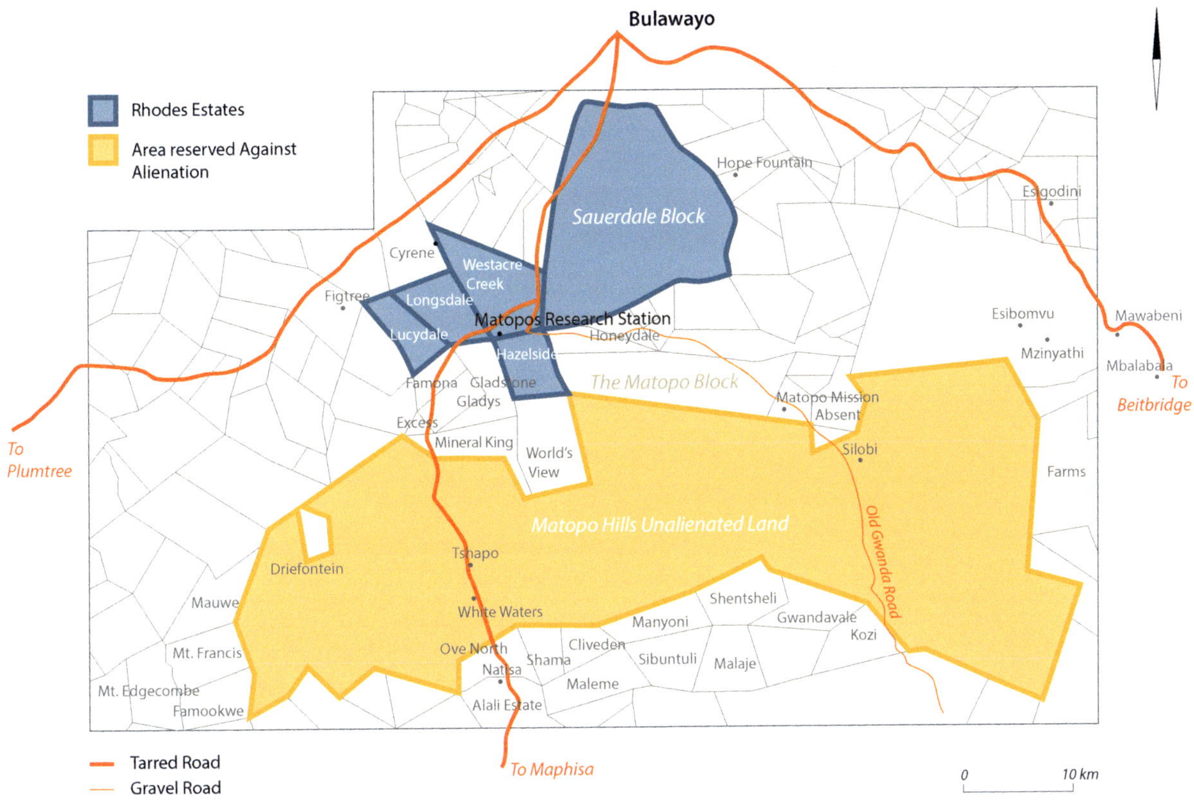

Fig. 5.1 A 1902 map of the Matobo Hills depicting a section of the area on which the national park was proposed. Surrounding the area is a subdivision of farms that were appropriated by the Europeans from the late19th century onwards (modified after Ashton 1981).

began to develop a plan to establish a national park which would encompass approximately one hundred thousand morgen of land (Nobbs 1920, 1924). The area proposed for a national park not only covered the whole of unclaimed land but also nine farms that had either not been claimed or had been returned to the BSACo as they were considered to be unsuitable for any agricultural pursuits in the Matobo Hills (Nobbs 1920; Ashton 1981, 5) (Fig. 5.1).

According to Nobbs (1920), the primary reason for establishing a national park in the Matobo Hills was for recreational purposes while the scientific research was of secondary importance. The development of the national park, as perceived by Nobbs, would be based on models such as the Yellowstone National Park in the United States of America, the National Reserve in the Blue Mountains in New South Wales in Australia, and the Mont aux Sources National Park in South Africa. In his plan, Nobbs proposed a national park in which "... the public could come and tour, trek or tramp according to their tastes and means, camp or stay at hotels and enjoy unique scenery and surroundings such as cannot be found in quite the same form or degree elsewhere in Africa" (Nobbs 1924, 65). Despite this grand plan by Nobbs, the Board of the BSACo initially rejected his proposal but later accepted it when Drummond Chaplin, who was the administrator of the Matobo Hills at that time, explained to the BSACo Board in 1920 that if the national park was to be established, the public could actually enjoy viewing areas of interests when roads and paths were properly developed (Ashton 1981). This approval did not, however, immediately culminate in the establishment of the park due to lack of funds and, perhaps, interest by the government. It was in 1926 that 224 000 acres (90 652 hectares) of land that adjoined Rhodes' estates of World's View and Hazelside was reserved for the purpose of establishing a national park and a game reserve

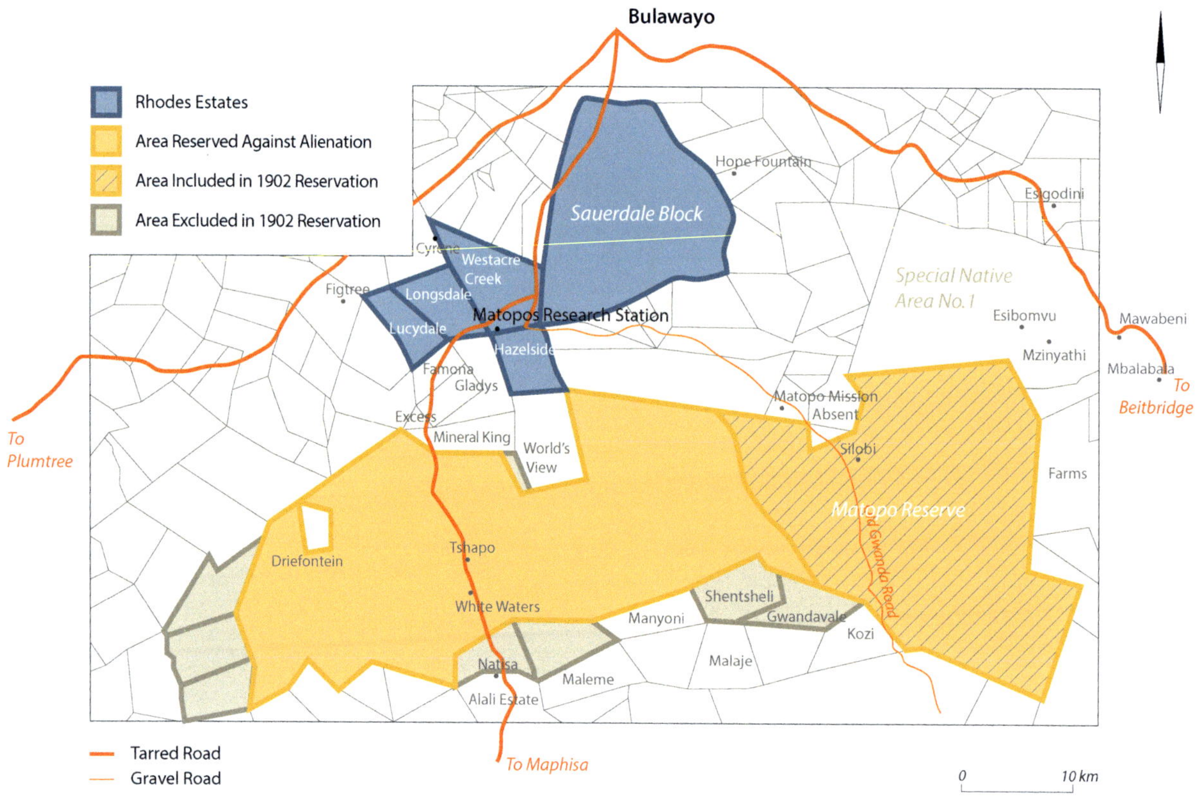

Fig. 5.2 A map of the national park in 1930. A number of farms were incorporated into the national park while the eastern portion of the Hills was omitted as Matopo Reserve (modified after Ashton 1981).

under the Game and Fish Preservation Act (Murray 1946; Grobler 1976). Following the proclamation, the section of the Hills on which the national park was established was left unmanaged and, as a result, several local indigenous communities began to settle in the national park while others began to also settle south and north of the area between 1924 and 1934 (Ashton 1981). As explained in the previous chapter, a number of local indigenous communities had permanently settled in the section on which the national park was declared during the 1896/7 war. A letter written by the Director of the Matopos School of Agriculture indicated that, by 1933, there were approximately 3000 people now living in the section of the Hills on which the national park was declared (Grobler 1976).

The Europeans who had already begun to administer the national park began to perceive the increase of local indigenous communities in the Matobo Hills and their traditional agricultural practices as abuse of the natural landscape. The forestry, irrigation, and natural resources departments began to invoke their legislations and prepare reports which stated that the local indigenous communities were indiscriminately cutting down trees as a result of their unscientific agricultural practices in the area. These reports also indicated that the cutting down of trees was resulting in the disappearance of wild animals from the Hills and was additionally spoiling the natural beauty of the entire landscape (Irrigation Department 1949; Ashton 1981). For these and other reasons, some of which are discussed below, and as argued by Ranger (1999), European notions of management began to dictate that the Matobo Hills must be preserved rather than used and that science was required to save the plants and wildlife from the aggression of local indigenous communities and their lack of sympathy. As a result, in 1930, the national park was re-proclaimed under the same Act, and its size was increased to 233 500 acres from 224 000 acres (Fig. 5.2). The re-proclamation of the national park was, retrospectively, a way of reaffirming its status which, according to the Europeans, was being threatened by the continuous entry of the local indigenous communities into the Hills.

SAVING THE MATOBO HILLS THROUGH SCIENTIFIC CONSERVATION

The concern about the increase of human population and livestock as well as the need to protect the Matobo Hills, however, stimulated a series of studies whereby the general objectives were to determine the maximum population size of people and animals that could be indefinitely sustained considering the food, habitat, water, and other resources available in the cultural landscape. The studies were also aimed at establishing the extent to which the Hills were being degraded by the local indigenous communities and their stock. As will be discussed, the eventual eviction of the local descent communities from a section of the Hills where the national park was established was extensively based on the results of these studies which are explored below.

The Adhoc Committee Survey

The first study was conducted by an Adhoc Committee. Adhoc Committees had been formed in the country to investigate if the existing local indigenous community areas had sufficient arable and grazing land, water, and timber. These Adhoc Committees consisted of the Provincial Native Commissioner, who was the chairman of the Committee, and two members of the Committee who were the Native Commissioner of the District and a nominee of the Director of Native Agriculture. The Committees were further required to precisely relate the type of areas on which the local indigenous communities lived in each district in terms of the land categories that the entire country was divided into:

1. Native Reserves
2. Native Purchase Areas
3. Those living in Crown Land who might be removed
4. Those living on European alienated land paying rent to the owner
5. Those living under labour agreements on European owned land
6. Unauthorised squatters on any land other than the Native Reserve or Native (Purchase) Area
7. Unassigned Area
8. Forest Area
9. Undetermined Area
10. Mission Area (Bhebe 1989, 22-23).

The study in the Matobo Hills was initiated by a group of Europeans who were concerned with the way the local indigenous communities were exploiting the area. Following a bitter complaint in 1933 by the Department of Agriculture on what it described as the high level of timber cutting, overgrazing, and uncontrolled cultivation by the local indigenous communities living in the Hills, the Adhoc Committee began its survey in 1944 (Lightfoot n.d). Subsequent to the investigation, the Adhoc Committee established that approximately 67 200 acres (30%) of the Matobo Hills was solid granite which was considered as waste land. Only 44 800 acres (20%) of the area was, however, regarded as suitable arable land while 112 000 acres (50%) was deemed to be suitable for grazing. This research, however, was later regarded as not comprehensive and conclusive. Therefore, it was decided that a new wide-ranging study be conducted that would establish the number of people and animals and the extent to which the Hills were being degraded. Decisions on how the Hills were to be administered in the future were going to be made on the basis of the outcome of the new study.

The Johan, H. Grobler Survey

The new research, which was carried out by Grobler, began in 1945 when Charles Murray, who was the Administrator and Pasture Officer for the Matobo Hills at that time, asked him to carry out the study. In this study, Grobler, who had just joined the national park as its first ranger, was asked to determine the following: (1) the number of males, females, and children living in the section of the Hills that was proclaimed as a national park; (2) the number of cattle, donkeys, sheep, and goats; (3) the total acreage of land suitable for farming purposes (arable and grazing land including vleis); (4) the total acreage of all arable land located away from vleis and where no degradation could be caused by cultivation; (5) the total acreage under cultivation in sections of the park where land should not be ploughed such as vleis; (6) the extent to which soil erosion has occurred and has affected the sponges and flow of streams and rivers; (7) the extent to which the area was overstocked and overpopulated; and (8) the suitability of the area for the construction of small weirs and dams (Ashton 1981).

To facilitate the study, Grobler either walked or rode a horse as he collected data in the field with the help of an interpreter. The results of the research were presented by Murray in 1946 and showed that there were 1 752 males, 1 559 females, and 4 327 children living in the area on which the national park was proclaimed. Of the 1 752 males, 1 042 were married while the remainder were either young men or aged persons living with their parents and relatives. The survey results also revealed that there were 11 399 cattle, 1 363 donkeys, 1 974 sheep, and 3 520 goats in the section of the Hills on which the park was proclaimed. Murray also reported that the high numbers of livestock in the park was causing overgrazing, and the numerous footpaths that were created by livestock as they grazed was also developing into gullies during the rainy seasons (Murray 1946).

Of the 224 000 acres of the park, only 60 499 acres (27%) were reported to be suitable for farming and, of these 60 499 acres, 11 785 acres (20%) of the land were considered to be vleis. Of the 11 785 acres of land, 2 457 acres (21%) were reported to be lands that were being cultivated by the local indigenous communities. The survey results also showed that, in addition to the 2 457 acres that were being cultivated, 6 260 acres were also under cultivation in sections of the park that were not vleis. Only 741 acres of arable land was not cultivated. The total acreage of arable land in the park, therefore, was 7 001 acres of which 6 260 acres were under cultivation. The 7 001 acres, which was only 20% of the 60 499 acres, was also considered to be suitable for farming. The remainder of the area consisting of granite ranges and kopjes covering 163 301 acres was considered to be useless for the purposes of either agriculture or grazing livestock (Murray 1946).

In this report, the local indigenous communities' traditional practices of farming were considerably criticised for causing the siltation of wet lands, streams, and rivers which originate from the Matobo Hills. Of particular concern was the increasing degradation of the Hills as an important water catchment area for European farms and communal lands situated south of the area (Murray 1946). Some of the areas that were reported to have been affected by the siltation of watercourses were Khumalo, Matopo, Tshatshani, Semukwe, Mbongolo, Gwaranyemba, Machuchuta, and Maramani (Lightfoot 1980a). It was necessary, according to Murray (1946), to immediately take measures to prevent further cultivation and overgrazing in the national park in order to save the Hills by conserving the water that was benefiting neighbouring areas south of the cultural landscape. Murray thus recommended the removal of 1 349 (77%) families and 9 771 (71%) livestock from the section of the Hills on which the national park was declared. Only 403 families and 4 030 livestock, which was considered to be enough for the carrying capacity of the park, were to remain in the area but under very strict conservation control (Table 5.1). The remaining families, as argued by Murray, would not only help manage the park but would also be an extra attraction to the tourists visiting the Hills. Additional land, however, was going to be needed elsewhere to relocate the excess families and their livestock. Murray also reported that the Matobo Hills were only suitable for livestock production and not for any other agricultural use since the soil was infertile and rainfall was low and erratic. He further recommended that the growing of maize and other grain crops should be discontinued as this caused soil erosion in the Hills. To prevent soil erosion and the growth of gullies, Murray further recommended that reclamation work should be performed in

	Present	Future	Number to be removed	Percentage to be removed
Native population	1 752	403	1 349	77%
Livestock population	13 801	4 030	9 771	71%

Table 5.1 Summary of people and animals in the park in 1945 and the numbers and percentages that were recommended by Charles Murray to be removed from the national park area (after Murray 1946).

areas where families were to be removed. He also recommended the construction of dams, dip tanks, and roads in the park, and these recommendations were to be implemented over a period of five years beginning in1946 (Murray 1946).

The proposal to displace a number of families from the Matobo Hills and the Europeans' disregard and ignorance of local cultural norms of managing the landscape infuriated the majority of the local indigenous communities. The situation, however, led to resentment and rivalry of identities which coincided with a racial division between Africans and Europeans related to the land: the Europeans regarding the natural landscape and the local indigenous communities the soil (Wels 2003). During the 1890s, the contradiction of ideas for managing the Matobo Hills and how to exploit them had actually led to open violence. Soon after the overthrow of the Ndebele State in 1893 by the BSACo, there was an ecological disaster of a prolonged drought, rinderpest, and locusts in the Matobo Hills and the rest of the Matabeleland region.

Consultations from the shrine priests revealed that these disasters were caused by the Europeans who had dominated the land and introduced alien laws and practices for managing the cultural landscape. Between 1896 and 1897, a war developed in Matabeleland and Mashonaland that was intended to remedy the calamity by fighting and forcing the non-indigineous people from the land. In the Matobo Hills, the war resulted in the killing of Europeans, and this eventually forced Rhodes to negotiate for a peace settlement during which time he is believed to have made promises to the local chiefs (Izinduna) as part of the agreement to end the war (Fig. 5.3). According to Ranger (1999), officials who participated in the negotiations contend that Rhodes made three promises to influential individuals and to local chiefs. The alleged promises included protecting the interests of local indigenous communities in the Hills; securing occupation of flat land for local indigenous communities if they emerged from the Hills "into the open", and that the majority of them would remain in the Hills undisturbed. Based on these assurances, the local indigenous communities agreed to end the war, and they hoped to be permanently settled in the lands that were provided and continue to farm and protect their shrines and lands using the traditional conservation practices as before. They also trusted and hoped that Rhodes' promises would be kept and fulfilled. However, the major problem of these promises was that they were never put in writing and, as indicated below, were later rejected by the European authorities when the local indigenous communities began to use them as support against their eviction from the Matobo Hills. As Ranger (1999) states, this idiom of orality later created enormous complications when the local indigenous communities attempted to use Rhodes' promises to fight expulsion from the Matobo Hills between the 1940s and 1960s. In 1946 when the local indigenous communities were first asked to be moved from the Matobo Hills to make way for the development of the national park as was recommended by Murray, they began to protest against the eviction. Their refusal to be moved from the Hills was partially based on the fact that they were traditionally and spiritually attached to the area. The plan to evict them from the Hills and from the national park, however, was designed to be in accordance with the dominant policy of the period which was preservation of national parks without human habitation and sometimes without the acknowledgement of the historic occupation of the areas (see also Meskell

Fig. 5.3 The brass-relief over the Fife Street entrance to the Bulawayo Municipal Offices depicting the first of the four indabas (meetings) held in the Matobo Hills between 21 August and 13 October 1896 when Rhodes and his small party met the Ndebele traditional leaders (Photo by Author).

2012). The local indigenous communities, however, resisted attempts to have their families evicted from the park and instead petitioned the government to establish a Commission of Enquiry to investigate the issue. By asking for a Commission of Enquiry, they had hoped that the government would correctly judge that they had a legal right to live in the Matobo Hills as was promised by Rhodes. However, without presenting an explanation and perhaps because of lack of funding, the government declined to form a Commission of Enquiry which resulted in protracted negotiations between the European administrators of the park and the local descent communities who were represented by a Bulawayo law firm. The negotiations, which later collapsed, forced the local indigenous communities to revert to their original plan of asking the government to set up a Commission of Enquiry. The much anticipated appeal was ultimately granted in 1949 when the Commission of Enquiry was finally established and led by Max Danzinger, a government official (Ashton 1981).

The Danzinger Commission Survey

The terms of reference, which were published in the government Gazette of 18th February 1949, stated that the Danzinger Commission was to:

(1) enquire into the origin and history of the occupation by the Ndebele people of the crown land known as the Matopos park; (2) examine whether it was necessary in the public interest that the said natives be moved from the said land; having due regard to (a) the de facto establishment of a national park, (b) the conservation of the natural resources of the said park, and (3) if the commissioners find that the movement of said natives from said land is necessary in the public interest, to make recommendations of the land to which they considered the natives should be moved.

To carry out a broad investigation of the issues concerned, the Danzinger Commission visited various parts of the Matobo Hills that were inhabited by the local indigenous communities. To help investigate the extent to which the Hills were being degraded by these communities and their livestock, a special committee comprised of six government officials was also appointed. Between the 16th and 24th of March 1949, the Danzinger Commission also held public sessions at the High Court in Bulawayo which were attended by more than 250 local indigenous communities. Additional sessions were held in Harare on the 18th of April and on the 13th of May of the same year (Danziger Commission 1949). The investigation by the Danzinger Commission established that, prior to the 1896-7 war, the area which was later declared the national park was sparsely populated by the Kalanga, Rozvi, and a few Ndebele people. According to the Danzinger Commission, the Ndebele only settled in the park area in enormous numbers just before and during the 1896-7 war when they had turned the Matobo Hills into their fortress. Prior to that time, the Ndebele were reported to be living in various settlements immediately north of the Matobo Hills. It was on the condition that they end the war that Rhodes invited

Reserve	Acreage	Families	Livestock	Capacity	
				Families	Livestock
Matopo	121 594	1 900	6 900	820	4 920
Shashani	55 500	1 040	4 000	531	3 200
Semokwe	288 070	3 180	15 296	2 613	15 680

Table 5.2 Shows the extent to which the Matopo, Shashani, and Semokwe reserves were overpopulated and overstocked in 1949 (after Danzinger Commission 1949).

some of the Ndebele chiefs and their subjects to live on farms he had recently purchased that were situated between the Matobo Hills and Bulawayo. These farms, some of which still have their original names, were Sauerdale Block, Westacre Creek, Longsdale, Lucydale, and Hazelside.

Although the local indigenous communities provided oral evidence during the court sessions in Bulawayo that they were allowed to live permanently on Rhodes' estates, the Danzinger Commission soundly rejected their claims as it argued that there was no proof of any promise made by Rhodes or by the BSACo that the farms were exclusively given to them to live in perpetuity. In its report, the Danzinger Commission argued that in his last Will, Rhodes actually gave his properties to the Trustees of the BSACo to use as experimental farms, and there was no reference in the Will as to the rights of the local indigenous communities to permanently live on the farms (see also Lightfoot 1980b). The Danzinger Commission's opinion was that the actual reasons why Rhodes invited them to live on his farms were to have the discontented chiefs live in one area so that their activities could be monitored and to also provide labour on the European farms (Danziger Commission 1949).

However, although the Danzinger Commission had argued that the Ndebele people were not the original occupants of the Matobo Hills, a considerable difference of opinion existed between its report and that of Grobler on the number of people living in the area. During its investigations, the Danzinger Commission approximated that 8 500 people were living in the Matobo Hills at that time. It was also estimated that these people possessed about 16 000 livestock units. Based on these figures and on past survey reports, the Danzinger Commission concluded that the area was overpopulated and overstocked. This was reportedly causing soil erosion and degradation of the entire landscape. As with the Grobler study, the Danzinger Commission also concluded that soil erosion was affecting the perennial flow of streams and rivers which was subsequently depriving water to non-indigineous farms and communal areas located adjacent the Matobo Hills (Danziger Commission 1949).

According to the findings of the Special Committee, of the 233 500 acres comprising the national park, only 72 385 acres was habitable, and 14 477 acres were vleis. The special committee also established that 49 222 acres were purely grazing land while 8 686 acres were arable land. The rest of the land consisting of kopjes and dwalas covering 161 115 acres was considered as useless for any agricultural pursuit (Special Committee 1949). Based on the findings of the Special Committee, the Danzinger Commission recommended that at least 500 families could be allowed to settle on 8 686 acres of arable land with a maximum of 4 000 livestock. Their security of tenure in the park, however, would be based on the condition that they were original inhabitants of the area and that they would observe the conservation guidelines established by the new administrators of the Hills. Each remaining family was thus entitled to 8 acres of land and 8 livestock units which would graze on 15 acres of land. The Commission further recommended that the remaining families and their

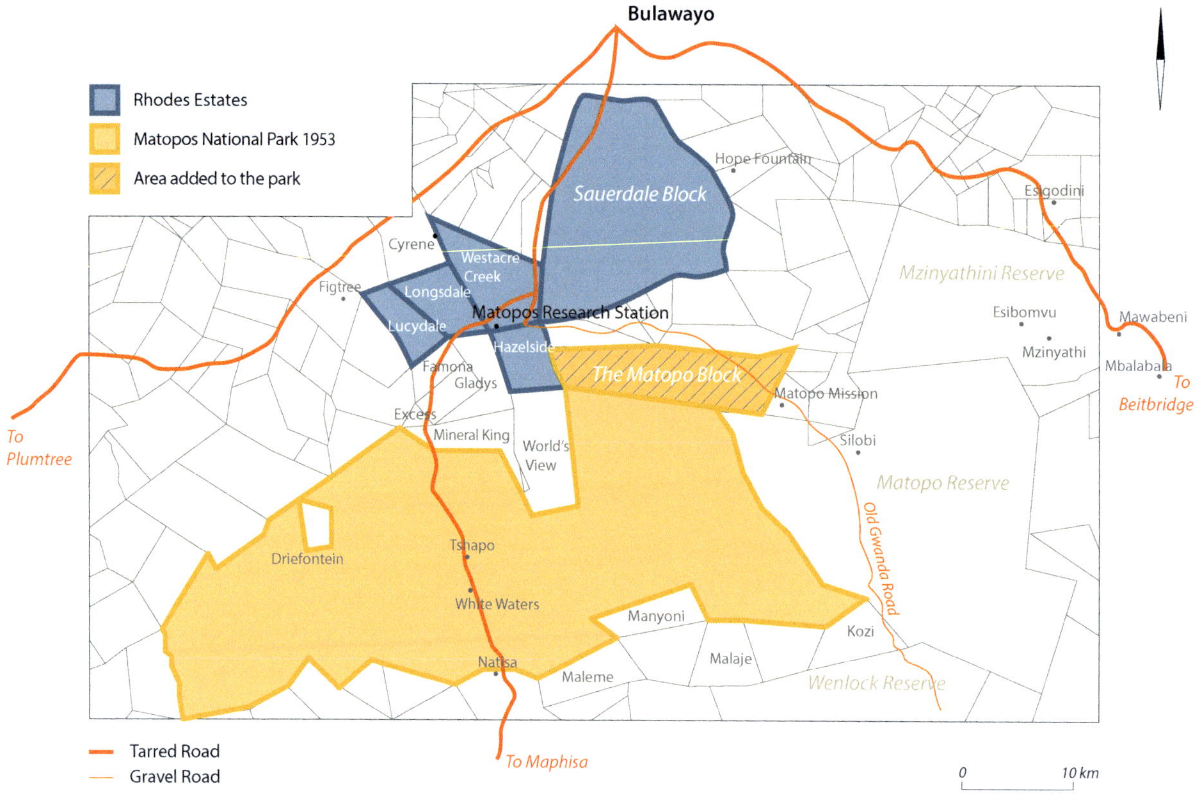

Fig. 5.4 A map depicting the proclaimed Federal National Park in 1953 whose size was enlarged by merging it with the Matopo Block Farm (modified after Ashton, 1981).

livestock be removed from the park area and be relocated to any suitable area in the Matabeleland region. Similar to the recommendation made by Murray in 1946, this exercise was going to be accomplished over a period of five years (Danziger Commission 1949).

Following the decision to evict excess families and their livestock from the national park, the Danzinger Commission's next task was to recommend the possible land to which the local indigenous people and their animals could be relocated. The initial enquiry from the Matobo District Native Commissioner of land that was not occupied showed that the Matopo, Shashani, and Semokwe reserves were already overpopulated and overstocked (Table 5.2). Further search for land by the Danzinger Commission also revealed that the Wenlock Block (165 000 acres) situated south of the Hills was also overcrowded at that time. The only possible area to which the families could be relocated was Prospect Ranch (134 290 acres), which adjoined the Semokwe reserve south of Gwanda. However, even though the area was considered not suitable for resettlement as it received very little rainfall, the Danzinger Commission made proposals that the government could buy the land, sink boreholes, and resettle at least 900 families on the farm. It was also recommended that no less than 140 families could join the 30 families already living in the Matopo Block (11 500 acres) situated just north east of the Hills. It was also suggested that the remaining 460 families be moved to farms which bordered the national park if the government could buy them. These farms were Mount Edgecombe to the west and Alalie, Ove South (later known as Canton Villa), Maleme, Manyani, Sibuntuli, Malaje, and Kozi to the south. Although these farms were claimed, they were not occupied and were used for farming and grazing by the few local descent people that were living on them. Alternatively, the remaining families were to be accommodated in Absent Farm which was situated east of the Hills and adjoining the national park (Danziger Commission 1949).

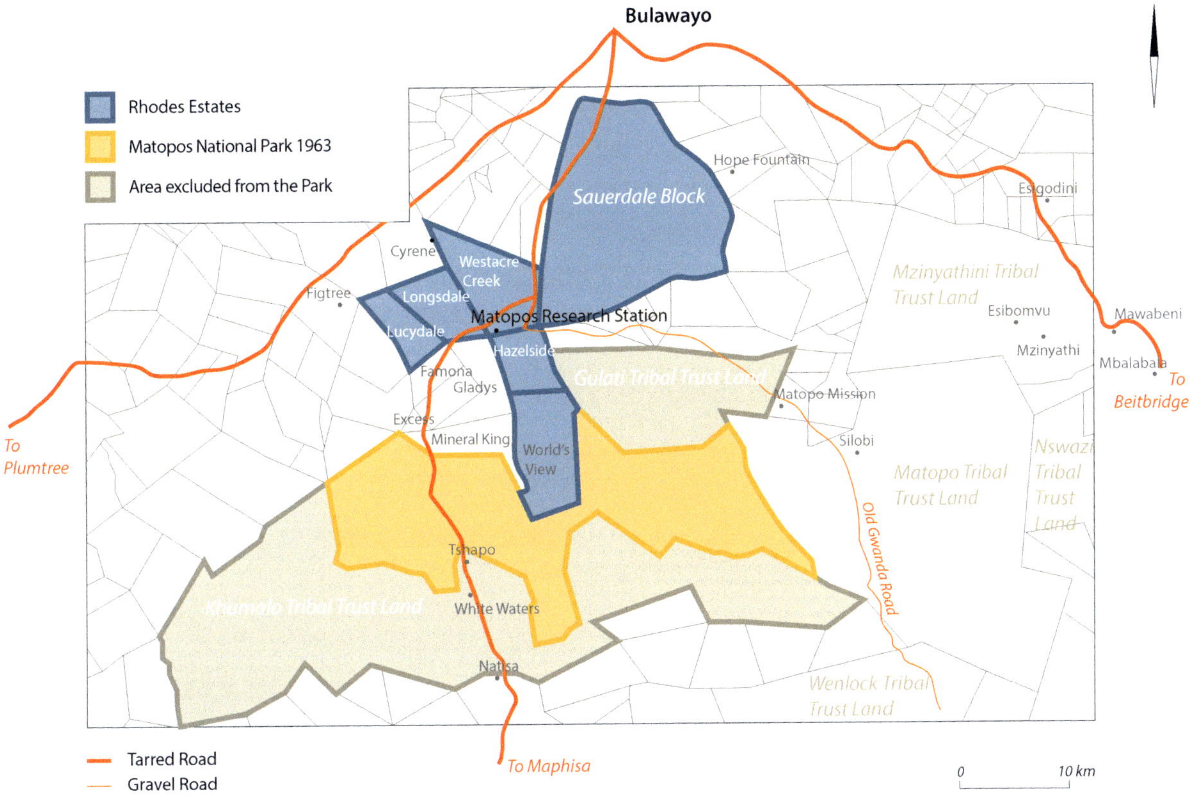

Fig. 5.5 A map showing the national park and areas that were excluded from it in 1963 (modified after Ashton 1981).

EVICTION OF THE LOCAL INDIGENOUS COMMUNITIES FROM THE NATIONAL PARK

When the government enquired about the availability of the farms recommended by the Danzinger Commission to resettle the local descent communities, it found out that most of them were not for sale as their owners had plans to develop them at some point in the future. In August 1949, however, the government purchased Prospect Farm to resettle 900 families as was recommended by the Danzinger Commission. Plans were also tabled to relocate several families to the arid lands of Lupane and Wankie (now Hwange) in northern Matabeleland and Nuanetsi (now Mwenezi) in southern Matabeleland. Some families that relocated to the Mwenezi area were nicknamed amadingindawo (literally meaning, those who look for a place to live), a term which is still currently being used. The government had, in fact, failed to acquire farms that were near the Matobo Hills which would have enabled the resettlement of the families close to their traditional lands, and this would have maintained their spiritual attachment with the cultural landscape.

The constant threats to evict the local indigenous communities from the Hills that began in the late 1940s, had led to their unrest and hopelessness. When they realised that their grievances were not going to be addressed, they resorted to protests and passively resisted the removals by ignoring eviction notices. Directed by their chiefs and prominent individuals, they also held several meetings to discuss possible ways that would stop the European authorities from evicting them from their traditional lands. An option, which they attempted without success, was to send a delegation to the High Commissioner in South Africa or to the king of Britain to impede the evictions (Ranger 1999). While the local indigenous communities were scheming to find ways of stopping the evictions, the Rhodesian government was also busy amending the 1930 Land Apportionment Act

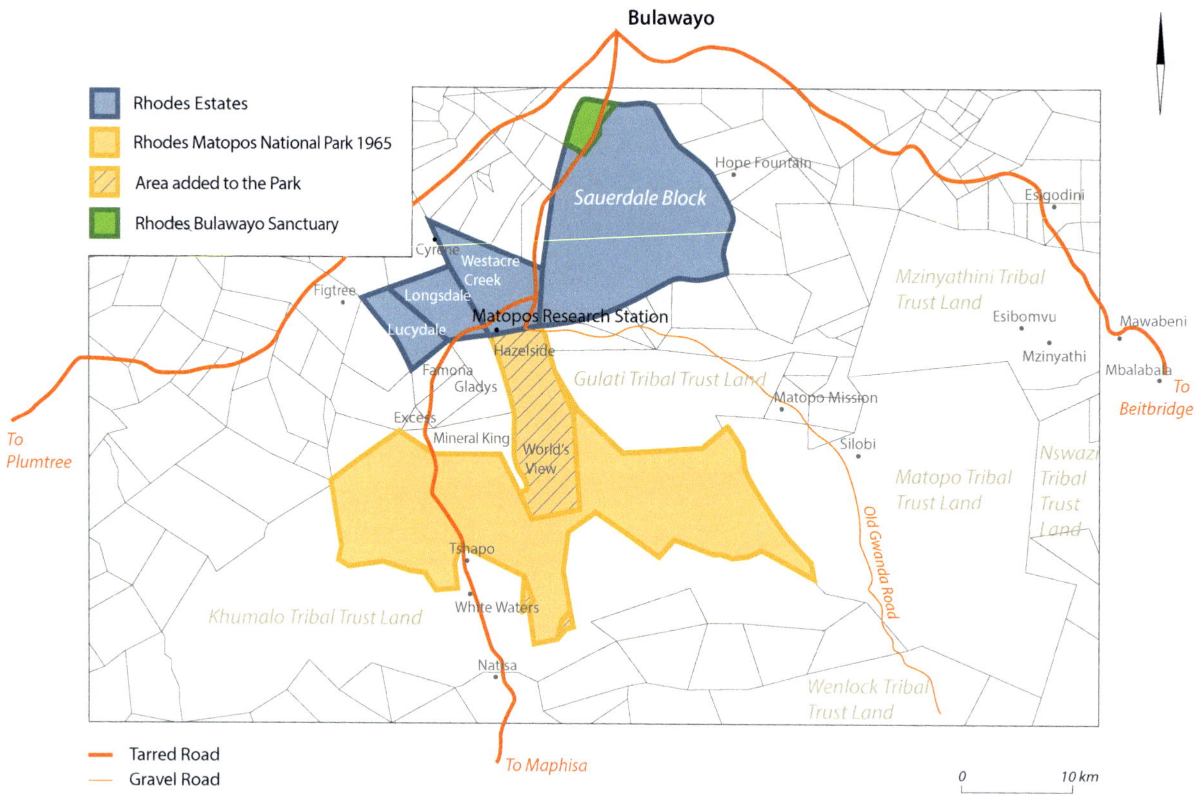

Fig. 5.6 A map illustrating the Matopos National Park in 1965 when two of Rhodes' estates were added, resulting in the renaming of the park as the Rhodes Matopos National Park (modified after Ashton 1981).

to include clauses that would make it feasible to enforce the evictions not only in the Matobo Hills but also in the rest of the country in areas that were now considered as European properties. This Act, as indicated in chapter 1, was intended to formalise legal separation of land between Africans and Europeans over the entire country. Between 1951 and 1952, the Act was amended to include a clause which specified that all Africans living on European land were to move into reserves within a period of six years (Kramer 1998).

In the Matobo Hills, as shown by Ranger (1999), remorseless evictions began to be effectively completed beginning in 1950 when 43 families volunteered to be relocated to the Prospect Farm while 140 families declined to be moved. In November of the same year, 17 more families were forcibly removed from the Matobo Hills to join the volunteers on the Prospect Ranch under the watchful eye of the British South Africa Police (BSAP). The BSAP had been formed as a paramilitary force in 1889 by the BSACo, from which it took its original name, the British South Africa Company's Police. Initially controlled directly by the company, it began to operate independently in 1896, at which time it also dropped "Company's" from its name. It served as the country's regular police force, retaining its name until 1980 when it was replaced by the Zimbabwe Republic Police (Gibbs, Phillips and Russel 2010). As Ranger further explained, from 1951 onwards, the evictions were also made possible by the passing of the 1951 Land Husbandry Act which was intended to enforce private ownership of land, destocking of livestock, and enforcing European conservation practices on local descent communities' traditional agricultural lands. In early 1951, more families received eviction notices from the local Native Commissioner. Subsequent to the notices, 210 families were removed from the national park to Prospect Ranch while a further 313 families were also forcibly removed from the Hills to the Lupane District in northern Matabeleland. In October of the same year, three kraal heads were also moved to

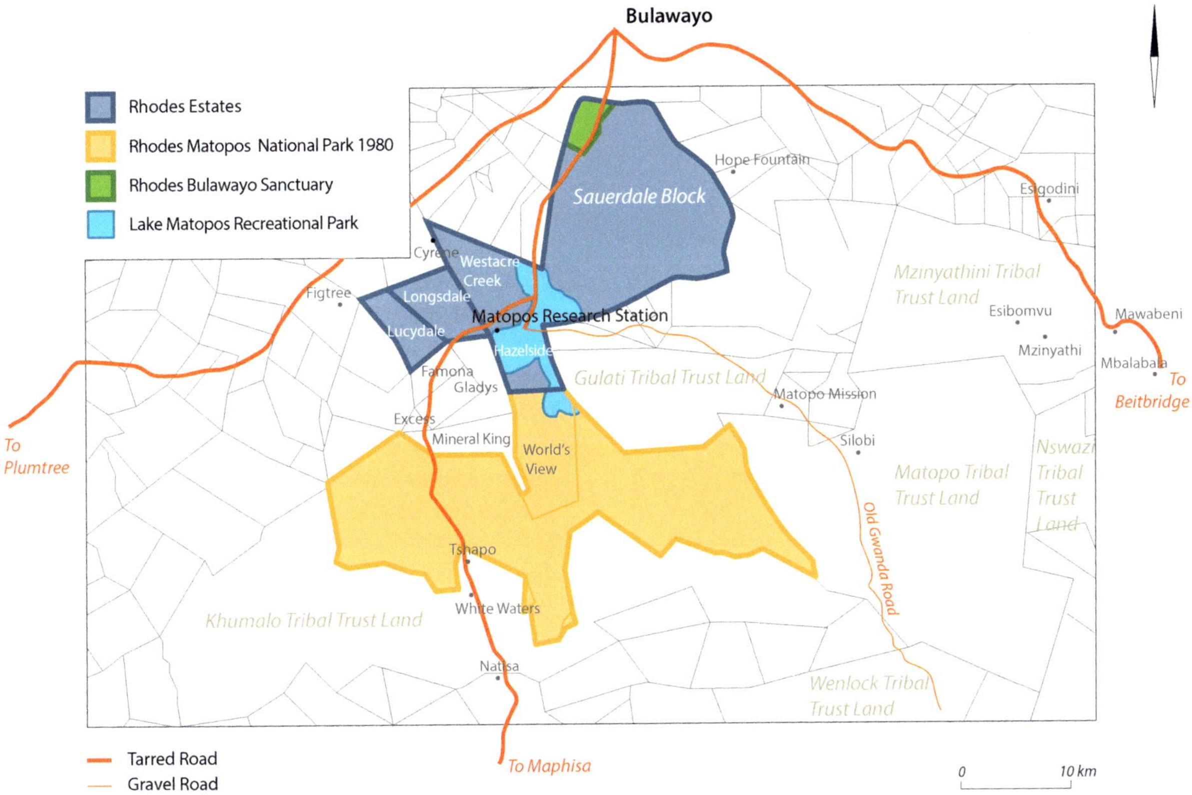

Fig. 5.7 A map of the Matopos National Park in 1980 showing the Tribal Trust Lands to which some of the local indigenous communities were finally resettled (modified after Ashton 1981).

the Prospect Farm. More evictions, however, were carried out in 1952 when 265 families were moved from the park to the Prospect Ranch while 150 more families were also relocated to Lupane. 268 families were also, at the same time, given notices of eviction. In September 1952, the police moved into the national park and in Whitewaters, an area which is located adjacent to the present national park, for a week of handcuffing and trucking more local indigenous communities to as far as the Hwange area (Ranger 1999).

Following the eviction of several families from the Hills, an area of 245 000 acres of land was re-proclaimed as a Federal National Park in 1953 (Fig. 5.4). This was in line with the colonial project of 1953 to amalgamate the colony of Southern Rhodesia (later Rhodesia and now Zimbabwe) and the territories of Northern Rhodesia (now Zambia) and Nyasaland (now Malawi) into an enormous and powerful economic unit in southern Africa. It was expected that the heightened visibility of the colony through the newly created Federation would promote trade and tourism in the country (Shutt and King 2005). One way of accomplishing this was through the development of national parks in the country. In the Matobo Hills, the size of the reproclaimed national park was thus enlarged as the Matopo Block Farm was merged with the park. During the same year, the department of national parks also took over from the irrigation department, which had run the park since 1946. Between 700 and 800 local indigenous families, however, were allowed to live in the park area but under very restrictive conservation conditions. This status quo remained until 1962 when it was decided to completely separate the different forms of conflicting land use in the park (Grobler 1976). The area was then divided into the picturesque core area of the Hills which became the national park while the rest of the area became Tribal Trust Lands (Ranger 1999). When the Federation collapsed in 1963, the park was further reproclaimed as the Matopos National Park and was reduced in size by 148.263 acres (Fig. 5.5). The remainder of the Hills was made available to the families who had remained in the park. In 1965, two of Rhodes' farms, specifically Hazelside and World's View, were added to the Matopos National Park, and it was renamed the Rhodes Matopos National Park (Fig. 5.6). The boundaries of the park which bordered non-indigenous farms in the north of the Hills were then fenced between 1965 and 1967 (Grobler 1976). Approximately 1 400 hectares of the western portion of the park, referred to as Whovi, had also been reserved for wild animals, and its southern section was subsequently fenced in as a game park in 1959. The original area of 1 400 hectares was enlarged to 2 600 hectares in 1967 and to the current 10 000 hectares in 1971 (Ashton 1981). A number of wild animals were then introduced, and this resulted in the replacement of the few remaining families who had continued to survive in the area. By introducing wildlife in the Whovi area, the park was thus converted into a wilderness, and its wildlife conservation value was enhanced and guaranteed (Makuvaza and Makuvaza 2012). In 1969, the Wildlife Commission recommended that there should be no cutting down of trees, livestock grazing, hunting, cultivation, or settlement in any national park in the country. These recommendations were later put into effect in the Parks and Wildlife Act of 1975 (Ranger 1999). These recommendations were also applied in the Rhodes Matopos National Park and, by the mid-1970s, the national park was completely reserved for tourists, most of which were of Caucasian descent, and wildlife (Lowry 2004; Maylam 2005). The entire national park was thus cleared of its human inhabitants regardless of whether they were original to the Hills or not. These families were settled in the communal areas of Gulati and Khumalo, which are now under the Matobo Rural District Council and in Nswazi, Matobo and Umzinyathini, which are also now under the Umzingwane Rural District Council (Fig. 5.7). Others were eventually settled as far away as Nkayi which is approximately 193 kilometers northeast from the Matobo Hills.

Following the eviction of the local indigenous communities and their livestock from the national park, comparative reports were made on the conservation of the park and the communal areas. These reports, however, were aimed at demonstrating that the park could be better managed and protected when there are no people living in it. In 1970, the Parks Commission reported that the natural beauty and vegetation of the park had now suffered less damage from human interference. Erosion scars were also reported to be in the process of healing while the basic scenic qualities of the park were now remarkably being preserved (Ashton 1981). In contrast, the condition of the communal lands neighbouring the national park were reported to be overpopulated and degraded. In Gulati and Khumalo, for example, stock numbers were reported to have doubled, and this was now causing overgrazing and soil erosion. Swamps were also reported to be drying up as a result of their continued use for market gardening (Lightfoot n.d).

The eventual establishment of the national park and the eviction of the local inhabitants from some sections of the Hills, however, meant that nature and culture was forcibly separated. The sharp and visible boundaries that were created were a sensitive expression of isolation of the local indigenous communities, and demarcating land created rival identities on either side of the borders (Makuvaza 2007). Although the size of the national park was reduced and parts of the Hills given to the local indigenous communities for settlement, the majority of the communities continued to demand that the park be further reduced in size or be completely abolished in order to provide more land for farming and for grazing their stock. When the evicted local indigenous communities realised that their grievances were not going to be addressed, they resorted to sabotage by destroying fences, poaching wildlife, setting fires in the park, and petrol bombing of Rhodes' grave (Ashton 1981; Ranger 1999). The bitterness, however, gradually worsened into national politics and later into a full-fledged war of liberation which was regarded as a civil war by the non-indigineous people (Fisher 2010). This does not mean that the war in Zimbabwe was caused only by the Matobo Hills local indigenous communities' anger over the appropriation of their land; this was however, one of the contributing factors to the war. The war, which began from the early 1970s and ended in 1980, was led by the Zimbabwe African People's Union (ZAPU) with its military wing, the

Zimbabwe People's Revolutionary Army (ZIPRA), under the leadership of Joshua Nkomo and by the Zimbabwe African National Union (ZANU) also with its military wing, the Zimbabwe African National Liberation Army (ZANLA), under the leadership of Robert Mugabe.

During the war, soldiers who engaged in guerrilla warfare in the Matobo Hills promised to abolish the national park and to resettle the indigenous people when the war was over. After the war and a victory by Robert Mugabe in the 1980 elections, the local indigenous communities in Matobo expected that the new ruling party and government would allow them to resettle in the national park and other parts of the Hills that were previously appropriated by the European settlers. After independence, however, the government failed to resettle the local indigenous communities and this, in part, resulted in civil fighting in the Matobo Hills and other parts of Matabeleland. The conflict is also believed to have been caused by forces loyal to Joshua Nkomo who could not accept the results of the 1980 elections. To suppress the conflict, the government deployed the police, Central Intelligence Organisation (CIO) personnel, and the hated North Korean trained Fifth Brigade army which resulted in the torture and death of many people in the Matobo Hills and other parts of the region (Eppel 2004). After nearly a decade of conflict, a unity accord was eventually signed between ZAPU and ZANU on 22 December 1987, and the new political party began to be known as Zimbabwe African National Union Patriotic Front (ZANU PF). Joshua Nkomo was elected as vice president of the country while several ZAPU politicians were given ministerial posts in the government thereby ending almost a decade of civil conflict.

THE LEGISLATION AND THE MANAGEMENT OF CULTURAL HERITAGE SITES IN THE MATOBO HILLS

In addition to appropriating land and establishing a national park, the Europeans had also begun to administer cultural heritage sites in the Matobo Hills. Through the introduction of legislation, the majority of the sites were subsequently proclaimed as national monuments. The designation, of which the primary purpose was to legally recognise sites of national significance, was aimed at protecting and developing some of them as tourist attractions in the Hills. The introduction of the legislation, however, as discussed below, also contributed partially to the elimination and disregarding of the local indigenous communities from traditionally managing their cultural heritage sites. This section will also demonstrate how the legislation weakened the local indigenous communities' involvement and capacity to manage the Matobo Hills through their traditional conservation practices as they did prior to the arrival of the Europeans in the area.

Formal laws to protect cultural heritage sites in the country were initiated when the Rhodesian Legislative Council enacted the Ancient Monuments Protection Ordinance in 1902 to stop European treasure hunters from mining dry stone ruins such as Rhodes had done when he formed a company called the Ancient Ruins Company. Dry stone wall sites such as Great Zimbabwe, Khami, Danan'ombe (Dhlodhlo) and others were, therefore, targeted for mining as they were falsely believed to be storage rooms for gold and other precious minerals (Mahachi and Ndoro 1997; Ndoro 2005).

While ruins had begun to be protected by law, it also became important to protect rock art sites from being destroyed by the Europeans who had developed an interest to study the hunter gatherer sites. The idea to protect rock art by means of legislation, however, appears to have also been significantly influenced by the introduction in South Africa of legislation that was aimed at protecting rock art from vandalism and theft (Ndoro 2005).

During the late 19th century and the first half of the 20th century, the interest to study rock art in South Africa had often resulted in the removal of panels which were then transported to newly established museums in the country and sometimes exported to certain European countries (Deacon 1993; Ndlovu 2005). In 1893, for example, Louis Tylor detached five paintings from Wildebeest Shelter in the Drakensberg Mountains which were later found in the Pitt Rivers Museum at Oxford University in

Britain (Vinnicombe 1966; Ward 1997). In 1910, several rock art panels were removed from Linton in the Eastern Cape and transported to the South African Museum in Cape Town for "safekeeping" (Deacon 1993). The rapid increase in the interest to study rock art, which had frequently resulted in the destruction of rock paintings, led to the enactment in 1911 of the Bushmen and Relics Protection Act in South Africa (Abrahams 1989). Although this Act required that a permit be obtained to export rock paintings or engravings, it was never effective in protecting rock art from being vandalised. The legislation also did not effectively halt the theft and wholesale export of rock art, therefore, this persisted in much of the 20th century (Deacon 1993). In Southern Rhodesia, a concern was raised following the theft and vandalism of rock art in South Africa that this unprofessional conduct would soon spread north of the Limpopo river and into the colony. To protect rock art from being vandalised, and following the South African example, the Southern Rhodesian Legislative Council also enacted the Bushmen Relics Ordinance in 1912. In this aspect, it may be argued that the protection of rock art in the Matobo Hills was very much in the forefront of those who promulgated the 1912 Bushmen and Relics Ordinance as the Hills were rapidly becoming popular for their distinctive rock art in the region and beyond. The enactment of this law was also influenced by the fact that the definition of ancient monuments was not initially included in the 1902 legislation (Ndoro 2005). Therefore, it was important to include the definition in the new legislation so that rock art sites could also be effectively protected by law.

In 1920, the Southern Rhodesia Legislative Council added a new law to protect monuments, vaults, tombstones, and graves. It could be construed that this law was enacted, to a very large extent, to protect the grave of Cecil John Rhodes which was later proclaimed as a national monument in the Matobo Hills (see also Muringaniza 2002). It would also seem that, by promulgating this law, the Rhodesian authorities had planned to protect other graves, vaults, and tombstones which would, in the future, be judged to be of national value for the country.

The improvement of the South African legislation seems to have persistently influenced the development of the legislation in the country. In 1923, a new law called the Natural Historical and Monuments Act was enacted in South Africa, and the old Bushmen Relics Protection Act of 1911 was repealed (Abrahams 1989; Deacon 1993). Following this development, the Rhodesian Legislative Council also repealed the 1902 and 1912 legislations, and these laws were replaced with a new and a comprehensive Act called the 1936 Natural Historical Monuments and Relics Act, CAP 64. The aim of this law was to provide for improved preservation of ancient, historical, and natural monuments, relics, and other objects of aesthetic, historic, archaeological, or scientific interest. In this Act, a monument was defined as (a) any area of land which is of archaeological or historical interest or contains objects of such interest; (b) any area of land which has distinctive or beautiful scenery or a distinctive geological formation; (c) any area of land containing rare or distinctive or beautiful flora or fauna; (d) any waterfall, cave, grotto, avenue of trees, old tree, or old building and; (e) any other object (whether natural or constructed by man) of aesthetic, archaeological, or scientific value or interest.

The new law also resulted in the establishment of the Commission for the Preservation of Natural and Historical Monuments and Relics, which was popularly known as the Monuments Commission and was headquartered in Bulawayo (Fothergill 1953). The Monuments Commission's mandate was to administer and implement the law. The 1936 Act, however, was later repealed and replaced with a new Act, CAP 313, after the Monuments Commission and the National Museums of Rhodesia were integrated in 1972 to establish the National Museums and Monuments of Rhodesia. Ndoro (2005) perceived this amalgamation as a positive development as it ensured that all cultural heritage sites must be categorised under a single administration. Chipunza (2005), however, saw the merger differently, arguing that the activities of the Monuments Commission to protect cultural heritage sites became limited as the inspection of monuments was no longer recognised as a profession. The new organisation was divided into five administrative regions and headquartered

No.	Name	Type of Monument	Government Notice	Year of Proclamation
4	World's View (Malindidzimu)	Historical	485	1937
7	Bambata Cave	Archaeological	485	1937
8	Nswatugi Cave	Archaeological	485	1937
19	Silozwane Cave	Archaeological	255	1938
20	Gulubahwe Cave	Archaeological	255	1938
29	World's View Farm	Archaeological	247	1939
39	Mzilikazi Memorial (Mhlahlandlela)	Historical	10	1942
41	Mzilikazi's Grave	Historical	469	1942
44	Mtshelele Valley Cave	Archaeological	541	1942
63	Rhodes Indaba Site	Historical	357	1949
78	Rhodes Summer House	Historical	75	1956
79	Rhodes' Stable	Historical	75	1956
71	Fort Umlugulu	Historical	622	1953
122	Amadzimba Cave	Archaeological	433	1969
116	Old Bulawayo	Historical	706	1966
133	Railway Terminus	Historical	523	1970
136	Orbicular granite site	Geological	985	1970
144	Mangwe Memorial	Historical	214	1972
159	Nanke (Manjenje) Cave	Archaeological	677	1976
47	Old Jesuit Mission	Historical	213	1943
50	Old Mangwe Fort	Historical	8	1945
83	John Lee's House	Historical	168	1957
87	Old Empandeni Ruins	Historical	4	1958
88	Fort Empandeni Earthworks	Historical	4	1958
97	Old Inyathi Mission Site	Historical	611	1959
89	Rhodes Hut	Historical	75	1958

Table 5.3 Cultural heritage sites that were proclaimed as national monuments within and near the Matobo Hills.

in Salisbury, and later Harare, and placed under the ministry of Internal Affairs. The organisation was then mandated to protect and present cultural heritage sites to the general public through museums. In Bulawayo, archaeological work by Neville Jones, a British missionary who was based at Hope Fountain, was then exhibited in the National Museum beginning from 1964 when it first opened to the public. In 1976, the 1972 Act was subsequently repealed and replaced with the National Museums and Monuments Act, CAP 313, which is now the NMMZ Act, CAP 25/11.

Although protective legislation was successfully introduced in the country, the recording and research of cultural heritage sites had already begun from as early as the 20th century. In the Matobo Hills, sites which were of interest to the European researchers were the caves and shelters in which rock art was painted by the hunter-gatherer indigenous communities. Nobbs (1924, 96) described these rock art sites as a "closed book to us... and once the key is found, the door of mystery may perhaps be partially opened behind which now lies hidden all knowledge of the social and religious notions of an ancient and primitive people". Thus, according to Nobbs, the sites were a promising field for research and required to be scientifically investigated.

With these words of encouragement by Nobbs, it did not take long before Arnold and Jones (1919) began to excavate and publish a report of their archaeological study of Bambata Cave, a rock art site located in the northern part of the Whovi area. Neville Jones, however, took further interest in studying the Stone Age of the Matobo Hills. He proposed the first local Stone Age sequence in the country (see Jones 1926). According to Walker (1995), the study of Bambata Cave by Arnold and Jones became so popular outside the country to the extent that overseas archaeologists began to arrive in the Matobo Hills to conduct additional research on rock art sites. As evidenced by their travelling long distances to study rock art in the Hills, the Europeans were most likely motivated by the lure of adventure and romance to explore a civilisation which they believed had long vanished. The arrival of Armstrong at the invitation of the University of Cape Town and the British Association for the Advancement of Science in the Matobo Hills led to the re-examination of Bambata Cave in 1929 (see Armstrong 1931). Subsequent to the re-examination of Bambata, an increasing number of excavations began to be conducted all over the country with the Matobo Hills now firmly established as the reference centre. This was also facilitated by the appointment of Jones as Keeper of Antiquities in the National Museum in Bulawayo (Walker 1995). Further archaeological work at Nswatugi Cave by Jones in 1930 led to the recovery of human remains that were dated to approximately 10 000 years, and this popularised the Matobo Hills as the country's cradle of humankind. From the 1950s onwards, Cran Cooke took over from Jones as the leading Stone Age archaeologist and began to also excavate Amadzimba, Pomongwe, and Tshangula Caves (see Cooke and Robinson 1954; Cooke 1963).

This research has revealed that it has become imperative that rock art sites be protected by law together with other important sites such as ruins, historic sites, and areas of scenic beauty as they were deemed to constitute a legacy that would be handed over to future generations. Accordingly, the Monuments Commission began to compile a list of rock paintings, ruins, historical sites, and locations of scenic beauty which were acquired through questionnaires distributed to non-indigineous farmers, mission stations, schools, native departments, and to the BSAP stations (Summers and Cooke 1959). A number of sites were located through publicity campaigns which were in the form of public lectures and television talk shows conducted by the members of the Monuments Commission. Some of the sites were also discovered through archaeological expeditions that were organised by the Matabeleland Rhodesian Schools Exploration Society (Armstrong 1929; Robinson 1961). Local descent communities were encouraged to report any sites that they knew existed in their village areas, however, in the Matobo Hills, the local indigenous communities refused to disclose some of their important sites to the Monuments Commission. According to Ranger (1999), while the Europeans were anxious to "discover" picturesque sites and paintings, they found resident elders very reluctant to allow their caves and shrines to become known and

Fig. 5.8 A brass plaque erected at World's View Hill in the Matobo Hills following the enactment of the Monuments and Relics Act in 1936. These plaques are still found at sites that are proclaimed as national monuments throughout the country today (Photo by Author).

even refused to provide information to their children who might have divulged the whereabouts of more secret places. Some sites that were found and whose values were considered to be of national importance were accordingly proclaimed as national monuments (see Table 5.3) and were then prioritised in terms of protection, research, and development. However, although important, the values of other sites were not considered to be of national importance, therefore, they were not prioritised for development.

Rock art sites were amongst some of the first cultural heritage sites to be proclaimed as national monuments in the country (Fothergill 1953). In the Matobo Hills, sites such as Silozwane, Bambata, and Nswatugi, which were also some of the significant shrines for the local indigenous communities, were then proclaimed as national monuments. Other rock art sites that were proclaimed as national monuments include Gulubahwe, Amadzimba, and Nanke. However, although Pomongwe and White Rhino are well known rock art sites in the Matobo Hills, these caves were never proclaimed as national monuments. In an email message of 26 January 2014, Paul Hubbard, a Zimbabwean archaeologist and an Associate Researcher in the Monuments and Antiquities Department at the Natural History Museum in Bulawayo, explained that the sites were probably not made national monuments because the rock art was of insufficient quality to justify their proclamation. He is of the opinion that the damage at Pomongwe during the 1920s had perhaps negatively impacted the aesthetic appeal for most visitors of the cave, and it was no longer impressive when compared with others that are found in the Matobo Hills (Hubbard, pers. comm., January 26, 2014). During the 1920s, experiments were conducted at Pomongwe with linseed oil as a preservative, and this darkened the paintings. White Rhino, on the other hand, was a public site, but damage from visitors and graffiti meant that it also lost its importance and could not, therefore, be proclaimed as a national

Registered Number	Name of Monument
1	Victoria Falls Reserve
4	World's View Hill-Matobo
9	Sinoia (Chinhoyi) Caves
10	Rhodes-Inyanga Estate
12	Pungwe Falls
29	World's View Farm-Nyanga
35	Chirinda Forest
42	Mtoa Ruins-Hwange
44	Mtshelele Valley Road Cave
46	Ewanrig Aloe Garden
51	Rupisi Hot Springs

Table 5.4 Monuments handed over to the National Parks Advisory Board in 1951 (Adapted from Makuvaza 2012).

monument. As further explained by Hubbard in the email, the Monuments Commission had also realised that the quantity of rock art sites in the Matobo Hills had far exceeded expectations, and it would have been impractical to proclaim all of them as national monuments (see also Fothergill 1953). Several smaller rock art sites such as Mtshelele, Matobo, and Buhwi were removed from the national monuments register during the 1950s because better sites had become known in the Matobo Hills. Sites that were deemed to be of historic significance began to be also proclaimed as national monuments. In the Matobo Hills, the World's View, King Mzilikazi and Rhodes' Graves, Rhodes' Indaba Site, Rhodes Summer House, Rhodes' Stable, Fort Umlugulu, and the Matopo Railway Terminus were all proclaimed as national monuments. Old mission stations that border the Matobo Hills such as Inyathi, Jesuit, and Empandeni were also declared national monuments. Most of these sites, however, were of colonial ancestry. According to Ndoro (2005), out of nearly 12 000 sites registered in the country, approximately 200 are of colonial ancestry and yet, of the 172 which are declared as national monuments, 143 of them

Registered Number	Name of Monument
2	Zimbabwe Ruins (Great Zimbabwe)
7	Bambata Cave
8	Nswatugi Cave
19	Silozwane Cave
20	Gulubahwe Cave

Table 5.5 Additional monuments transferred to the Parks Advisory Board after further agreement was made in 1961 and were to be co-managed by the Monuments Commission (Adapted from Makuvaza 2012).

are related to colonial history. The proclamation of these sites as national monuments was perhaps a way that Europeans could legitimise their presence in a cultural landscape where the majority of the people were local and indigenous to the area. It was also perhaps a way of asserting their identity and to institutionalise their administration of the Matobo Hills and the rest of the country.

Following the proclamation of several cultural heritage sites as national monuments, the Monuments Commission also began to mount photographic displays and erect brass plaques in suitable locations to notify the public that the sites were now formally protected by law (see Fig. 5.8). The mounting of photographic displays was also a way of presenting the sites to the public and to also promote tourism in the Hills. These displays were accordingly mounted at World's View, Old Bulawayo, Rhodes Summer House, and at the Government House in Bulawayo. In addition to the displays, small site museums and interpretive centres were also constructed at the foothills of Pomongwe and Nswatugi Caves. The information that is displayed in these site museums came from excavations that were performed earlier at Nswatugi by Jones during the 1930s and at Pomongwe by Cooke during the 1950s. By-laws were made and entrance fees were introduced to regulate access to the majority of the monuments in order to reduce their degradation by visitors. Excavations began to be regulated and penalties for contravening the provisions of the Act were also introduced. Activities such as archaeological excavations, alteration, defacing or removal, and exporting of an ancient monuments or relics were not permitted without the written consent of the Monuments Commission (Fothergill 1953).

Fig. 5.9 A member of the local indigenous community employed to look after Nswatugi Cave and Site Museum in the Matobo Hills, circa 1970 (Source: Monuments Department, Natural History Museum, Bulawayo).

During its early formation, the Monuments Commission had felt that the enactment of the legislation was not adequate for a comprehensive protection of sites in the country. Physical intervention, therefore, was required in cases where sites would collapse or were vandalised. An inspection program was established, and the work included conducting regular monitoring of all monuments including their maintenance and repair (Fothergill 1953). All national monuments and other sites were to be inspected at least once a year or more regularly when possible. The Monuments Commission also employed an inspector of monuments who was responsible for sites in the Matobo Hills and the rest of Matabeleland. Inspection reports, which outlined the conservation requirements of cultural heritage sites, were also introduced as a component of the program. However, much of the early conservation work was technical and unsystematic and only involved seasonal clearing of vegetation, restoration, and provision of access to the visiting public. This approach, however, focused more on the protection of physical elements of the sites while the protection of intangible aspects was, at that time, not of major concern (Pwiti 1997). A major challenge during the formative years of the Monuments Commission was insufficient staff and equipment to carry out maintenance work on proclaimed monuments and other sites. Following an agreement with the National Parks Advisory Board in 1951, Victoria Falls, Sinoa (now Chinhoyi) Caves, Rhodes-Inyanga Estate, Pungwe Falls, World's View Farm-Nyanga, Chirinda Forest, Mtoa Ruins-Hwange, Ewanrigg Aloe Garden, Rupisi Hot Springs, and the Zimbabwe Ruins (Great Zimbabwe) were temporarily transferred to the Parks Board for management. In the Matobo Hills, sites that were transferred to the Parks Board were the World's View and Mtshelele Valley Cave (Table 5.4). Additional monuments, the majority of which were in the Matobo Hills, were transferred to the Parks authorities after further agreement was reached in 1961. These sites included Bambata, Nswatugi, Silozwane, and Gulubahwe Caves which were to be co-managed by the Monuments Commission and the Parks Board (Table 5.5). The hope of the Monuments Commission was that these monuments would be transferred back in the future when adequate staff members were employed and more equipment was acquired. Great Zimbabwe, Bambata, Nswatugi, Silozwane, Mtshelele, and Gulubahwe Caves were returned in 1975, however, the remainder including Victoria Falls and Chinhoyi Caves remained under the current ZPWMA. As will be seen later in chapter 7, attempts to take over the management of Victoria Falls and some of the sites from the parks authorities by the NMMZ in recent years have caused considerable disputes between the two organisations which is affecting the management of the Matobo Hills. Many sites that were proclaimed as national monuments, especially those in the Matobo National Park, were subsequently fenced off while archaeological research continued in some of them. Fencing was one of the methods that the Monuments Commission had put into practice to protect the sites from being vandalised. The fencing of sites, however, only served to relegate the local indigenous communities who once used a number of them as centres for various cultural activities. The local indigenous communities, however, resisted fencing the vleis and shrines as their survival was hinged on the communities (Ranger 1999). Sign posts also began to be erected to provide directions for tourists who wished to visit the sites. This increased the number of visitors to the sites, even to some sites which were considered sacred by the local indigenous communities in the Matobo Hills. The archaeological research, which did not involve the local indigenous communities, and the erection of directional signs quickly resulted in the debasement of the sites. Sacred objects such as clay potsherds, bone tools, and ostrich egg shell beads were removed from Bambata, Pomongwe and Tshangula caves while human remains were also removed from Nswatugi in the name of archaeological research. Some of these objects were taken to the Natural History Museum in Bulawayo where they were publicly displayed.

To provide security at national monuments, the Monuments Commission also began to employ site custodians which were selectively chosen from members of the local descent communities (Fothergill 1953) for archaeological sites such as Silozwane, Nswatugi, Bambata, Pomongwe, and World's View Hill which resulted in locals monitoring the sites. These custodians were asked to put on traditional Ndebele war regalia and would wear an ostrich head gear, hold an ihawu (war shield), umkhonto (spear) and an induku (knob carry) to impersonate an ibutho (warrior) guarding a very important shrine (Fig. 5.9). While keeping these sites, the custodians themselves had also become objects of attraction to the inquisitive non-indigineous visitors of the Matobo Hills. By employing the custodians, the Monuments Commission had ironically substituted the traditional custodians that were appointed by the local indigenous communities to monitor the sites before the Hills were tamed by the Europeans.

The proclamation of sites as national monuments signified that the local indigenous communities were no longer able to freely manage or access shrines which were now regarded as government property. To access the sites, they were now required to go through bureaucratic state systems in order to obtain permission to use them. During the pre-colonial era, consent to access sites was directly sought and obtained from traditional leaders such as chiefs and shrine priests. The protective laws that were introduced in the Hills by the Europeans had left the local indigenous communities with only minimal or no control over the cultural sites which they had long considered as theirs. This disappointed them, therefore, they fiercely resented attempts to declare shrines outside the national park such as Njelele, Dula, and Zhilo as national monuments. Refusing attempts to proclaim these sites as national monuments, the local indigenous communities argued that they would care for them through traditional conservation practices as was the case before the arrival of the Europeans in the Hills (Makuvaza 2008).

The management of cultural heritage sites and the development of infrastructure, however, made the Matobo Hills a preferred tourist destination near the city of Bulawayo. The building of rest camps and hotels in 1902 as well as the construction of roads and a railway line from Bulawayo to the Matobo Hills in 1903 ensured that the cultural heritage sites and other scenic locations could now be easily accessed by a greater number of people. Recreational pursuits such as angling, sailing, bird watching, camping, photography, picnicking, rock climbing, and walking were also introduced to aid tourism in the Hills. As a result of these developments, excursions to the World's View became very popular with tourists from Bulawayo and from other parts of the country as well as the rest of southern Africa. In 1959, the World's View attracted 159 000 tourists and was second only to Lake Mcllwaine National Park, which is now Lake Chivero, located about 40 kilometres west of Harare. The graves at World's View Hill had become a place of memory and pilgrimage for the non-indigineous Rhodesians. The Whovi game park also became popular and, in 1973, received 205 000 visitors (Ashton 1981). The number of tourists visiting the Matobo cultural landscape, however, began to increase every year, and the Hills became the third largest tourist attraction in the country after Victoria Falls and Great Zimbabwe. The Matobo National Park was thus successfully converted into a playground to photograph and barbecue meat (Ranger 1999; Wels, 2003).

POST COLONIAL MANAGEMENT OF CULTURAL HERITAGE SITES IN THE MATOBO HILLS

After independence, the local indigenous communities living in communal areas around the national park made efforts to return and settle in sections of the Matobo Hills from which they had been evicted during the colonial period as they felt that they needed to return and settle in the ancestral lands where they were born and where their forefathers were buried (Ashton 1981). Through their traditional leaders, they began to complain that the establishment of the national park during the colonial period had taken much of their land, and they were not benefiting from the protection of the Hills and conservation of the cultural heritage sites (Ranger 1999). They further complained that the protection of the Hills and the management of cultural heritage sites was a luxury that the country could not afford and must be relinquished for practical development from which they could also benefit. In addition, they also felt that there was a need to fulfil the promises that had been made by the soldiers that the park would be abolished and given to them when the war was over (Makuvaza and Makuvaza 2012). The local indigenous communities also wanted the stringent laws which protected the Hills to be relaxed or even removed and replaced with the traditional conservation practices that would allow them to access and use their traditional shrines as was the case before the colonial period. According to Ranger (1999), there was some reason to believe that, in the new Zimbabwe, the populist interest was going to win over environmentalists or non-indigineous farmers who were continuing to farm in areas around the Matobo Hills. However, contrary to their expectation, the new Zimbabwean government began to consolidate state institutions and legislations to govern national parks and game reserves in the country. ZAPU members who were now holding political posts in the new Zimbabwean government and representing the Matobo area began to explain to the local indigenous communities that the national park and the game reserve could not be abolished as they were important not only for indigineous people but also for the country for tourism reasons (Ashton 1981; Ranger 1999).

While the local indigenous communities were pressing diligently to return to their ancestral lands, the methods used to manage cultural heritage in the Matobo Hills were also not changing as they expected after independence. The displays that were mounted in site museums such as at Pomongwe and Nswatugi Caves were never reviewed to reflect the local indigenous communities' views and knowledge about how the Hills were traditionally managed. Thus, following independence, the presentation of major monuments in the Matobo Hills had largely remained targeted at non-indigeneous foreign tourists. As Ranger argued, even after independence, the imperatives of international tourism have ensured that the Matobo Hills presented much the same symbolic face as they did under the settler rule (Ranger 1999). The national park, therefore, continued as a "wilderness" area for tourists while the previous history of settlement by the local indigenous communities, farming, and traditional management of the entire Matobo Hills area continued to be disregarded (Ranger 1996; Makuvaza and Makuvaza 2012).

In the early 1990s, a masterplan for the conservation, management and presentation of national monuments in Zimbabwe was developed by UNESCO for the government of Zimbabwe. This plan was to encourage growth of tourism in Zimbabwe, thereby increasing the economic benefits derived from the monuments. In addition to the cultural and educational importance of the preservation of a country's archaeological heritage, there was also a realisation that the past is a commodity which can be marketed to the public as a way of generating revenue through entrance fees, selling of souvenirs and refreshments. Among other things, the masterplan was also aimed at improving the quality of life in the surrounding rural areas in which most of the monuments are located (Collet 1992).

Following the doner's conference that was held in July 1992, various projects were kick started in the country after the Zimbabwean government endorsed the NMMZ's masterplan document for the

Fig. 5.10 Local indigenous people, mostly from Silozwe and Gulati communal lands, selling souvenirs and crafts at EJikweni turnoff to the World's View Hill in the Matobo National Park.

development of archaeological heritage. The plan involved the selection of monuments in the country, which were ranked in terms of their educational significance and their potential to generate revenue through local and international tourism. The development programs were designed in such a way that they would consider local sensitivities and cultural needs as an important part of the effort not to alienate cultural heritage management from the people to whom it belongs (Pwiti 1997). The Shona Village at Great Zimbabwe, Dambarare, Jumbo Mine, Domboshava rock art site, Khami, Old Bulawayo and various monuments in the Matobo Hills were identified as some of the monuments that required developement. Of these monuments, Great Zimbabwe, Domboshava, Khami and Old Bulawayo were at the beginning selected for development. Although Domboshava and Old Bulawayo were all developed, Domboshava was later vandalised by paint that was splashed on the rock art (Pwiti and Mvenge 1996; Taruvinga and Ndoro 2003) while Old Bulawayo was destroyed by fire in 2010 (Makuvaza and Burrett 2011). Other sites such as Dambarare, Jumbo Mine and monuments in the Matobo Hills were never developed as part of the objectives of the masterplan while Khami and the Shona Village at Great Zimbabwe were partially developed. Even though the implementation of the master Plan can be commented, its objective appear to have not been fully realised as a result of various factors some of which are discussed in chapter 7.

PROCLAMATION OF THE MATOBO HILLS AS A WORLD HERITAGE CULTURAL LANDSCAPE

In 1995 during the "first UNESCO Global Strategy Meeting" to discuss "African cultural heritage", it was noted that a new definition for "cultural landscape" was required. In defining the cultural landscape, the old approach that emphasised monumentality needed to address the social, symbolic, religious, and economic context of sites to be inscribed as a WHL (Ranger 1999; UNESCO 1995). The case made at the meeting was unquestionably that Africa's "living heritage" should be recognised, and the Matobo Hills were indicated as a good example. It was the entire Matobo Hills that were considered for nomination and not just the national park and commercial farms for inscription as a WHL. It was, in fact, the communal areas and their shrines that made the case for the Hills as an African World Heritage Cultural Landscape (Munjeri, et al. 1995).

Following this meeting, in 1998, the then Zimbabwean minister of Home Affairs, Dumiso Dabengwa, announced at a gathering in Matobo Hills that the area was to be nominated as a World Heritage Site. The meeting was attended by government officials, traditional chiefs, and the local indigenous communities to solve the Njelele priesthood and custodianship. The local indigenous communities had already been involved in a contest for priesthood and custodianship of Njelele (see Ranger 1999; Makuvaza 2008). At the meeting, Dabengwa relayed to the people that he had begun to work with the local traditional chiefs to have Njelele and other shrines included in the area which was to be proclaimed as a World Heritage Site.

The new UNESCO approach, together with the backing of powerful government officials and traditional chiefs, raised new hopes that, if the Hills were successfully nominated as a World Heritage Site, the local indigenous communities would be reattached with the shrines, several of which are now archaeological sites located in the national park, after two decades of further alienation by the post-colonial government. It was explained to them by

Fig. 5.11 Harvesting of thatching grass in the Matobo Hills National Park.

the Technical Team working on the nomination of the Hills that the UNESCO Operational Guidelines require the indigineous communities to participate in order to facilitate shared responsibility with the State Party in the maintenance of the property (see UNESCO 2008). The local indigenous communities also expected that this requirement would now allow them to link shrines in the park with those located outside its boundary. They had also hoped to benefit from tourism ventures in the park which, for a very long time, have been dominated by government departments managing the national park and private players. The Matobo people also looked forward to access wildlife for meat and other animal products through the CAMPFIRE projects which, as previously discussed, focus towards community participation and benefits. For the Matobo people's hopes to be fulfilled, the ZPWMA offered them trade opportunities through the selling of souvenirs and crafts in the park, harvesting of thatching grass and wood for construction, and pastures for domestic livestock (Figs 5.10 and 5.11). The ZPWMA and the Forestry Commission would also assist the local indigenous communities by issuing permits to them so that they could harvest grey mukwa (Pterocarpus angolensis) for curio making (see Technical Committee 2004). It was proposed that, under such a management system, the local indigenous communities as the main beneficiaries would start traditional conservation initiatives in the Matobo Hills. This approach was to ensure sustainable management of the natural and cultural heritage of the Hills.

The involvement of the local indigenous communities in the nomination process of the Hills in the WHL began to inculcate the sense of ownership of a cultural landscape which had long been eroded by the colonial and post colonial governments. However, the local indigenous communities hoped that these objectives would be implemented and achieved as was now guaranteed by their own local politicians, traditional chiefs, and UNESCO requirements. As a result, the nomination document and the Site Management Plan were successfully documented and submitted to the UNESCO World Heritage Committee which subsequently declared the Matobo Hills as a world heritage cultural landscape. The Site Management Plan was to be implemented over a period of five years beginning from 2003 to 2007.

Through representative democracy, a local Site Management Committee chaired by Effort Nkomo, a ZANU PF local politician and deputised by the ZPWMA with the NMMZ taking the secretariat position and a traditional chief coming in as one of the committee members and representing the local indigenous people was elected into office (Makuvaza 2012). The Committee was tasked to implement the Site Management Plan, and to solicit funds to finance some of the conservation initiatives in the new world heritage cultural landscape.

SUMMARY

This chapter has illustrated how the colonial authorities perceived the Matobo Hills on their arrival in the area and how they established European farms and the national park as well as how they evicted the local inhabitants from several locations of the cultural landscape. The appropriation of the Hills, however, meant that the local indigenous communities were forcibly separated from their cultural landscape. The introduction of legislation to protect cultural heritage sites has directly and indirectly undermined the traditional conservation practices of the local indigenous communities which had been argued to have been very effective in managing the Hills. The de-emphasising of the traditional conservation practices for protecting the cultural landscape and the argument by the Europeans that the Hills required science to be properly protected could have been driven, to some extent, more by genuine conservation considerations even though the mechanism by which these goals were attaned was indeed imperialistic. This was only meant to facilitate development and administrative agendas in the Matobo Hills which otherwise could have been well protected by traditional conservation means well before the introduction of European derived laws of conservation. The development of state departments meant to implement state laws in the Matobo Hills also significantly undermined and diminished the ability of local indigenous institutions to continue effecting traditional conservation practices of protecting the Hills because these practices had become part of the responsibility of the state, and this marked the beginning of the loss of the local indigenous communities' power to look after the Matobo Hills. The roles of local indigenous communities to safeguard the Matobo Hills were thus re-defined and converted to that of the state system. The promises made by Rhodes to resettle people in lands that he had purchased in Matobo were not genuine as they were actually only a temporary solution to end the 1896-7 war. The failure by local indigenous communities to use Rhodes' promises to challenge their eviction from the Hills demonstrated that their traditional attachment to the Hills was now nullified and completely replaced by European concepts of landscape value. The traditional priests' job of taking pilgrims and messengers to shrines for cultural reasons was also now controlled by the state for recreational purposes. Consequently, the sacredness of shrines in Matobo was ruined as they were now exposed and visited by people whose cultures were not related to them. The embracing of the principles of international conservation by the new Zimbabwean government after independence meant that the war time promise to abolish the park and the local descent people's hopes of resettling in it was no longer going to be feasible. Thus, the socio-political transformations at independence did not bring much institutional change in the Matobo Hills as was hoped by the local indigenous peoples.

6. The Traditional Conservation Practices of the Matobo Hills

INTRODUCTION

This chapter presents the traditional conservation practices of the Matobo Hills and explores how the local indigenous communities use these practices to manage their cultural landscape. By exploring the practices, the chapter is intended to address one of the objectives of this study which is to establish if there are traditional conservation practices that are locally distinct and evident that can be reinstated or restored after they were disregarded during the colonial period when the European authorities domineered the cultural landscape. While the traditional conservation practices of the Matobo Hills are examined in this study, it was not feasible to identify and examine all the practices that may have existed or that still currently survive in this world heritage cultural landscape considering the complexity and extent of the area. This is because the informants who were interviewed and who engaged in discussions during the fieldwork may have failed to remember several practices since, as explained below, by their nature, they are ingrained in memory and not written down.

UNDERSTANDING TRADITIONAL CONSERVATION PRACTICES

Chapter 1 argued that interest in the traditional conservation practices of world heritage cultural landscapes has been increasing in recent years. This is partially due to the assumption that such practices can contribute to the effective conservation of world heritage cultural landscapes. For this reason, traditional conservation practices have been a subject of discussion among archaeologists, anthropologists, cultural heritage managers, ecologists, and other scholars primarily for conservation reasons. In an effort to ascertain a suitable term that best describes traditional conservation practices, scholars have derived a number of terms whose meanings are closely related such as traditional conservation methods (Makuvaza and Makuvaza 2012, 2014), customary laws (Chiwaura 2005; Jimoh et al. 2012), indigenous knowledge systems (Mapara 2009), traditional ecological knowledge (Berkes 1999; Berkes, Colding and Folke 2000), and traditional conservation practices (Boaten 1998; Folke and Colding 2001). However, although all of these terms generally refer to the traditional knowledge that is embedded in the cultural traditions of local indigenous communities, referring to this knowledge as traditional conservation methods or laws, as some scholars have done, is not appropriate. Instead, in accordance with scholars who perceive traditional knowledge of conservation as practice supports the argument that the term best describes the norms, customs, myths, legends, stories, beliefs, and taboos that were or are a component of everyday initiatives by the local indigenous communities to manage their cultural landscapes.

According to Ohmagari and Berkes (1997), traditional knowledge of conservation may be holistic in outlook and adaptive by nature and accumulated over generations by observers whose lives depended on this information and its use. Ohmagari and Berkes further contended that this knowledge often accumulates incrementally, is tested by trial-and-error, and transmitted to future generations orally or through shared practical experiences. Thus, traditional knowledge of conservation entails norms or customs, myths, legends, stories, beliefs, and taboos that are typically perceived as practices of indigenous communities (see also Adams and Hulme 2001). The term methods, however, refers to procedures which are usually carried out according to definite, established, logical, or systematic plans. It is a way of doing certain things that can be repeated by others in similar conditions (Urbina 2002). The term laws refers to a standardised system of written formal rules which a country or community recognises as regulating the actions of its members or citizens (Reynolds 1983). In this case, laws are enforced by the police and applied by trained judicial officers in a public court whereas traditional conservation practices are enforced by community leaders and applied by chiefs or headmen at a traditional court. Methods and laws are inscribed whereas traditional conservation practices are not; they are learned and performed within the local indigenous communities, in the public realm, in daily work, and at home. Conversely, methods and laws are studied at a formal institution of education such as a university or college.

The term conservation can simply be described as the act of managing and protecting a cultural landscape from being destroyed or damaged. Broadly, it involves the management of both the tangible and the intangible aspects of a cultural landscape and the changes that may affect it. Typically, this involves taking corrective measures by restoring or eliminating existing damage and by reducing or preventing any future changes.

Based on the above approach, traditional conservation practices should be defined as cumulative bodies of traditional knowledge, stories, and beliefs that are produced, preserved, and transmitted from one generation to the next through the word of mouth for the purposes of protecting a cultural landscape. Unlike methods and laws, traditional conservation practices have no formalised structures since they are handed down from one generation to the next through the word of mouth. Since they are not written down, they are primarily mental cognisance. They also do not have detectable external influences or outside interventions with new conservation practices with which people were unacquainted (Jopela 2010, 2011). Traditional conservation practices are, therefore, understood through day to day norms, folklore, oral traditions and songs, and they are enforced or applied through prohibitions in the form of taboos. Taboos were or are social or religious customs that prohibit or restrict a particular practice or association with a particular person, place, animal, bird, or object. The purpose of taboos was to instil fear into people to discourage them from performing immoral acts. For that reason, taboos threatened severe penalties and misfortune for anyone who violated them (Masaka and Chemhuru 2011). In terms of conserving cultural landscapes, taboos informed moral values that emphasised profound environmental awareness even though they may give the impression on the surface to have been straight forward prohibitions on the use of archaeological sites, sacred sites, mountains, rivers, caves, water pools, and wildlife within a cultural landscape.

Traditional conservation practices can also be regarded as intangible cultural heritage which local indigenous communities inscribe on their cultural landscapes. Intangible cultural heritage encompasses customs, languages, songs, stories, beliefs, and many other cultural practices that cannot be touched or interacted with (Boswell 2008). It is commonly the intangible cultural heritage that provides information about the history, identity, and ways of living of the local indigenous people surviving in cultural landscapes (Andrews and Buggey 2008). Just as with traditional conservation practices, intangible cultural heritage, therefore, provides an enormous amount of information on how local indigenous communities perceived, symbolised, and ascribed meaning to their cultural landscapes for conservation reasons. Without intangible cultural heritage, cultural landscapes on their own contain no essential cultural value in and of themselves. Rather, they can only be considered to have cultural value if the intangible elements that give them context and meaning are embraced (Bradshaw, Bryant and Cohen 2012). Intangible cultural heritage, therefore, cannot be mutually exclusive from cultural landscapes. There is always an association between intangible and tangible values and a dynamic relationship between nature and culture in a cultural landscape (Mitchell 2008).

According to the Heritage Foundation of Newfoundland and Labrador (2008), it is not only inherited "old" traditional knowledge of conservation that comprises intangible cultural heritage. Modern-day customs and traditions practiced by local indigenous communities in cultural landscapes can also be considered as intangible cultural heritage. Some scholars refer to this type of intangible cultural heritage as "living religious heritage", "living heritage" or "living cultural heritage" (Stovel, Stanely-Price and Killick 2005; Bwasiri 2008; Kreps 2012). To be considered living, intangible cultural heritage is deemed as alive, ongoing, and regularly practiced and is also seen as practices in everyday life.

Living implies a type of cultural heritage that is still in use (Inaba 2005). Intangible cultural heritage as "living cultural heritage" was also incorporated into the initiatives of the local indigenous communities for conserving their cultural landscapes.

Intangible cultural heritage can be used to define and claim land rights by local indigenous communities. In cases where land was inherited from ancestors, it is regarded as heritage (see Mararike 2001), and intangible cultural heritage together with archaeological sites located on the land are, at times, used by local indigenous people as evidence of ownership when reclaiming ancestral lands. In eastern Zimbabwe, for example, according to Mupira (2013), upon independence of the country, the Chikukwa people demanded the return and re-erection of the Nzvinzvi sacred shrine, a typical archaeological site with double concentric stone enclosures located on a spur ridge southeast of the Hangani primary school. The shrine is believed to be the burial place of the founding fathers of the SaUngweme people who had once settled in the area. The Chikukwa people have also been claiming the restoration of the portion of Martin Forest in which a number of archaeological sites and shrines are located. In the Limpopo-Shashe valley on the South African side, several Venda clans have also been claiming some parts of the Mapungubwe cultural landscape using archaeological sites (Pikirayi 2011). In addition to these examples, there are many other cases across the globe where local indigenous communities have used archaeological sites and intangible cultural heritage in the form of stories, myths, and legends to claim their ancestral lands.

One important thing to note about traditional conservation practices is that they were and are not static. They were constantly recreated by the local indigenous communities in response to their needs as they interacted with cultural landscapes. This process also continues in contemporary times. These changes are usually influenced by internal and external factors which have an effect on how the local indigenous communities managed their cultural landscapes. Traditional conservation practices were thus created and recreated depending on the values that the local indigenous communities wished to protect or inscribe on their cultural landscapes. This means that there could be, in a cultural landscape, diverse versions of myths, legends, beliefs and stories of protecting the area, archaeological sites, or shrines which could be explained as layers of history. As discussed in the next chapter, traditional conservation practices, therefore, are also continually in the process of being shaped and reshaped by social, economic, political, cultural, and natural forces that have an effect on their meanings. In that aspect, traditional practices of conservation that were considered no longer relevant were probably disregarded while new ones that were considered relevant were created or modified to suit the existing needs of the local indigenous communities for protecting their cultural landscapes. This resulted in the establishment of new sets of social, religious, and political values which subsequently added a new layer of meaning or meanings on a cultural landscape.

THE TRADITIONAL CONSERVATION PRACTICES OF THE MATOBO HILLS

The traditional conservation practices of the Matobo Hills were a range of beliefs, customs, folklores, and taboos which regulated the conduct of the local indigenous communities on how they utilised the cultural landscape. In the Matobo Hills, taboos comprised activities that were or are prohibited or sacred based on the religious beliefs and morals of the indigenous people. The traditional conservation practices, however, formed an integral part of the local indigenous communities' moral values in the Matobo Hills. They had a fundamental ethical role towards the wellbeing of both the individual and of the local indigenous people living in the entire cultural landscape. As a knowledge practice-belief complex (see Berkes 1999), traditional conservation practices in the Matobo Hills accordingly included an unwritten body of long standing customs, world view, and religious beliefs of the local indigenous communities. As in many other cultural landscapes in southern Africa, the traditional conservation practices in the Matobo Hills did not, therefore, have any discernible foreign influences or persuasions. Their main objective was, by and large, to promote sustainable use and conservation of both the natural and cultural values of the Hills. In many ways, traditional conservation practices were intangible cultural values that the local indigenous communities of Matobo had attached to their ancestral lands which they regard as heritage.

In the Matobo Hills, the traditional chiefs and political authorities worked together in shaping and maintaining the traditional conservation practices of the area (Ranger 1999). The cooperation of the political and religious authorities served to generate taboos which ensured that the surroundings as well as the economic and cultural traditions in the Hills were always kept intact and protected. In principal, these traditional conservation practices, therefore, were espoused by the shrines which advanced an ideology of conservation and ensured the balance of the ecosystem. The shrines derived their importance not only from their historical significance but also from the perceived influence that they had over the people and the contiguous environment (Nyathi and Ndiweni 2005).

The following paragraphs will present the traditional conservation practices of the Matobo Hills, some of which, according to the informants I interviewed and had discussions with during fieldwork, are still currently being practiced. However, given the multiplicity of the local indigenous communities in the Matobo Hills as seen in chapter 4, I did not attempt to identify and classify the traditional conservation practices according to their types or according to the local indigenous communities that practice or value them. The main reason for not categorising them is that the local indigenous people of the Matobo Hills observe homogeneous traditional conservation practices.

While conducting the fieldwork, I observed that the local indigenous communities had developed practical traditional conservation systems that were significantly influenced by religious beliefs and economic requirements to conserve vegetation in the entire cultural landscape. The majority of informants stated that trees continue to play an important function in shaping the general temperament of the Matobo Hills. The informants also indicated that, prior to the arrival of the Europeans in the area and the subsequent introduction of formal laws to protect trees, there were taboos and beliefs which proscribed the unsanctioned cutting down of trees in the cultural landscape.

According to Pathisa Nyathi, certain tree species were not supposed to be cut as it was one way of protecting the Matobo Hills, and the local indigenous communities associated them with a range of cultural practices (P. Nyathi, pers. comm., 10 March, 2014). These trees include the umphafa or umlahlabantu [Ziziphus mauritiana] whose branches were cut and placed on the grave of a person soon after burial as a death seal (see also, Bozongwana 1983). The ichithamuzi or idungamuzi [Philenoptera violacea] was also not supposed to be cut or used as firewood because it was believed that doing so would destroy one's homestead by causing conflict among the family members. The Umnondo [Burkea Africana] tree, which does not produce ash when burnt and was typically used for iron smelting by the early farming communities in the Matobo Hills, was also not supposed to be cut. This was because the leaves were the only food source for edible caterpillars or mopane worms, amacimbi, which are harvested during the rainy season, mainly in January and February, in the Matobo Hills and the surrounding environments. These caterpillars are an important source of protein and are dried for consumption later in the year.

The bark of the Burkea africana tree was used to dye the fiber which is woven into baskets. The roots were used to treat stomach pains and toothaches. For both treatments, the outer skin of the roots was scraped away, and the roots were cut into small pieces and boiled for five to ten minutes. For stomach pains, the mixture was cooled and three cups were taken per day. For toothaches, the mixture was rinsed while warm in the mouth around the aching tooth for approximately three minutes and then spat out. This was repeated three times a day, once in the morning, afternoon, and in the evening just before going to bed. The bark of Burkea africana tree was also used as traditional medicine in many parts of southern Africa (see Palmer and Pitman 1972; Palmer 1977). Wild fruit trees from which both people and wild animals such as baboons, monkeys, and birds depended on for food were also not supposed to be cut. A number of wild fruits such as umbumbulu, [Mimusops zeyheri], amaxakuxaku [Azanza garckeana], umngono [Strychnos spinosa], umtshwankela [Vitex payos], umqokolo [Flacourtia indica], umkhiwa [Ficus sur/capensis] and many others are abundant in the Matobo Hills. Community leaders in the Matobo Hills prescribed traditional ways of harvesting wild fruits and other tree by-products. Members of the local indigenous communities were dissuaded from collecting more wild fruits than was necessary as this was regarded as a sign of disrespect and greed. Only ripe fruits that would have fallen to the ground were supposed to be collected. It was taboo to curse or to pass a negative comment on the quality or taste of wild fruits, for example, remarking on their bad taste. The belief was that one could become insane or disappear in the forests of the Matobo Hills. For the offending individual to return, the ancestral spirits had to be appeased usually by offering an animal to them.

It was taboo to cut down trees in areas that were considered sacred places of the Matobo Hills such as caves, forests, and hills. This was because the local indigenous people believed that their ancestral spirits reside in forests, hills, caves, hollowed trees, and in water pools (Nyathi and Ndiweni 2005). Ancestors were believed to symbolise the past and were considered to be individuals who deserve a higher order of being. Chief Mathe from Silobi stated that these ancestors were often referred to as Izinyoka (snakes) and were believed to have established high standards of moral excellence that succeeding generations living in the Matobo Hills were expected to embrace and practice (Chief Mathe, pers. comm., August 16, 2014). Cutting down trees in the Matobo Hills, therefore, was tantamount to exposing ancestors and Mwari/Mwali in the open. The local indigenous communities attached great respect to the Hills because they believed that, by desecrating the cultural landscape, they deprived their ancestors and the spirits of a home to live in. If anyone had a project with the land and planned to cut down trees in the forest or a shrine area, permission had to be sought from the Mwari/Mwali priest or priestess providing convincing reasons why trees had to be cut from that piece of land (Ranger 1999; Technical Committee 2004). Trees that were struck by lightning during the previous rainy season had to be removed as part of cleansing the Matobo Hills. As further explained by Nyathi, land was considered barren until it was watered and had to be cleansed before the rains came in September or October (P. Nyathi, pers. comm., March 10, 2014).

During the pre-colonial era, the local indigenous communities of the Matobo Hills depended on swampy areas for farming. Cultivation of crops, however, was not allowed on certain swampy areas that were considered to be sacred in the Matobo Hills (Ranger 1999). Traditionally, the swampy areas and other sources of water symbolised the socio-ecological well-being and stability of all the local indigenous communities in the cultural landscape. They also provided important habitat for a wide variety of wildlife species. The swampy areas were known as nuta or goba (P. Nyathi, pers. comm., March 10, 2014) and also as amaxaphozi (S. Sibanda, pers. comm., August 15, 2014).

Obtaining drinking water using a black vessel was not allowed in swampy areas that were considered to be sacred places. Women experiencing their menstrual cycles were also not allowed to fetch water from sacred swamp areas. It was one way of promoting hygienic standards of water sources while simultaneously managing the welfare of the natural environment in the Matobo Hills (W. Moyo, pers. comm., April 8, 2014). The belief was that failure to observe the above moral codes would lead to the swampy areas drying out.

In the Matobo Hills, wild animals were allowed to drink at swampy areas where people would not fetch drinking water. Domesticated animals such as cattle, goats, and sheep were rotated and allowed to graze in swampy areas during the dry months of the year. However, after harvesting in July, the animals were moved from the wetland areas to graze on cereal stalks left in the crop fields. During the rainy season beginning in October or November when the swampy areas began to become waterlogged and the lands cultivated, they were moved back to the summer grazing areas. Bedding and ridging systems were also practiced during farming in order to retain moisture and to prevent stream and gully erosion (Ranger 1999).

Fig. 6.1 Dula Hill in south eastern Matobo as viewed from the south in which the shrine is said to be located (Photo by Author).

These swampy areas and other water sources were also believed to have been protected by the injuzu (mermaids) (see Ranger 1999, 2001) who are believed to live in the sacred permanent water pools which persist even through the driest seasons of the year. The myths associated with injuzu are widely held among many indigenous communities in Zimbabwe and in many southern African countries. The mythology is featured very strongly among the local indigenous communities of southern Africa including the Venda, Sotho, Ndebele, Tswana, Kalanga and the Shona.

According to Bernard (2003), it is believed that injuzu could submerge a person under water for hours, days, or even up to a number of years after which the individual would emerge as a skilled traditional healer. Relatives of the person taken by the injuzu were not supposed to mourn or demonstrate any indications of grief as that would make the person who was taken disappear forever. It was also believed that the submerged person is taken to a dry area under the water pool where the ancestors or water spirits live and have a lifestyle similar to people who live on earth. The relatives of the submerged person had to perform a ritual libation by pouring an offering on the ground and telling the spirits that the person has gone to the spirit world and that the spirits should look after the person while under the water pool (Aschwanden 1989). Individuals who have had such experiences commonly report to have visualised snakes, mermaids, or even their ancestors while under the water pool (Bernard 2003).

The local indigenous communities in the Matobo Hills still believe that injuzu live in swampy areas, water pools, and in shrine caves. In Matobo, Mwali adepts are said to have gone down into the water pools for years on end to be taught by the injuzu and learning, among other things, how the Hills should be conserved and protected. For instance, at Dula, a shrine that is located in the south eastern part of

Fig. 6.2 A Khami-type site, which was once a shrine and sacred to the local indigenous communities in the Fumugwe area (Photo by Author).

the Hills (Fig. 6.1), prophetess Juliana claims to have been taken by the injuzu and lived under water for four years. During this period, she was instructed to go back and teach people to live according to law and order so that it will rain in the whole of the Matobo Hills (Ranger 1999, 284, 2001). Given the belief in injuzu, there is a wide variety of taboos which surround the access and use of water sources in the Matobo Hills. The use of soap to wash clothes or to bathe in water or cave pools was not allowed in the cultural landscape as this would pollute the water. In the same way, metal containers could not be used to draw water from the rivers or pools believed to be inhabited by injuzu. Only gourd cups called inkezo were used to obtain water from these water sources. Great care was thus taken in the Hills to avoid disturbing or angering injuzu. Respect of injuzu means respect for water pools, caves in which rock art was painted, and rivers where they are thought to have been living and, for this reason, water sources and archaeological sites were safeguarded in the Matobo Hills. In the Matobo Hills, local indigenous people would keep rock art sites and shrines as a secret that were considered to be sacred. One such site which the Nyubi people kept as secret was a Khami-type site (Fig. 6.2) found in the south western part of the Matobo Hills and is approximately 2 kilometers west of Fumugwe Township. It is located at the summit of a low-lying granite hill called Sixobeni in Phumuzamaphiko village. There are a number of stone cairns at the site which are believed to be "graves" of people who previously settled at the site (M. Dube, pers. comm., April 8, 2014). These graves are marked by the iminyela [Commiphora africana] trees that are planted on graves according to the cultural practice of the local indigenous communities in the Matobo Hills (Fig. 6.3). Planting iminyela trees on graves is also widely practised in much of the Matabeleland region even up to the present day. A study of the archaeological site data base at the Natural History Museum in Bulawayo indicates that the site was never officially documented or reported

Fig. 6.3 Misheck Dube pointing at a stone cairn that he asserted is one of the "graves" of people who once resided at the site (Photo by Author).

to the NMMZ. This could be part of the reason why it is still currently well protected. Also, the conservation of wildlife in Matobo was steeped in taboos, customs, clanship, ancestors, and spirituality of the local indigenous communities. During a group discussion at Fumugwe Township in the western end of Matobo Hills, informants stated that the local descent people in the the cultural landscape still believe and value the idea of totems and clans (Fig. 6.4). The informants also said that each individual belongs to a clan which claims descent from a common ancestor and has its own particular isitemo (totem). These totems, they said, are a shared identity marker that they are still following and respecting in the cultural landscape today. The informants further indicated that these totems vary throughout the Matobo Hills and that the majority of the items forming the main element of totems are terrestrial and aquatic animals as well as birds. They attach a taboo to the totem animal or to a certain part of its body, and members of the totem animal are not supposed to eat the animal or a particular part of its body. Terrestrial totem animals that were not to be eaten or a particular part of their body include impofu (eland), ingulungundu (warthog), inyathi (buffalo), idube (zebra), indlovu (elephant), and many others. Aquatic totem animals, which were likewise not to be eaten, include the hippopotamus, crocodile, and fish. The consumption of animals that stand for a clan was strongly discouraged in the Matobo Hills (O. Ngwenya, pers. comm., April 8, 2014). Ngwenya further said that he cannot, for instance, eat a crocodile as it is his totem animal. J. Moyo (Pers. comm., April 8, 2014) remarked that he may not eat the heart of any animal whether it is domesticated or not since his totem is moyo (heart). Similarly, as the informants further added, those who fall under the nyoni (bird) totem will not, in the same vein, eat birds. Also, these animals were not to be killed as they were sacred to the local indigenous people (N. Sibanda, pers. comm., April 8, 2014). Going against such practices was believed to cause illness or the loss of the offender's teeth.

The local indigenous people in the Matobo Hills practiced selective hunting to safeguard their wild animals. They would not kill animals that were young or those that were in the gestation period; these were left to grow and reproduce (L. Dube, pers. comm., April 8, 2014). During traditional hunting in the Matobo Hills, when a wild animal escaped into the forest, the chase was immediately called off as it was considered to be part of the sacred herd and was not, therefore, supposed to be pursued and killed. Wild animals in the sacred areas did not belong to an individual and, as a result, no one could hunt them with impunity. This way, wildlife was protected in the Matobo Hills (Technical Committee 2004). There are many other taboos and beliefs that are associated with totems, however, some of them, such as the one that forbids people of the same totem to marry, were not associated with the conservation of the Matobo Hills and lie outside the scope of this thesis.

The informants further indicated that Wednesday is respected as the resting day in the Matobo Hills. It is known as izilo and is also considered as a day of ancestors (T. Mahlangu, pers. comm., April 8, 2014). During this day, no one is allowed to do any work in the fields (see also, Ranger 1999, 24). The informants added that all the shrines in the Matobo Hills are accessible throughout the week except on Wednesday. Those who disobey and do not comply with the observance of the day, it was believed, would be struck by lightning (if it is during the rains season), bitten by a snake, or chased away from the fields by a male baboon (Bozongwana 1983). Anyone who breaks the rules is brought before the traditional chief, tried at a traditional court and, if found to be noncompliant, are fined (Makuvaza 2008).

Fig. 6.4 A group discussion at Fumugwe Township with some members of the local descent communities.

Several informants also said that rain making is one of the cultural practices that is still linked to the fertility of the land and to the conservation of the entire Matobo Hills cultural landscape. The practice is still being followed and venerated in the area. The informants also stated that there were and are many shrines where rain making ceremonies are still being performed in the the cultural landscape. Before the national park was established, some of these shrines were located in an area that is now a national park while others were outside of the area. In the eastern part of Matobo Hills, there was Khozi, Zhilo, and Dula. Lunuwa was in the western part of the Matobo Hills while Mashakambayi was in the national park. Except for Dula and Zhilo, all the other shrines are no longer active, especially those that were located in the national park (M. Dube, pers. comm., April 4, 2014). Dube further said that the shrines were distributed in such a way that those people who live near Khozi could travel to Khozi, those near Mashakambayi would go to Mashakambayi, and those near Lunuwa would go to Lunuwa. Dube also said that, even though the shrines were not similar to the modern churches that were introduced in the Hills by the European missionaries and later by the Pentecostal Churches, they considered these shrines as their churches.

Njelele remains the main shrine where everyone travels for the rain making ceremony every year towards the beginning of the rainy season between August and September. Asking for rain from ancestors has always been a way of looking after the Matobo Hills since it is known that, when it rains, animals, insects, trees, grass, and everything else would be able to survive (M. Dube, pers. comm., April 4, 2014). Njelele as the central shrine is still associated with the cultivation of crops and conservation of the entire cultural landscape. According to Ranger (1999, 24), the shrine "lay(s) it down when planting

Fig. 6.5 Lucydale Farm signpost located in the north western section of the Matobo Hills just west of Matopos Research Station (Photo by Author).

can start and where; where fire could be used for clearing the farm land and where not; what days to rest and when harvesting shall commence". People visit the Matobo Hills from all over the country on a regular basis to consult the shrines, especially Njelele, on issues which affect their personal lives.

Rain making spirit mediums, which are known as amawosana, also continue to play a very significant role in the protection and conservation of the Matobo Hills. According to Cecilia Malinga, an iwosana living at Lucydale Farm (Fig. 6.5), the rain making spirit mediums are intermediaries between the world of the living and the world of the spirit. They can make oracular pronouncements and perform traditional ceremonies that can ensure good rain and crops in the whole of the Matobo Hills. Malinga also said that, as an iwosana, her job is to converse with the existing local indigenous communities through traditional chiefs regarding any grievances that the ancestors may have about the misuse of the Hills, pollution of water sources, or other environmental exploitations that can anger the spirit guardians and could cause drought or late rains in the cultural landscape. The spirit medium further noted that the conservation of the Matobo Hills is ensured by the rain making ceremonies, which are still being peformed in the cultural landscape. She also said that the amawosana who dance for rain are still currently found in much of the Matobo Hills. In the western part of the Hills, they are found at the Manyangwa and Ntogwa shrines (C. Malinga, pers. comm., April 8, 2014). Manyangwa is a well known rain making shrine and is actually located about thirty kilometers from the border town of Plumtree to the northwest in chief Mpini's area while Ntogwa is in the Ramokwebana area across the border in the north eastern part of Botswana. Both shrines are intrinsically linked to Njelele in matters of rainmaking and the general traditional conservation of the Matobo Hills (see Werbner 1989; Nthoi 2006). In the Lushumbe area, amawosana are found at shrines in the south central and eastern parts of the Hills such as at Msekesa, Dula, and Zhilo (T. Moyo, pers. comm., June 21, 2014).

Malinga further narrated the roles that the shrine custodians play in the administration of the Matobo Hills. She said that the custodians ensure that the environment around the religious shrines is safely protected and that they also preside over the rituals that are performed at the sites. Pilgrims are not allowed to visit shrines or their vicinity alone without a shrine custodian. The spirit medium also pointed out that these practices were not static; they were also occasionally changed, especially as a result of the introduction of objects of European origin in the Matobo Hills. When entering a shrine or its environs, the acceptable behaviour is to remove and leave objects of European origin such as shoes, wrist watches, and money outside the sacred area. Visitors to the shrines are expected to leave these items at the residence of the custodian. Failure to observe these customary practices, it is believed, can result in individuals or their families or the entire local descent communities being punished by the aggrieved ancestral spirits. The ancestral punishment could come in the form of diseases, pestilence, poor harvests, or severe drought in the rest of the Matobo Hills. One of the common traditional ways of conservation still found in the Hills, as Malinga recounted, is that only shrine custodians are allowed a limited annual allocation of firewood from the forest for personal use. Ordinary people are not allowed to retrieve firewood in areas around shrine areas (C. Malinga, pers. comm., April 8, 2014). Also, some hills in the Matobo area were said to have a magical significance and could not be pointed at with a forefinger (see also, Cooke 1965). Pointing at a sacred hill with a finger was believed to invoke bad luck. This behaviour was most likely meant to protect the sacredness of the hills and shrines and to prevent their defilement by pilgrims. It was also a sign of respect for the entire Matobo Hills cultural landscape area.

In the Matobo Hills, the local indigenous communities also believed in the existence of spirits called amalinda. They believed that when aged people die, their spirits return to dwell among their descendants, and they become the guardian spirits of the area. These ancestral spirits, especially those of former traditional chiefs, are thought to often take the physical form of lions. The actual amalinda spirit mediums are believed to be men and women who lead ordinary lives as members of the local indigenous communities. They concern themselves with the welfare of their descendants and with maintaining harmonious relations between people and their natural and cultural environment. They are also believed to possess the power to heal and protect people against misfortunes (C. Malinga, pers. comm., April 8, 2014). Before the Europeans arrived in the Matobo Hills, shrines such as Njelele are indicated as having been guarded by the amalinda spirits (see Ranger 1999).

In the north eastern part of the Matobo Hills, folklores were relayed that helped protect and conserve rock art sites. One such archaeological site that is extensively featured in the folklore of the cultural landscape is Ntunjambili Cave (Fig. 6.6). The cave is said to have been an important rain making shrine controlled by a male priest called Dada and later by his daughter Nhlangiso Mmeke (Ranger 2001). Before the colonial period, the cave is said to have been the dwelling place of the amazimu who were believed to be giant human beings driven to cannibalism by famine and were eating human flesh. With the story of amazimu being told to children, no one would enter the cave and, as a result, the paintings in the cave were completely protected (W. Masuku, pers. comm., August 15, 2014). Masuku, however, recalls that this changed with the coming of the Europeans to establish the nearby Matopo Mission in 1898. The missionaries would take school children into the cave labyrinths using lamps so that they could track back to the entrances of the cave. As a result of the school excursions, the amazimu story of Ntunjambili Cave was then realised to be just folklore meant

Fig. 6.6 Ntunjambili Cave in the north east of the Matobo Hills (Photo by Author).

to discourage people from visiting the site. It is probably for this reason that the site eventually lost its sacredness as, soon after that, the cave was turned into a common visitor consumer site, and all of the paintings were affected by fading. According to Masuku, the local descent people refused to have the site proclaimed as a national monument as they thought that its sacredness could be ruined as was the case with other similar sites that were already appropriated from them. The Disappearance of the paintings was also one of the reasons why the Monuments Commission did not proclaim Ntunjambili as a national monument.

SUMMARY

This chapter has explained the meaning of the term traditional conservation practices and argued that scholars use the term differently depending on the subject of study although, in actual fact, the terms all refer to traditional knowledge of conservation which embraces norms, customs, myths, legends, beliefs and taboos that the local indigenous communities used to conserve their cultural landscapes, shrines, and archaeological sites. As explained in this chapter, the traditional conservation practices were learned within the communities, memorised, and passed orally from one generation to the next. For this reason, they were thus considered to be part of the world views, social, economic, and belief systems of local indigenous communities surviving in the cultural landscapes.

This chapter also demonstrates that, prior to the introduction of European management systems in the Matobo Hills, the supervision of the area was deeply rooted in traditional conservation practices and beliefs which the local indigenous communities were using to safeguard their cultural landscape. These traditional conservation practices constituted an integral element of the cultural identity of the local indigenous communities in the Matobo Hills while their knowledge of managing the cultural landscape was embodied in the wealth of experiences they had gained through direct practices and was transmitted orally from one generation to the next. Consequently, as seen in this chapter, a number of the traditional conservation practices still currently survive in the area. It appears, however, that after the eviction of the local indigenous communities from some parts of the Matobo Hills during the colonial era, several traditional conservation practices were revived or continued in the communal areas in which people were now residing. It is in the communal areas where the surviving traditional conservation practices, therefore, were transmitted orally from generation to generation up to the present times. It would also appear that these traditional conservation practices were completely discontinued or abandoned in the national park and on private farms due to the introduction of European approaches of management. As seen in the previous chapter, the local indigenous communities no longer had access to the national park and private farms which means that they could not continue to manage these portions of the Matobo Hills through their traditional conservation practices. It also appears that, even if some traditional conservation practices are still surviving in the Matobo Hills, they are no longer valued or practiced and some of them are gradually dying a natural death.

7. Perspectives of Local Indigenous Communities Introduction

INTRODUCTION

Chapter 1 explains why the category of world heritage cultural landscapes was adopted by the World Heritage Committee in 1992. It also discusses that, subsequent to the acceptance, several archaeologists and heritage managers began to contend that several world heritage management documents ignore other social and existing values that may be important within these areas. As indicated, these scholars went on to argue that local indigenous communities should be involved in the management of cultural landscapes and that some of their traditional conservation practices should be considered in the management ethos of these areas. Questions that arise from these proposals include: Is it possible to bring traditional conservation practices back into the management of world heritage cultural landscapes, and especially in the Matobo Hills where it has been evicenced that they were disregarded during the colonial period and further ignored during the post colonial period when the government began to impose its own management approaches as well? Can local indigenous communities be successfully involved in the management of cultural landscapes such as the Matobo Hills in which there are other actors who conceivably have competing interests in the cultural landscape? Is it possible to bring traditional conservation practices back into a cultural landscape where social and other values are always shifting and where there are official laws which already govern the area?

The above questions were answered using data collected in the field and by presenting the opinions and experiences of the local indigenous communities in the Matobo Hills. The previous chapter demonstrated that traditional conservation practices are the defining elements of the local indigenous communities' ethos and world view in the world heritage cultural landscape. It is, therefore, prudent in this chapter to present their views and experiences on the suggestion that traditional conservation practices should be considered in the management of the world heritage cultural landscape and that they should be involved in its management as local indigenous communities. In my view, this is important because it is the local indigenous peoples themselves who can judge whether or not the idea could work as they understand the practices and the cultural landscape that require protection and management. In addition, it is also the local indigenous communities who put into practice the traditional conservation approaches of managing the Matobo Hills.

As will be discussed in the chapter, the views of the local indigenous communities are based on their experiences, knowledge, dilemmas, and wishes of living in the Matobo Hills and of managing their part in it. In many ways, the chapter also reflects on the socio-politics and religious ideologies of the area which is interwoven in a setting of conflicting meanings, ownership, interests, and administration of the cultural landscape. As will be discussed further in the chapter, the question of bringing traditional conservation practices back into the Matobo Hills remains inseparable from the welfare, socio-politics, and religious faiths of the local indigenous communities in the cultural landscape. The following information will explore each of the several thematic categories evidenced during the data analysis of interviews and discussions with the local descent people of the Matobo Hills.

EMPLOYMENT, TOURISM AND THE RENAISSANCE OF TRADITIONAL CONSERVATION PRACTICES

When asked whether or not it is possible to return to some of their traditional conservation practices and involve them in the management of the Matobo Hills World Heritage Cultural Landscape, the reaction by informants was mixed. Several considered that the idea is likely to be embraced in the communal areas where traditional conservation practices are commonly understood and valued while others believed that the idea may not work in the national park and in private commercial areas which are managed through formal state laws and by modern conservation approaches. Others, however, queried the ability of the practices to conserve the cultural landscape while some argued that it is no longer possible to bring back or maintain traditional conservation practices in the Hills as they are losing value and meaning due to a range of reasons, some of which will be explored in detail later in the chapter.

Tha Lunga, an employee at Amagugu International Heritage Center, stated that not all traditional conservation practices may need to be considered in the Hills. Lunga said that there are certain traditional conservation practices that are still surviving in the cultural landscape today, therefore, do not need to be revived. According to Lunga, only conservation practices that are declining and are believed to be in danger are the ones that may need to be considered, especially in the communal areas since that is where they are most relevant and where the majority of people who understand them are living. In places such as the national park and private commercial farms, as Lunga further argued, reintroduction of traditional conservation practices may be difficult as these areas are currently being managed or owned by people who do not understand the deep rooted methods of caring for the Matobo Hills (T. Lunga, pers. comm., April 7, 2014).

Fili Tshimba Ncube, a souvenir maker at Amagugu, like Lunga, viewed the return of traditional conservation practices in the national park and in private commercial farms as something that may be very difficult to achieve. He concurred with Lunga that the idea could probably work better in the communal areas where the majority of the indigenous people are living than in protected areas where the residents are not completely original to the Hills. He thus viewed the idea of reintroducing traditional conservation practices in the protected areas as a futile exercise since, according to him, employees in these areas are not necessarily engaged from the neighbouring communal areas, therefore, would not possess intimate traditional knowledge of protecting the cultural landscape. According to Ncube, workers in the national park and safari lodges as well as on private commercial farms will never respect or understand the traditional conservation practices of the Matobo Hills even if the practices would be returned to these protected areas. As Ncube argued, it may be a waste of time and energy to discuss such an exercise in these areas. The majority of workers, as he further argued, are not from the Matobo Hills, and they may not appreciate the genuine motive behind bringing back the traditional conservation practices in the sections of the Hills in which they work or involving them in their management (T. Ncube, pers. comm., April 7, 2014).

To bring about traditional conservation practices in the Matobo Hills, Sipho Dube, a villager from near Tshapo Business Center suggested that the ZPWMA, the NMMZ, and the private sector could employ some of their workers from the adjoining communal areas and encourage them to promote traditional practices of conservation. Dube went on to explain that this would keep the traditional conservation practices alive and commonly practiced and learned within the local indigenous communities and between generations since employees from the contiguous communal areas are familiar with and understand the local values of the Hills. According to Dube, employment can provide the local indigenous people with a sense of ownership of the Matobo Hills which they lost during the colonial period. For this reason, they could enthusiastically support the idea of being involved in the management of the Hills when they know that they will somehow benefit from their management (S. Dube, pers. comm., April 7, 2014). However, Gilbert Pwiti, a Professor of archaeology at the University of Zimbabwe, indicated that, although he agrees with the idea of employing site custododians from neighbouring communities, there is no policy that compels the ZPWMA or other public and private organisations to employ workers from communities that are adjacent to national parks in the country. Pwiti went on to make an important observation that this position differs from that of the NMMZ which has an unwritten understanding to employ site custodians from nearby communities in cases where some cultural heritage sites are located in the communal areas (G. Pwiti, pers. comm., August 6, 2014). Administratively, this idea works well for the NMMZ as the employees can work from their rural homes, and this gives them a sense of ownership of the cultural heritage sites which they will be caring for. Although this arrangement can be successfully implemented at some cultural heritage sites such as Great Zimbabwe where a number of the workers are employed from the adjoining local indigenous communities, the same cannot be applied in the whole of the Matobo Hills due to its size and the number of cultural heritage sites that may require traditional custodianship.

Considering this situation, a villager from Mazhayimbe commented that, as local indigenous communities, it will always be difficult for them to become employed in the national park and lodges or in the private commercial farms and push for their cultural practices in these portions of the Hills. The villager concluded that some parts of the Hills, especially the national park and private commercial farms, will never be theirs as they are owned by the government and certain individuals with power and money. Another villager from the same area remarked that the sections of the Hills that they feel to be truly theirs and where they have the autonomy to use traditional ways of conservation are only the communal lands.

Regarding the relationship between the national park, private commercial farms, hoteliers, and the local indigenous communities, Pathisa Nyathi said that the majority of people in the communal areas no longer have a sense of ownership of several sections of the Matobo Hills, especially the protected areas as they feel that they have continued to be disregarded by both the colonial and post colonial management systems. Nyathi argued that the idea of employing some of the workers from the surrounding communities so that they could promote traditional conservation practices in the Hills is certainly not going to change the long held view by the ZPWMA authorities that the local indigenous communities are trespassers and poachers. As Nyathi further argued, since the proclamation of the Hills as a World Heritage Site in 2003, the ZPWMA has continued to adiminister its own affairs independently from the communal areas and the commercial farms. According to Nyathi, contrary to the local indigenous communities' expectations that the proclamation of the Hills as a World Heritage Site would bring the park, private commercial farms, and the communal areas together and promote tourism in the area, this has not happened (P. Nyathi, pers. comm., March 10, 2014).

Fig. 7.1 A rock art site near Tshapo Business Center opened to encourage tourism in the communal areas of the Matobo Hills (Photo by Author).

Concurring with Nyathi, a villager selling souvenirs at the foothills of Silozwane Mountain said that tourism begins and ends in the national park. According to the villager, there is no tourism evidenced in the communal areas of the Matobo Hills. A member of the Cecil John Rhodes Campfire Community Cultural Village attributed the failure of their project to low tourism arrivals in the Lushumbe communal area. She said that few tourists would choose to spend much of their recreational time in the national park instead of in the communal areas. The member also explained that since few tourists venture into the communal areas, the development of the project that they had hoped to expand through revenue generated from tourism has also been affected. The villager further stated that they had hoped to promote tourism in their communal area by opening to tourists a few rock art sites that are close to the cultural village but this did not help them much. As a way of promoting tourism in the communal areas, the Amagugu International Heritage Center has actually opened a rock art site that is less than one kilometer from Tshapo Township (Fig. 7.1). A female informant selling souvenirs at EJikweni complained that their engagement in the tourism business has always been that of mere souvenir sellers, and they do not make much money by selling their objects of art to tourists.

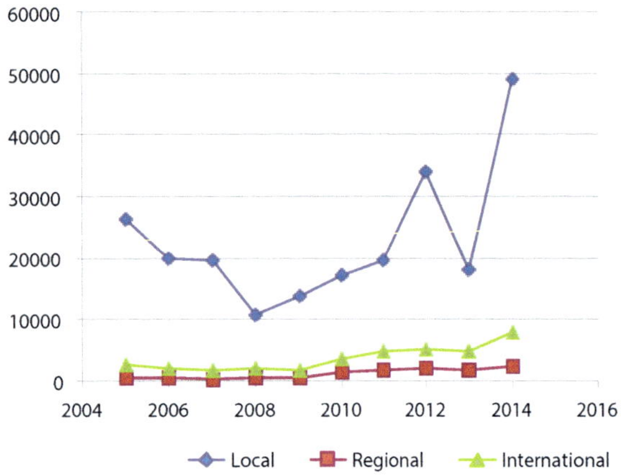

Fig. 7.2 Visitor trends in the Matobo National Park.

Other informant souvenir sellers at EJikweni, however, attributed this to diminished tourism in the Matobo Hills in recent years. They indicated that, in the past, they had many tourists coming to the Hills. They also said that there are few international tourists who visit the Matobo Hills and that most of the tourists they receive are local, and these tourists do not purchase very many of their works of art.

A study of visitor trends in the Matobo Hills shows that tourists from the Southern African Development Community (SADC) region and beyond began to decline from about 2004 and reached the lowest levels between 2005 and 2009 (Fig. 7.2). Low tourism in the Matobo Hills during this period could be attributed to the unfavorable publicity of the country following the imposition of sanctions and the subsequent collapse of the economy. However, tourism began to improve again from about 2009, perhaps in part as a result of the formation of a Zimbabwean Unity Government after the disputed elections of 2008 between ZANU PF and the opposition parties.

In the Lushumbe area, informants were also concerned that, over the years, tourists who visit the communal areas are those that want to avoid paying park entry fees. The informants, however, blamed tour operators who they contend organise "cultural tours" and divert tourists from the park to communal areas where entry fees are not charged (see also Chronicle, 6 September 1999). One informant from the area beleived that Tour Operators who organise cultural tours in their communal areas make money. The informant also said that the Tour Operators never offer anyone money or help promote traditional conservation practices even though their business is thriving on the conservation of the cultural landscape. The activities of tour operators were also condemned by Gavin Stephens, Chairman of the Matobo Conservation Society and a Bulawayo conservationist, during a course on the Conservation and Management of Rock Art Sites in Southern Africa (COMRASA) which was held in the Hills from July to August 1999 (cf. Deacon 2006). According to Stephens, the uncontrolled visits by tour operators in the communal areas damage important archaeological deposits and rock paintings in the caves (Chronicle, 6 September 1999).

A female informant selling souvenirs at Silozwane Cave, which is one of the archaeological sites visited most often by tourists outside the park, explained that, as local indigenous communities in the Matobo Hills, they have no authority to stop tour operators from bringing tourists to the cave or to care for it with their traditional conservation practices since, by law, the cave does not belong to them (Fig. 7.3). The informant also stated that they have no authority to charge entrance fees at the site even though the cave is located in their village. The infomant further said that their interest is only to sell souvenirs to tourists who visit the site and not look after the cave using traditional conservation practices even though they are aware that it was once used by their elders as a rain making shrine. A full moon ceremony at the cave is indicated to have been last witnessed in approximately 1942, and it continued to be used as a shrine until about 1950 (Murray 2013; see also Ranger 1999, 20).

REVENUE GENERATION, DEVELOPMENT OF THE MATOBO DISTRICT AND THE SUPPORT OF TOURISM

In the late 1990s, a local member of parliament, Ananias Nyathi, began to campaign that the Matobo Rural District Council should receive a percentage of the annual earnings from the park and from the Rhodes Matopos estates in order to fund development projects in the district. Lobbying for

Fig. 7.3 Villagers selling souvenirs to visitors at the foothill of Silozwe Mountain (Photo by Author).

the returns, Ananias Nyathi argued that revenue generated from these parts of the Hills should benefit the local indigenous communities as compensation for their loss of ancestral lands and shrines during the colonial period (Sunday News, 13 September 1998). Following the campaign, the Chief Executive Officer of the Matobo Rural District Council instructed Silozwe villagers to charge entrance fees at the Silozwane rock art site so that they could raise funds for developing their district. The directive was, however, immediately opposed by the Executive Director of the NMMZ who responded through a local newspaper and warned that revenue collection from tourists visiting the archaeological site was unlawful. The Executive Director also cautioned that charging entrance fees at the cave by the villagers was a violation of the NMMZ Act which is the only organisation authorised to collect entrance fees at such sites. For fear of being arrested, the villagers halted charging entrance fees at Silozwane Cave, but they continued to sell souvenirs to tourists who visited the site. Knowing that their attempts to benefit from the cave had failed, several local indigenous communities began to contest the threats of the removal of Rhodes' grave from World's View Hill contending that this would economically disadvantage them as the tourists who buy their souvenirs would stop coming to the park (Sunday News, 6 September 1998).

During the late 1990s, a Harare based pressure group called Sangano Munhumutapa and led by Lawrence Chakaredza had threatened to exhume Rhodes' remains and throw them in the Zambezi River if the British would not come and take them away (Muringaniza 2002). During the crusade to dig up the grave, Chakaredza argued that the presence of Rhodes' remains in Matobo Hills was disrespectful to ancestors who were stripped of their political, economic, and social dignity during the colonial period (Sunday News, 13 December 1998). He also argued that, by removing the grave, he was seeking to restore the Hill to its former glory as a traditional shrine for the local indigenous people of the

Matobo Hills. To achieve his objective, Lawrence Chakaredza even sought the support of ZANU PF politicians to remove Rhodes' grave from the Matobo Hills (Maylam 2005). The attempt by Chakaredza to remove Rhodes' grave from Malindidzimu Hill, which is believed to have been sacred, was ironically contested by villagers mostly from Silozwane and Gulati whose cultural practices he wanted to defend. Mloyiswa Moyo from Silozwane, who vividly recalled the 1951 land evictions, used a combination of economic and weather explanations to contest the removal of Rhodes' grave from the Matobo Hills. He argued that the Matobo Hills area is arid and rainfall is erratic, therefore, there is little opportunity to benefit from the Hills. Moyo further argued that they depend on selling sculptures, baskets, mats, and wall hangings to tourists who visit the grave. Moyo also went on to explain that his family had survived on tourism through selling souvenirs in the park for nearly 30 years (Sunday News, 6 September 1998). Keli Ndlovu from Gulati also felt that, as local indigenous communities of the area, they should be consulted first on such matters since they depend on the grave for their survival in the Hills (Sunday News, 6 September 1998). Aware that local indigenous communities benefit from tourists who visit the grave, the Governor of Matabeleland South Province, Stephen Nkomo, also objected to its removal, arguing that Chakaredza should not fight a war which is not his and that he should concentrate on the politics of Mashonaland where he comes from. The Executive Director of the NMMZ further warned that, if Chakaredza did go ahead and remove Rhodes' grave from the Matobo Hills, he would be arrested as it is fully protected by the law (Sunday News, 6 September 1998; Maylam 2005).

The struggle by Chakaredza to exhume Rhodes' bones from the Matobo Hills appears to have ended when President Robert Mugabe publicly supported its preservation during the 14th General Assembly and Scientific Symposium of the International Council on Monuments and Sites (ICOMOS) in Victoria Falls in 2003. During his keynote address, President Mugabe encouraged European foreign delegates to take the opportunity of the conference and travel to the Matobo Hills to see how the country is caring for the grave. "But of course you have to pay in order to see it," said President Mugabe, "...and that way, he [Rhodes] would be paying for the sins he committed to this country" (see also Ranger 2004).

It would seem, however, that the call to remove Rhodes' grave from the Matobo Hills did not end with Chakaredza. The Zimbabwean liberation war veterans also continued to push for the removal of the grave, blaming it for the lack of rain in the cultural landscape. Demands to remove Rhodes' grave from the Matobo Hills appears to have also been recently rekindled following the insistence by Cape Town University students in South Africa to remove Rhodes' statue from the Company's Garden, the heritage site where it was erected in 1908. On a recent visit to South Africa, President Mugabe also appeared to be against the idea to remove Rhode's grave when he scornfully but diplomatically told the South Africans that "We are looking after the corpse. You have the statue of him," Mugabe said. "I don't know what you think we should do-dig him up? Perhaps his spirit might rise again." Although Rhodes' grave has survived in the Matobo Hills in Zimbabwe, in South Africa, the University of Cape Town eventually relented to student demands and removed the memorial of the prominent British imperialist.

Several local indigenous communities were also concerned that they have never benefited from the CAMPFIRE project in the Matobo Hills. They argued that they never had the opportunity to manage wildlife resources in the Hills as was originally planned. A villager remarked that the project has never quite been realised in the Matobo Hills because there is not much wildlife in the park when compared to Hwange or Zambezi national park. The failure of the CAMPFIRE project in the Matobo Hills was also caused by several other factors. The economic collapse in Zimbabwe and the withdrawal of the donor funds following the land reform programme since 2000 has greatly affected the effectiveness of CAMPFIRE projects in the country including the once successful Mahenye CAMPFIRE project in south eastern Zimbabwe along the border with Mozambique (see Balint and Mashinya 2006; Gandiwa, et al. 2013). Local governance failure also contributed to the collapse of the CAMPFIRE project in the Matobo Hills.

SHARING OF FINANCIAL BENEFITS

Mark Ncube, a former archivist in Bulawayo and also a former member of the Matobo Conservation Society, suggested that, if local indigenous communities cannot directly benefit from cultural heritage sites and if benefiting from them could positively influence the return of traditional conservation practices, there may be a need to introduce a Community Share Ownership Trust (CSOT) in the Matobo Hills (M. Ncube, pers. comm., March 13, 2014). The CSOT suggested by Mark Ncube is a concept that was introduced by the Zimbabwean Government in 2011 through the Ministry of Youth, Indigenisation, and Economic Empowerment. The idea behind the introduction of the CSOT is that the communities must have a share of the commercial exploitation of natural resources, including minerals, that occurs in their ancestral lands. The CSOT was introduced in addition to the Indigenisation and Economic Empowerment Act which now compels foreign owned companies, especially mining companies operating in Zimbabwe, to relinquish a 51 percent stake to locals with at least 10 percent spared for the local indigenous communities in which the companies operate. Money accruing to the scheme from the mining companies is then expected to be used for the provision of social and economic infrastructure in accordance with the priorities of the local indigenous communities concerned (Matsa and Masimbiti 2014).

The establishment of the CSOT in the mining sector was based on the historical observation that mineral resources had not benefited the local indigenous people in the communal areas wherein foreign companies operate. Launching the Mhondoro-Ngezi, Chegutu-Zvimba Trust in central north-west Zimbabwe, President Mugabe lamented the exploitation of resources by foreign mining companies with little benefits accrued by communities (Guvamatanga 2014). "Zimbabwe is well endowed with natural resources that are of a finite nature, particularly in the mining sector. These natural resources have, over the years, been exploited largely for the benefit of multinational corporations and other foreign business entities," said President Mugabe. He went on to argue that there is no meaningful revenue accrued by the local authorities responsible in these areas, let alone the vast majority who fall under the traditional leadership in the communal and resettlement areas.

Mark Ncube's idea to introduce a CSOT in the Matobo Hills is, in fact, based on the long observation that revenue generated in the park, and particularly from archaeological sites, has never really made its way back to the local indigenous communities to compensate them for the loss of their ancestral lands and shrines during the land evictions of the 1950s and 1960s. Consequently, several informants that I interviewed accepted it as true that revenue generated in the park merely benefits the ZPWMA, the NMMZ, and the private sector companies that mostly manage lodges and conduct tour guides in the cultural landscape.

However, the question to answer is that, if part of the money generated by these organisations does not benefit the local indigenous communities of the Matobo Hills, where does it go? An informant in the ZPWMA stated that their organisation no longer depends on government funds for conservation in all of its national parks throughout the country. This followed the reorganisation of the ZPWMA in 2004 from a department to an authority, therefore, it operates on a profit making basis and fund its own operations. Originally, the ZPWMA was the Department of National Parks and Wildlife Management and all of its operations were largely funded by the government. The establishment of the authority was a response by the government to the negative macro economic growth, high inflation, high unemployment, massive foreign exchange shortages, and other economic ills that were afflicting the economy subsequent to the sanctions that were imposed on the country by the European Union countries and the United States of America. The sanctions were imposed on the country as a punitive method of forcing the Zimbabwean Government to stop what they regarded as an unwarranted land reform programme and human rights abuses during elections. The sanctions, however, strained the funding for agriculture, health, education, archaeological resources, tourism, and other sectors of the economy (Murimbika and Moyo 2008; Makuvaza and Makuvaza 2013; Makuvaza 2014).

As a result of sanctions, the Zimbabwean government was required to critically re-examine the performance of some of its state owned enterprises, and it established that several of them were experiencing losses and were heavily draining the fiscus. It was thus decided as one of the turn around strategies to reorganise some parastatals and convert them to authorities so that they would operate on a profit making basis. Following this exercise, the ZPWMA is now retaining revenue and funding operations such as the maintenance of roads, construction of lodges, and supplies for rangers who patrol the parks. According to the informant, this leaves the park with very little money that can be given to the local indigenous communities as CSOT.

An NMMZ informant indicated that they collect an average of US$4500.00 per month in the Matobo Hills which they remit together with revenue they collect at the Natural History Museum to their head office in Harare. The staff informant also stated that they retain only 40% of the total amount they submit to their head office for conservation and other administrative requirements. The NMMZ, like the ZPWMA, is also no longer supported by the government for its operations and conservation obligations. However, the informant further said that, as a result of the current difficult economic times, there is very little that can be spared for local indigenous communities as contribution to the idea of the CSOT.

Apart from the ZPWMA and the NMMZ, there are also a number of private players in the Matobo Hills that could contribute to the idea of the CSOT and these include lodges, tour operators, and commercial farmers. According to Ranger (1999, 271), a number of lodges that were originally non-indigineous owned farms and previously thriving as agricultural or grazing units are now blossoming forth as safari lodges. As Ranger further argued, although the private sector arranges “cultural village trips” and even though the farms were originally intended for exploitation rather than the preservation of the environment, they now, by and large, represent the Matobo Hills as a natural landscape and exploit this value for profit making.

Well known private players include the Matobo Conservation Society which was founded in 1993 and whose objective is to foster all natural and cultural aspects of conservation in the Matobo Hills and the Dambari Wildlife Trust established in 1997 whose objective is to conduct research, outreach, and conservation programmes for three primary groups of animals, specifically: small African antelopes and carnivores-primarily cheetahs, and the rhinoceros. Membership of these associations is open to any person with an interest in the conservation of the Matobo Hills. Other associations with branches in Bulawayo include Birdlife Zimbabwe, Wildlife and Environment Zimbabwe, and the Aloe, Cactus and Succulent Society of Zimbabwe.

Although the general objectives of the private sector, and specifically conservation associations, is to support the conservation of both the natural and cultural attributes of the Matobo Hills, the discussions that I had with informants indicate that their activities are not supportive of traditional conservation practices. First, I observed during fieldwork that the majority of local indigenous people in the Matobo Hills are not aware of the existence of these associations and, secondly, that there are no representatives of local indigenous people in the associations. For instance, since it was established, the membership of the Matobo Conservation Society has largely remained comprised of non-indigenous people mostly from the city of Bulawayo.

When I interviewed Mark Ncube about his opinion regarding the membership of the Matobo Conservation Society, he strongly criticised it for remaining primarily non-indigenous in its composition of members. He argued that the broad objective of the Matobo Conservation Society and of other associations cannot be realised if they continue to ignore the local indigenous communities whose ancestral lands they want to conserve. He also asked how the Society can seek to take care of the communal areas and the park without involving the local descent communities of the area (M. Ncube, pers. comm., March 13, 2014).

An informant who is also a member of the Matobo Conservation Society, however, viewed the issue differently when he said that he does not see any problem with the composition of the Society whereby membership is largely non-indigenous. He argued that, if there are local indigenous people in the communal areas who are interested in joining the Society, they should look for it and join since its membership is open to anyone with an interest in the conservation of the cultural landscape. However, perhaps it is the Society that should introduce itself to the local indigenous people so that they could confidently join it. This makes sense considering that it is the Society that has volunteered to help the communal areas conserve the natural and cultural values of the Matobo Hills and not the other way around.

Gavin Stephens acknowledged the unrepresented local indigenous ideas of conservation in the Matobo Conservation Society. He attributed this problem to the lack of resources to popularise the Society in the communal areas of the Matobo Hills. He also pointed out that, in as much as he would like communal people to join the Society, it is difficult to convince them since there are no tangible benefits that are associated with membership. Stephens however, went on to argue that local indigenous people are welcome if they want to join, however, they should not join with the idea of monetary benefits in mind as the Society does not have money (G. Stephens, pers. comm., August 8, 2014).

Although the Matobo Conservation Society has taken major strides to promote the Matobo Hills as a world heritage cultural landscape by erecting world heritage sign posts, other conservation associations have generally tended to limit and confine their activities to research in the national park. However, organisations such as hoteliers consider that, since they pay fees to operate in the Matobo Hills, it is the duty of the government through the ZPWMA and the NMMZ to retain a portion of the revenue generated by these groups in the park to support the idea of CSOT.

In 1995, the deputy minister of Environment and Tourism, Chindori Chininga, under which the ZPWMA belonged at that time, complained that his ministry did not have information about the operations of the independent conservation societies and trusts which source funds in the name of conservation in the Matobo Hills but ultimately use the money for other purposes. However, he further encouraged private players to be transparent with regards to funds which they raise for conservation in the cultural landscape (Chronicle, 11 November 1995). Peter Mundy, a Professor of Forest Resources and Wildlife Management at the University of Science and Technology and former Principal Ecologist in the Matobo National Park, argued that it is in the interest of the private sectors that operate within the Matobo Hills to support the idea of bringing back traditional conservation practices and of involving local indigenous communities in their management as their business largely thrives on these values (P. Mundy, pers. comm., June 6, 2014).

RECLAIMING OF ANCESTRAL LANDS

Given the above struggles to control and benefit from cultural heritage sites, several informants wondered how it could be possible to return to traditional conservation practices in the Hills and be involved in their management when attempting to retain their ancestral lands had failed. The informants stated that local indigenous people had expected that, upon independence, they would return to their ancestral lands where they would continue to look after the Hills with their traditional conservation practices. The informants also said that one of the main reasons why the local indigenous people supported the liberation struggle in the Matobo Hills was to reclaim their ancestral lands that were taken away from them during the colonial period. The informants further indicated that, when they received independence, they were betrayed by their own leaders who denied them a chance to return to their ancestral lands and to manage them through their traditional conservation practices.

From the early 1980s to the late 1990s, the local indigenous communities in the Matobo Hills attempted to return to some sections of the national park and commercial farms where they had hoped to continue with their traditional ways of living. According to Ranger (1999), they began by initiating different combinations of official and unofficial ways of repossessing their lost ancestral lands. Ranger writes that, soon after independence, village heads (known as kraal heads during the colonial period) in Gulati sent a memorandum to the warden of the park explaining that a large area of the park east of the Mtshelele River was their ancestral land and should be returned to them. This request was made based on the knowledge that, previously, additional local indigenous people's ancestral land was granted to the park. Ranger also writes that, informally, the local indigenous communities began to cut timber indiscriminately, poach and snare animals, and graze their livestock in the peripheral sections of non-indigineous commercial farms and the park.

Despite efforts by local indigenous communities to reclaim their ancestral lands, the position of the new Zimbabwean government was that no resettlement would be allowed in the park or on the commercial farms. As Ranger further writes, the political tensions between ZAPU and ZANU which were fueled by the South African agents (see Scarnecchia 2011), the fighting between ex-ZIPRA and ex-ZANLA soldiers, the emergence of armed dissidents in Matabeleland and the huge deployment of state forces to quell dissidents, and the attacks on local indigenous people by the Fifth Brigade army, the CIO, and police resulted in no development in the Matobo Hills between 1982 and 1988. During this period, a number of non-indigenous farmers who had retained farms in the Hills after independence were killed. For security reasons, however, others abandoned their farms south of the Hills, and the farms were subsequently taken over by the government. Fearing for their own safety also ended any hopes that the local descent communities had of reclaiming their ancestral lands and of restoring traditional conservation practices in the cultural landscape (Ranger 1999).

Muzi Khumalo vividly remembered that, as local descent people, they feared attempting to reclaim their ancestral lands in the Matobo Hills (M. Khumalo, pers. comm., August 15, 2014). The dissidents would either harass or kill villagers who would not support them, therefore, no one wanted to live on farms that were close to the national park and risk the fury of either the dissidents or of the government security agents who had interpreted local demands for ancestral lands as subversive (Alexander 1991). It was safer to continue living in the communal lands together with other villagers. Even after independence, some local indigenous people did not wish to move back to their ancestral lands in the park and on commercial farms as they were now war weary. They wanted to remain where they had settled during the colonial period (M. Khumalo, pers. comm., August 15, 2014).

Surprisingly, even though the local indigenous communities in the Matobo Hills were reclaiming their ancestral lands, they were not interested in the resettlement programme, which was introduced in the country by the government in the early 1980s. The resettlement programme was a post colonial plan and an organised movement of rural people to state-acquired former commercial lands that were previously reserved for non-indigineous farmers (Kinsey 1983; Geza 1986). The programme was focused on ensuring a more equitable racial distribution of land and extending the livelihood opportunities for the poorest communities, including the landless and those who were displaced during the colonial period. It was also aimed at reducing population pressure in the communal lands (Elliott, Kinsey and Kwesha 2006). The British had agreed at the Lancaster House Conference in 1979 to fund the land reform on a willing seller/willing buyer principle where non-indigineous farmers who were unwilling to stay in the country could be bought out by funds provided by the British government through the Zimbabwe Government. The conference was organised to discuss how to reach an agreement on how to end the war of liberation in Zimbabwe as well as to craft a new constitution for the country.

The resettlement programme comprised Models, A, B, C and D. Model A involved intensive village settlements with individual allocations of arable land of five hectares per family and communal grazing areas allocated on the basis of a variable number of livestock units depending upon agro-ecological zone (Kinsey 1983). Model B involved the formation of enterprises to manage farms on a cooperative basis. Model C was based on the nucleus of a commercial estate while households had their own individual plots but acted as out-growers. Model D was intended for low rainfall areas in natural regions IV and V and involved the use of ranches for grazing of the herds owned by communal people (Mudege 2008). Being in region IV, the Matobo Hills, therefore, was more suited for the Model D resettlement programme. Families settled in one of these models were required to renounce any land claim elsewhere in Zimbabwe. They were not given ownership of the land on which they were settled but were instead given permits covering residential and farm plots. In theory, these permits could be withdrawn if beneficiaries failed to follow the guidance of government appointed resettlement officers, who were teaching farmers how to farm, and adjudicated in cases of conflict between or among resettled people (Elliot, Kinsey and Kwesha 2006).

Due to the nature of its implementation, the resettlement programme did not address the plight of the Matobo Hills' local indigenous people who wanted to reclaim their original ancestral lands without any conditions attached so they could return to their traditional ways of living. Although a number of farms between the Matobo Hills and the southern communal areas had become available for resettlement, none of the resettlement models were successfully implemented in the Matobo Hills. As an alternative, it was decided that the land should be leased from the non-indigineous owners for five years at an annual rate of six per cent of an agreed valuation with an option for the government to buy it at the end of the five year period. Until that time, the land was to be managed by the Agricultural and Rural Development Authority (ARDA) (Ranger 1999, 252).

The conditions that were established for the resettlement were not popular among the local indigenous people of the Matobo Hills as they did not support the people being involved in the management of the cultural landscape and the return of traditional conservation practices in the Hills. The issue with the resettlement programme was that it discouraged unstructured settlements and attempts to revert to old practices of managing the Hills as was the case in communal areas (M. Moyo, pers. comm., August 15, 2014). Moyo also explained that the conditions of the resettlement programme were such that the resettlement areas were to be managed by leaders who were selected through democratic procedures. As Moyo further argued, the idea to return to traditional conservation practices, therefore, could not have succeeded since the popularly elected leaders did not have traditional knowledge of managing the resettlement areas. In addition, the composition of resettled people which incorporated people from ex-communal areas, ex-farm labourers, ex-urban workers, inter-provincial migrants, returning refugees from neighbouring countries, and others (see Geza 1986) meant that, with the influx of new inhabitants, the remaining traditional conservation practices in the Matobo Hills were also going to be adulterated.

In 1987, a unity accord that ended political tensions between ZANU and ZAPU was signed, and this once again brought peace to the Matobo Hills and the rest of the Matabeleland region. Soon after the unity accord, the local indigenous people began to make fresh demands to reclaim some of their ancestral lands. In reclaiming their ancestral lands, they also began to argue that the social use of the park should be negotiated and that the government should buy farms which they should give to the indigenous people without any conditions attached. Earlier, the failure of the resettlement programe in the Matobo Hills was also a result of the appropriation of 22 ARDA farms by top government officials and business people which also denied the local indigenous people a chance to reclaim their ancestral lands and to return to their traditional ways of managing the area (Chikuhwa 2006).

This led, in 1995, to a protest by more than 900 members of a pressure group called Inqama who moved on to the Honeydale and Matopo Vale estates which had been purchased by top government officials. The group demanded that the estates be given to them as the ancestral land was, in actual fact, their heritage. The land lay adjacent to the Matobo Research Station and to the Gulati communal lands. The farms had been sold to top government officials by the Chennells family. The Chennells family had lived at Three Sisters farm for free, producing crops such as oats, lucerne, potatoes and beans. The family was also involved in dairy farming (Nobbs 1924). The Inqama people, which claimed 4000 members at

Fig. 7.4 The Inqama pressure group reclaiming a section of Sauersdale Farm (Photo: Sunday News, 18 July 1998).

that time and was led by Jonathan Moyo, a Bulawayo accountant, were arrested and fined Z$30 each for demanding their ancestral land back (Ranger 1999). In October 1996, another group of 200 local indigenous people who had lost confidence in the government sponsored resettlement programme decided to resettle on the idle Lucydale farm which is adjacent to the Matobo Research Station. Some families were, as a result, eventually allowed to reside in the south western section of the farm. Following the occupation of Lucydale farm, Chikuhwa (2006, 12) remarked that the anger of the local indigenous communities was no longer only targeted at addressing the colonial injustice of land appropriation but was also now targeted at senior government officials who had begun to seize farms acquired by the state for resettlement purposes.

Two years later, in 1998, more than 100 Inqama people led by Faniya Masuku also unsuccessfully attempted to occupy a section of Sauersdale farm where the Mzilikazi Memorial and Grave and Old Bulawayo cultural heritage sites are located, arguing that it is their ancestral land (Fig. 7.4). Before the 1896/7 war, the Inqama regiment had lived along the northern edges of the Matobo Hills, and this area had come to be known as Inqama (Ranger 1999). "We have come back to our ancestral homes where our forefathers were unfairly evicted by the white people. We have old people among us who can still pin-point where their homesteads were located, which proves wrong all assertions that there was never any settlement of people here," announced Faniya Masuku. The Inqama people also said that, by settling in the Sauersdale block, they would take on the responsibility of reviving local customs of managing the area (Sunday News, 18 July 1998). The majority of people who had come to settle in the section of Sauersdale farm were non-local descent communities from Tsholotsho and Nkayi while others were local descent communities from the communal areas of the Matobo Hills themselves. After three months, approximately 25 local indigenous people who had remained in the farm were removed by Stephen Nkomo who told them to go back to their respective districts and wait for the government to properly allocate them land. To remove the Inqama people from Sauersdale, the Governor was accompanied by officials from the ZPWMA, the Matopos Research Station, the police, and the Matobo District Administrator, Stanley Bhebhe (Chronicle, 15 October 1998).

It is surprising that local indigenous communities in the Matobo Hills did not attempt to reclaim their ancestral land during the so called "fast track" land reform programme in Zimbabwe. Beginning in early 2000, the Zimbabwean government embarked on a compulsory fast track acquisition of non-indigineous owned farms and redistributed them to "landless" Zimbabweans. The fast track land reform programme was most likely a direct response to the British government which had reneged on funding the earlier resettlement programme as was agreed at the Lancaster house conference (Welz 2013). However, this land reform initiative could have been a populist move that was designed to strengthen the support of ZANU PF among the poor rural people (Balint and Mashinya 2006).

Just as with the organised resettlement programme before it, the fast track land reform programme purported to redress and complete the settler-colonial land dispossessions and the agrarian inequalities that the minority government had created during the colonial era (Moyo 2013). The reasons why the local indigenous communities in the Matobo Hills did not take the opportunity to reclaim their ancestral lands were very difficult to obtain during the fieldwork as informants were not willing to discuss the subject. However, it could have been that they did not want to be part of the controversial land reform programme which they believed was being used by the ZANU PF government to garner support during the 2002 and 2008 elections. Chief Masuku stated that only four families, including his, moved from Natisa and settled in the south east portion of Westacre Creek farm (Chief Masuku, pers. comm., March 7, 2015). Chief Masuku settled between the Matopos Dam and Mthwakazi Township on a farm that was previously owned by Charles Chenole, a non-indigineous dairy farmer. The chief's move from Natisa to the farm, however, was criticised by some of the informants that I interviewed who indicated that he ran away from leading his people and from his duties of protecting the Hills using traditional conservation ways. They also said that he had transformed himself into a city chief by moving close to Bulawayo.

It is interesting to note that, prior to the fast track land reform programme, the local indigenous communities who were organising themselves to reclaim their ancestral lands did so without much support from their traditional chiefs. The non-involvement of traditional chiefs in reclaiming ancestral lands in the Matobo Hills was cited by many informants during the interviews as one of several factors that make the idea to reintroduce traditional conservation practices and their involvement in the management of the cultural landscape problematic. The informants largely attributed this problem to the loss of authority by their traditional leaders, especially the chiefs and their headmen. To understand the link between the loss of power by traditional chiefs and the challenges of incorporating traditional conservation practices in the management of the Matobo Hills will require an understanding of colonial and post colonial politics and chieftaincy in the cultural landscape.

POLITICS AND THE BREAKDOWN OF TRADITIONAL LEADERS' AUTHORITY

Chapter 1 stated that, during the pre-colonial period in southern Africa, traditional leaders played a very important role in the management of cultural landscapes as they were the custodians of cultural landscapes in the region. It is also important to point out that chiefs and clan heads were selected and appointed based on the customary procedures of the local indigenous communities and that there were also customary procedures which specified the dismissal of traditional chiefs from leadership. Usually, these individuals were appointed on the basis of the custom that was governed by heredity and not on modern elective democratic principles. It is not necessary to provide details of these procedures here; what is important is to examine how the selection of chiefs contributed to the loss of legitimacy by some traditional leaders in the Matobo Hills.

In Zimbabwe, as in much of southern Africa, the traditional structure of leadership had the head chief as the leader of the entire communal area and a headman (sub-chief) followed by the village head. The headman would control a clan or lineage with different clans making up an ethnic group while the village head controlled an extended family or a village comprising close blood related people (Mukamuri, Campbell and Kowero 2003). He would also assist the chief to carry out his duties and had identical powers in many respects which he exercised within the ethnic group. Similarly, village heads assisted the headmen and chiefs. With the advent of colonialism, the organisation of traditional chiefs began to be intensely interfered with, and this affected the protection of cultural landscapes with traditional conservation practices. In the Matobo Hills, the breakdown of traditional authority began during the colonial period as a result of political interference on the way chiefs were selected. Native Commissioners began to assume the duty of selecting and appointing traditional chiefs who supported the colonial system of administration. They also began to remunerate them so that they continue to pay allegiance to the colonial government. The selected chiefs, however, were not customarily appropriate for the new positions that they were now holding. This has, according to the informants I interviewed, resulted in the loss of legitimacy of several traditional leaders in the cultural landscape (Bhebe 1989).

Following the 1896-7 war, the colonial authorities feared that another war might break out in the Matobo Hills if the traditional chiefs were permitted to reorganise their military regiments and followers. To avert this threat, the Native Commissioners began to take it upon themselves to select and appoint traditional leaders and particularly chiefs. The colonial administrators also began to split Ndebele regimental units so that the Matobo Hills area could be more governable. They did this by substituting the pre-colonial chiefs with new ones who could hold both civil and criminal courts and who could collect court fees from their subjects.

According to Ranger, four Ngameni influential men from the Wenlock ranch, specifically Dhliso Mathema, Nkonkobela Khumalo, Mtuwani Dlodlo, and Hluganiso, were all appointed as new chiefs in March 1897. During the reign of Lobengula, all of the four men had played important roles. Dhliso was active in the northern part of the Hills during the 1896-7 fighting while Hluganiso was active in the eastern part. Nkonkobela was a successful military commander while Mtuwani was believed to possess a special association with the shrines. To pacify them, upon their appointment as chiefs, Hluganiso, Nkonkobela, and Mtuwani began to be paid a monthly subsidy of £2 while Dhliso's salary was designated at £5 as he was promoted to the position of the head chief for the entire Matobo Hills district. However, Dhliso's remuneration was later reduced to £3 as he did not want to be involved in the collection of taxes, sending his people out to European farms and to mines as labourers, nor to disarm them after the 1896-7 war (Ranger 1999).

Msindo (2012, 72-73) who examined the Kalanga chieftaincy in the western precincts of the Matobo Hills writes that there were several other Ndebele chiefs who were promoted in lieu of Kalanga chiefs. According to Msindo, these chiefs include Gampu of Igabha, Mpini Ndiweni of Usaba (Zimnyama), and Sindisa Mpofu of the Mpande regiment. As a result of their elevation, the Kalanga chiefs began to be marginalised and were now required to report to the government through the Ndebele chiefs. Msindo also writes that Gampu Sithole, who collaborated with the BSACo in the 1896-97 war, was immediately promoted to become head chief of the Bulilima Mangwe district and began to be paid a subsidy of £5 per month. According to Msindo, the colonial authorities began to install more Ndebele chiefs such as Ngazi (Wasi), Mbambeleli, Mahlathini, and Mazwi whose area later became part of the Bulawayo district. Loyal Kalanga chiefs such as Tategulu, Nkolomana (Nyiga), Magama, Malaba, Luswina (Tjingababili) Mate, and Sangulube were also recognised. Msindo further argued that several customarily important pre-colonial Kalanga chiefs, some of which even had more followers and villages than their appointed counterparts, were never officially recognised. These chiefs include Mengwe, Nswazwi, Matundume, Bango, Gonde Tshuma, Mninigau (Hikwa), Mlevu, Soluswe (Solusi), Sinete, Nkaki, Langabi (Langapi), and Sitshungulwana of Mahlabatini.

The colonial authorities however, began to introduce administrative structures and legislative laws that reduced the position of traditional chiefs to that of state officials. For instance, after the power to allocate land was usurped by the Europeans during the early years of colonialism, this authority was only returned to selected chiefs through the enactment of the Tribal Trust Lands Act of 1967. Powers to try some cases were also returned to the selected chiefs through the Tribal Courts Act of 1969 while they were also granted executive and administrative powers through the African Councils Act (Amended) of 1973 (Weinrich 1973; Chatiza 2010).

The selection and installation of chiefs by the colonial authorities created a host of problems for other local indigenous communities in the Matobo Hills area, especially for the Nyubi and the Kalanga people who were already identified with and paying allegiance to their own customarily selected traditional chiefs. The first issue was that this created an impression that the Ndebele chiefs were the rightful rulers of the entire Matobo area, and the Kalanga, Nyubi, and other local indigenous communities were subordinates who should recognise their authority (Msindo 2010, 2012). The second problem was that the appointed Ndebele chiefs began to promote a broad Ndebele identity which was sustained by deliberately balancing the forces of tradition and modernity in the cultural landscape (Ranger 1999). Nonetheless, in a cultural landscape where chieftainship was being redefined and the local indigenous people were being forced to move from the park into newly established communal areas, the popularity of the appointed chiefs, as Msindo (2012) argued, would have significantly depended on the extent to which they protected their people against a repressive government that had begun to effect management changes in the entire Matobo Hills cultural landscape. Jeffrey Ndlovu, a Kalanga informant, argued that the imposition of Ndebele chiefs by the colonial government in the Matobo Hills has led to the misplacement of traditional conservation practices in the area. He further argued that the appointed chiefs, and especially the Ndebele chiefs, had no understanding of the cultural traditions of the Hills since they were only recent immigrants to the area (J. Ndlovu, pers. comm., August 20, 2014). A Nyubi informant also said that the selection of traditional chiefs and the loss of their authority in the Matobo Hills meant that they had become victims of colonial injustice. The informant further stated that they began to doubt the legitimacy of the Ndebele chiefs to lead them and to conserve the Matobo Hills as they were now acting as government agencies to manage the ancestral lands.

The colonial state's policy of exercising direct control over traditional leaders, however, continued into the post-colonial era even though the new Zimbabwean Government had initially relegated them. On attainment of independence, the government had to rapidly construct a different system of rural government aimed at fostering development at the local level. As a result, the government began to disregard the institution of traditional authority and especially that of chieftainship because the traditional leaders were perceived as having colluded with the government during the colonial era (Chatiza 2010; Makumbe 2010). For this reason, most of the powers that the traditional chiefs had prior to independence were divested through the enactment of the Chiefs and Headmen Act [Chapter 29:01] of 1982, which, in general, excluded them from rural governance (Chakaipa 2010). The powers of the chiefs were further reduced in 1984 through the Prime Minister's directive which introduced the concept of Village Development Committees (VIDCOs) and Ward Development Committees (WADCOs). This instruction was meant to address the problems of the colonial administration which was highly centralised, deeply authoritarian, and which had ensured that basic public services were not accessible to indigenous people who were the majority in the country. During the colonial era, the rural areas were administered by Rural Councils which were exclusively meant to serve the European communities and by the African Councils that were responsible for the Tribal Trust Lands and African Purchase Areas (Mangiza 1986). The position of chiefs, in particular, was consolidated in 1957 through the enactment of the African Councils Act. This Act enabled the chiefs to be appointed as vice-presidents and the District Commissioners as presidents of the African Councils. The empowering of the African Councils was intended to counteract the emerging threat of nationalism which was becoming established in the country (Chakaipa 2010). This arrangement of managing rural areas was racial and discriminatory and did not involve the local indigenous communities in the planning and development of their areas. The Prime Minister's directive, therefore, was intended to involve the rural communities in the development of their areas through the decentralisation process. The decentralisation reform in Zimbabwe was a decision taken by the government in the early 1980s to transfer responsibilities, resources, and power from the higher to the lower levels of government. The rationale behind decentralisation was based on the belief that the implementation of projects would be improved through better coordination by the decentralised government structures (Halaar and Olthof 1994; Manhokwe 2010).

The VIDCO, which is the lowest development-planning unit in the district, was designed to represent one hundred households while the WADCO was planned to represent six villages. A number of wards then form a district. Each district is headed by a District Administrator who is appointed by the Public Service Commission. However, representation on the VIDCO and WADCO was based on the "democratic" voting system (Mukamuri, Campbell and Kowero 2003). The VIDCO is represented by a chairperson while the WADCO is represented by an elected ward councilor who also becomes its chairperson. The WADCO consists of all of the secretaries and chairpersons of all of the VIDCOs in the ward. After consultation between the villagers and the VIDCO regarding developments, the VIDCO is supposed to submit development plans annually to the WADCO. The WADCO then coordinates the proposed plans from all of the VIDCOs and submits them to the District Development Committee (DDC) which would then incorporate ward plans together with government departments' plans into an integrated district plan for approval by the District Council. The plans would further be submitted to the Provincial Development Committee (PDC) and to the Provincial Council (PC) (Fig. 7.5) who would then submit to the ministry of Local Government Urban and Rural Development. The Rural District Council comprises the elected ward councilors and the District Administrator and is headed by a Chief Executive Officer. The management of local government falls directly under the ministry of Local Government, Urban and Rural Development (Halaar and Olthof 1994; Manhokwe 2010).

In 1999, the then minister of local government, John Landa Nkomo, announced plans to bring back the authority of chiefs in communal areas. President Mugabe then followed and publicly apologised for ignoring chiefs since independence (Ranger 2001). Following efforts to recognise the institution of chieftaincy in the country, the Traditional Leader's Act was enacted in 2000, and their powers were eventually "returned". Chiefs were given powers to lead development programmes in their areas of jurisdiction including the distribution of land to their subjects. They were also tasked with the role of promoting cultural values and norms within their communities (Makahamadze, Grand and Tavuyanago 2009). The institution of traditional leadership is now provided for in the country's constitution. Chiefs are appointed by the President in accordance with Chapter 15 of the Constitution of Zimbabwe and Section 3 of the Chiefs and Headmen Act. The president also has the power to remove a chief from office. Additionally, the appointed chiefs are now legally paid an allowance or salary by the state that is decided by the government through an act of parliament. The constitution also states that the traditional leaders must uphold cultural values and, in particular, promote sound family values. In addition, they must also, in accordance with the constitution, take measures to preserve the culture, traditions, history, and heritage of their communities including sacred shrines. The constitution further states that, except as provided by an act of parliament, traditional leaders have authority, jurisdiction, and control over communal land or other areas for which they have been appointed and over persons within those communal lands or areas.

Several informants that I have interviewed, however, did not discern any difference between traditional chiefs of the colonial era and those that were appointed after the independence of the country. The informants said that, like the chiefs that were appointed during the colonial period, post indipendence chiefs have no authority over their land and people. They argued that they are political figures whose interest is only money and not the conservation of their ancestral lands.

Chief Mathe admitted that, as chiefs, they have lost their traditional authority because of government interference in the selection of chiefs. However, he denied that he is manipulated by politics or money to consider the return of traditional conservation practices in the Matobo Hills and the involvement of his subjects into the management of the world heritage cultural landscape. Instead, he blamed human rights laws for making it difficult to keep traditional conservation practices in the Matobo Hills when he stated that, in theory, they have power but, in practice, they do not. Chief Mathe also explained that, in the past, they could inflict corporal punishment on anyone who would have violated traditional conservation practices in the Hills, especially toward children. Currently, any attempts to use corporal punishment can be interpreted as child abuse, and they can be arrested and tried even if they are traditional chiefs (Chief Mathe, pers. comm., August 16, 2014).

Headman Zibuyeni Ncube who assists Chief Tshitshi Mpofu and lives near Empandeni Mission, admitted that, although they still have authority, their powers are not sufficient enough to enforce the return of traditional conservation practices in the Matobo Hills. The headman also argued that, although the Traditional Leaders' Act grants them powers to promote cultural values within their communities, it does not specify what cultural values should be promoted. He also argued that the understanding of the Traditional Leaders' Act and how it should

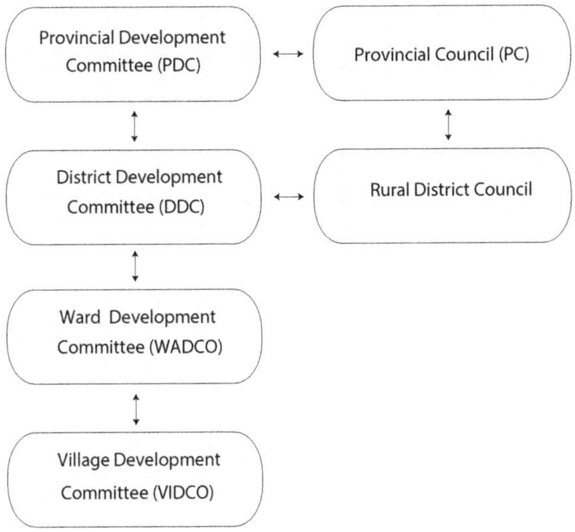

Fig. 7.5 Structure of the decentralised local government in Zimbabwe.

be implemented is understood differently from one chief to another throughout the whole of the Matobo Hills and the rest of the country. Headman Ncube also went on to assert that the involvement of the local indigenous people in the management of the Hills as a World Heritage Site requires negotiation as this is not enshrined in the Traditional Leaders' Act (Z. Ncube, pers. comm., August 20, 2014).

Chief Malaki Masuku, however, attributed the difficulty of integrating traditional conservation practices in the management of the Matobo Hills to the local indigenous communities who have disregarded their traditional cultural practices. Chief Masuku argued that the local indigenous people in the Matobo Hills have since disregaded their cultural practices and are now following other people's cultures (Chief Masuku, pers. comm., March, 2015).

Several informants also blamed traditional chiefs and their headmen for contributing to the failure of reintroducing traditional conservation practices in the Matobo Hills as they gave land to people who do not originally come from the area. The informants argued that the population is increasing in the Hills as result of these people who are being given this land. Some swampy areas and watercourses around the Silozwane area have dried up as a result of demand of land for farming and grazing due to population increase (S. Ndlovu, pers. comm., June 26, 2014). Micah Moyo argued that the increase of population in the Matobo Hills is also fashioning a new cultural landscape with people who have different identities and beliefs. According to Moyo, these people are perceived as not supporting the original cultural practices in the Matobo Hills. The majority of them, as Moyo further exaplined, bring or end up going to churches which place unfamiliar values in the communal areas. As Micah Moyo further asserted, the increase in population has tremendously contributed to the erosion of cultural practices in the Matobo Hills (M. Moyo, pers. comm., June 26, 2014).

All of the informants including the traditional leaders also largely blamed church organisations for seriously contributing to the breakdown of traditional conservation practices in the Matobo Hills. The chiefs argued that, even though they are quite aware that church organisations are destroying their cultural practices in the Matobo Hills, they cannot prevent their establishment in the cultural landscape as they respect the freedom of worship for their subjects. To understand how church organisations have contributed or are contributing to the destruction of traditional conservation practices and the involvement of local indigenous people in the management of the Matobo Hills, the activities of Christian churches in the Matobo Hills will be elucidated.

CHRISTIANITY AND THE BREAKDOWN OF TRADITIONAL CONSERVATION PRACTICES

Chapter 4 states that Christianity was introduced in the Matobo Hills by European missionaries beginning in the mid 19th century onwards. However, while European missionary churches eventually made their way into the Hills, the African Initiated Churches also began to gain considerable prominence in the lives of the local indigenous communities in the cultural landscape. These African Initiated Churches, which are also known as African Instituted Churches, African Independent Churches or Pentecostal Churches, are Christian Churches which were established by the Africans without the assistance of European missionaries (da Silva 1993; Oduro 2006). Several critics argue that these churches were created as a result of racial bias, politics, and theological dominance of early Missionary Churches. These critics also argue that these churches were established to address the needs of the local indigenous communities' socio-cultural needs and theological interpretive disparities in the religious spiritual world (see, for example, Chitando 2006; Oduro 2006).

In Zimbabwe, the largest African Initiated Churches which have penetrated the Matobo Hills are the Apostolic Faith Church (Figs 7.6), the Zion Christian Church (ZCC) and the Zimbabwe Assemblies of God Africa (ZAOGA). Other Missionary Churches that have also found their way in the cultural landscape include the Kingdom of Jehovah's Witness (Fig. 7.7), Seventh Day Adventist (SDA), which is commonly known in the area as Savada/ Sabatha (Sabbath) and the Salvation Army. The detail of how and when these churches penetrated the Matobo Hills is beyond the scope of this study and will not be discussed. However, it is noteworthy that these churches have had a tremendous impact on the lives of the local indigenous communities, and they have nurtured a new brand of Christians which hold disparate views towards the use of traditional conservation practices in the Matobo Hills and involvement in their management. These churches have introduced concepts which are often in sharp contrast with those that are embraced by the traditional institutions of conservation in this world heritage cultural landscape. The Apostolic Faith and the SDA Church, for instance, intermingle African traditional religion and Christianity, and they also promote Old Testament practices. Nkomazana (2006) describes this fusion as syncretism, which is a type of Christianity that blends the gospel with indigenous cultural and religious practices. The faith of these Christian churches is centered on umoya oyingcwele (Holy Spirit) and on Biblical movements which draw their preaching primarily from the Old and New Testaments. Unlike Missionary Churches, African Independent Churches are fundamentally united by their theological thrust which is the preaching of the ilizwi elingcwele (Good News) and the healing and casting out of umoya omubi (demons) using the power of the Holy Spirit. They are also based on the doctrine of being "born again".

Both the Apostolic Faith and the SDA churches take on a number of symbols and practices of Judaism which forbid eating pork, drinking alcohol, and smoking tobacco, and they dictate Saturday as their Sabatha (Sabbath) day. They also emphasise healing and prophecy, holding their prayers in the wilderness or in open spaces, fasting, and performing all night prayers in hills or mountains. The Zion Churches, like the Apostolic Faith Churches, also take on some symbols and practices of Judaism which forbid eating pork, amacimbi, drinking alcohol, and smoking tobacco. They also conduct their prayers on hills and mountains or in open spaces, and they also prophesy and use water to cast out demons from afflicted people. However, unlike the Apostolic Faith Churches, the Zionists dictate Sunday as their day of prayer.

Charles Ncube, who lives in the Mapani area just south west of Natisa Township, blamed Pentecostal Churches for making it difficult to return to traditional conservation practices in the Matobo Hills. Without referring to a specific Pentecostal Church in the Matobo Hills, Ncube argued that these churches are preaching the gospel of abandoning culture and stopping veneration of ancestors in the Matobo Hills. Ncube went on to explain that these churches also associate the veneration of ancestors with the worshiping of evil spirits. Ncube further stated this is the reason why he does not want to attend church (C. Ncube, pes. comm. April 14, 2014). Zweli Mthunzi was even more concerned with the fact that children now listen much more to church pastors and to prophets than they do to their elders. Mthunzi said they now regard the traditional knowledge of conservation as izinto zabadala (things of the old people) (Z. Mthunzi, pers. comm., August 16, 2014). Ndawana Sibanda, who is a traditional healer and lives in the Ezinyangeni village near Matopo Mission, said that although he is a devoted SDA member, his church regards traditional healers and those who believe in traditional religious practices as amahedeni (hidden) people. Sibanda, however, denied that, although he is a traditional healer, he is not hidden. He stated that he even prays to God before administering his traditional medicines to patients. He further said that he follows this procedure because he believes that the medicines he administers to patients are from God (N. Sibanda, pers. comm., August 15, 2014). Another informant, Mabuthelela Sibanda, who is also a traditional healer and lives in the same village with Ndawana Sibanda, indicated that the way some local indigenous people believe in church is such that they now regard it as their ancestors. She also said that, in the past, she used to dance for rain in the Hills, however, she has since stopped the practice because some villagers had started labeling her as a witch (umthakhati) (M. Sibanda, pers. comm., August 15, 2014).

Headman Ncube, who lives near to Ntunjambili Cave, also blamed the church for "killing" their cultural practices in the Matobo Hills. He said that some church members, especially those of the SDA, work on Wednesday which is observed as the day of ancestors in the whole of Matobo Hills. During the interview, the Headman mentioned Cleopas Mpofu and Albert Mkandla as some of the SDA members who are violating cultural practices of the Matobo Hills by working on Wednesday. Headman Ncube also said that, although they work with neighbourhood police to ensure that people comply with the cultural norms of the Hills, prosecuting them has proved to be difficult as there is no law that forbids people to work on Wednesday (Headman Ncube, pers. comm., August 15, 2014).

When I asked Cleopas Mpofu why he works on Wednesday, he said that he is a devout SDA and cannot follow cultural traditions he does not believe in. Explaining further, Mpofu went on to quote Exodus 20: verse 8-11 in the Bible, "For in six days the Lord made the heavens and the earth, the sea, and all that is in them, and rested on the seventh day; therefore the Lord blessed the Sabbath day and made it a holy day." According to Mpofu, the seventh day on which the Lord rested falls on a Saturday. "Now tell me where it is written in the Bible that people should not work on Wednesday?" asked Mpofu. Mpofu went on to argue that if other villagers want him to stop working on Wednesday, traditional chiefs and their headman should also tell commercial farmers and people who work in the national park to stop working on Wednesday (C. Mpofu, pers. comm., August 15, 2014). Mpofu's argument is based on the observation that people in commercial farms and in the national park work on Wednesday, yet the traditional chiefs and their headman have not attempted to refrain them from violating this cultural practice.

Several Pentecostal Church members share Cleopas Mpofu's views while others like Ndawana Sibanda value both the church and the cultural practices. Timothy Mahlangu confirmed this when he said that he has no issues in observing cultural practices even though he was an ordained pastor in a local SDA church. Mahlangu also argued that this is not strange because Christianity and cultural practices have existed side by side in the Matobo Hills since the arrival of missionaries in the area. He further argued that he easily mixes the two and views them as sources of divine authority and spirituality. He also said that he draws his strength and protection from both sources. Mahlangu further argued that going to church and respecting cultural and religious practices is quite a common practice among the local descent people of the Matobo Hills (T. Mahlangu, pers. comm., April 8, 2014). It would appear that, although it is now common practice in the Matobo Hills that local indigenous people would like to have both the church and traditional religious practices, the church has continued to be viewed as the main hindrance to the idea of reintroducing traditional conservation practices and involving people in the management of the world heritage cultural landscape. Several local indigenous people in the Matobo Hills also thought of Pentecostal Churches as businesses that are designed to enrich their owners (prophets and pastors) who take advantage of the gullibility of their followers by asking them to give to God as a way of asking for blessings. One informant said that, in this business game, followers are instructed to render their cultural practices and sinful ways to Satan (the devil) and to give part of their income to God so that they can receive blessings in return. The informant argued that the idea of reintroducing traditional conservation practices and of involving local indigenous people in the management of the Hills can be interpreted by those who attend Pentecostal Churches as a defeat by the devil. The informant further argued that when interpreted this way, many people are unlikely to support the idea of returning traditional conservation practices and being involved in the management of the cultural landscape.

Fig. 7.6 An Apostolic Faith Church center in Lushumbe communal area (Photo by Author).

POWER STRUGGLES IN THE MATOBO HILLS

One of the key issues that affects the return of traditional conservation practices and the involvement of local indigenous people in the management of the Matobo Hills is the differences of opinion between the NMMZ and the ZPWMA regarding the management of the world heritage cultural landscape, and especially the national park. The disagreement began when the NMMZ proposed to take over the management of the Special Area (404 hectares) at Victoria Falls, a Transboundary World Heritage Site shared between Zambia and Zimbabwe (see Makuvaza 2010, 2012). The dispute has its origins from the late 1980s as part of the government of Zimbabwe's efforts to stop parastatal organisations from depending entirely on government funding for their operations and salaries. To address this problem, the NMMZ quickly decided to directly engage in commercial operations in the tourism sector, then a growing and perceived profitable part of the country's economy (Makuvaza and Burret 2011). The NMMZ then approached the ZPWMA and proposed to take over the management of the Special Area, arguing that it is the country's first national monument, which was declared in 1937 under the existing Commission for the Natural and Historical Monuments and Relics. The Special Area is part of the Victoria Falls National Park and consists of a rain forest, several islands, and the downstream gorges (Makuvaza 2010, 2012).

The NMMZ further asserted that, as is the case with other national monuments that are located in national park lands nationwide, the land category in which the Special Area is located does not affect its national monument status. Based on the definition of a national monument, the NMMZ argued that the Special Area remains its property. The NMMZ also asserted that its responsibility of managing the

Special Area together with the duty of the ZPWMA of managing the surrounding environments was acknowledged by the World Heritage Committee when the site was proclaimed as a World Heritage Site in 1989. It further argued that, in terms of managing Transboundary World Heritage Sites, the 1972 World Heritage Convention requires that they be administered by the states parties that are concerned: that is, in the case of the Victoria Falls, by Zambia and Zimbabwe. On the basis of this requirement, the NMMZ further contended that the Zambian side of the Victoria Falls is managed by a state agent, i.e., the National Heritage Conservation Commission, a counterpart and sister organisation of the NMMZ. Considering its experience in managing world heritage sites in the country, it is the most appropriate to jointly administer the site with its Zambian counterpart (Makuvaza 2010, 2012).

The ZPWMA refused to surrender the management of the Special Area to the NMMZ, counter-arguing that, as a government organisation, it has managed the area ever since the Victoria Falls National Park was established in 1952. The ZPWMA Act considers any botanical garden, recreational park, safari area, or sanctuary as a park. Its objectives are to make provision for the preservation, conservation, propagation, or control of the wildlife, fish, and plants of Zimbabwe and the protection of the natural landscape and scenery. Based on this definition, the park's authorities argued that the land in which the Special Area (a natural landscape) is located is part of the national park, therefore, the administration of the site is its legislative responsibility under the Act; hence, the status quo should be accepted as a fait accompli (Makuvaza 2010, 2012).

Negotiations to change the administration of the area from the ZPWMA to the NMMZ resulted in a stalemate, and the dispute quickly amplified to include the Matobo Hills where, as seen in chapter 5, certain cultural heritage sites are located in the national park. However, prior to the dispute in the mid 1990s, the NMMZ had begun to charge admission fees at some of its cultural heritage sites located in the Matobo National Park as a way of raising revenue. The decision created a double ticketing system for tourists entering the park who wished to visit rock art

Fig. 7.7 Kingdom Hall of Jehovah's Witnesses Church at Tshapo Business Center near Whitewaters school (Photo by Author).

sites. This meant that visitors were now required to pay entrance fees twice, first at the main gates when entering the park and, second, if they wished to view rock art caves and other cultural heritage sites located in the park. As relations between the ZPWMA and the NMMZ were favorable at that time, the NMMZ site custodians were accommodated at the Maleme main camp. The ZPWMA also helped maintain gravel roads that led to rock art sites to make it easier to visit the archaeological sites.

However, with the introduction of the new payment arrangement, many visitors began to complain that they were being double ticketed to enter the same park and being cheated out of their money. The Matobo Conservation Society began to also argue that the dual ticketing system was making the park the most expensive in the country which resulted in fewer tourists visiting the Hills. According to the Society, tour operators were now diverting tourists to rock art sites that are located in the communal areas to avoid the double ticketing system. The Society began to urge the ZPWMA and the NMMZ to find a lasting solution to the problem by coming up with single paying points when entering the park (see Chronicle, 22 August 1995; Chronicle, 31 October 1995).

According to a NMMZ informant, to solve the problem of double ticketing, the ZPWMA and the NMMZ agreed in July 1995 that the NMMZ should be allowed to move to the main entrance gates of the park so that they could charge entry fees to tourists who would like to visit rock art sites from there. Although this arrangement ensured that visitors could now pay to enter the park and to see cultural heritage sites at single entry points, this did not eliminate the double ticketing system as the ZPWMA and the NMMZ continued to charge separate entry fees to visitors. This arrangement, however, soon created managerial problems as some visitors still did not understand why they were being issued with two different tickets when, in fact, they were entering the same national park. According to one of the NMMZ staff members who once collected revenue at the park's main entrance gate, many visitors preferred to pay to see cultural heritage sites that are managed by the NMMZ rather than paying for the ZPWMA which only offers accommodation and camping facilities to tourists who would like to spend a night in the park (see also Chronicle, 11 November 1995). As the NMMZ informant explained, this soon created competition for customers at the park's main gates between the ZPWMA and the NMMZ. As rivalry for customers strengthened, the ZPWMA reneged on the agreement to have NMMZ staff collect revenue at the main park entrance gates.

With NMMZ once again collecting revenue at its cultural heritage sites, demands were again made to solve the double ticketing system in the park. One suggestion to resolve the problem was that the two contesting organisations should charge a single entry fee into the park and then negotiate sharing the proceeds (see Chronicle, 21 October 1995). Although this was agreed in principle, the suggestion was never implemented. The two organisations continued to charge tourists two separate fees, one to enter the park and the other to visit rock art paintings and other cultural heritage sites that are located in the park (Chronicle, 18 October 1995; Chronicle, 11 November 1995). The problem of double ticketing visitors has even now remain unsolved.

The rapport between the ZPWMA and the NMMZ appears to have deteriorated when the NMMZ attempted to take over the management of the Special Area at Victoria Falls in 2000 by establishing its physical presence at the site. Although an agreement was later reached that the NMMZ should halt all attempts to take over the Special Area to allow for an amicable solution to the problem, the ZPWMA responded by temporarily ejecting the NMMZ site custodians who were earlier offered accommodation at Maleme, arguing that the houses were required to accommodate the park staff members. The ZPWMA also halted regular maintenance of the roads leading to rock art sites and other cultural heritage sites citing lack of funding and equipment.

A NMMZ informant said that, although they use a portion of the 40% of the money they submit to their Head office to perform conservation work, they have not been able to maintain roads leading to rock art sites in recent years due to the financial problems they are experiencing as an organisation. A ZPWMA informant complained that, as a result of the NMMZ's failure to maintain roads leading to cultural heritage sites, the park authorities are now being blamed by tourists for failing to maintain them. The informant also argued that the NMMZ should be able to maintain the roads since they are collecting revenue from those archaeological sites. The ecologist responded that they cannot maintain these roads as there is no budget for that.

The rift between the ZPWMA and the NMMZ later became more apparent when as the main players in the management of the Hills failed to support the renewal of traditional conservation practices and the involvement of local indigenous communities in the management of the World Heritage Site as outlined in the Site Management Plan. The two organisations, however, as seen in chapter 3, ironically chaired the Site Management Committee or Site Steering Group and were to implement the Site Management Plan. The ZPWMA and the NMMZ were expected to also work cohesively with both the traditional and elected leadership and specifically with the local indigenous communities to properly manage the Matobo Hills. The two organisations were thus mandated to promote the preservation of local traditional culture such as rain making ceremonies and dances (Technical Committee 2004, 26-36).

At a meeting on 26 October 2009 to review the Site Management Plan, tempers flared as the representatives of the local indigenous communities took turns to castigate the Site Management Committee for failing to arrange regular meetings to monitor the progress of implementing the Site Management Plan. The ZPWMA was criticised for reneging on the relaxing of stringent state policies which prevent the local indigenous communities from benefitting from the park's resources. The NMMZ was also equally criticised for being only interested in the collection of revenue from national monuments located in the park without investing any of it back into conservation and maintenance of the roads leading to rock art sites. The local indigenous communities also argued that the proclamation of the Hills as a World Heritage Site had not helped to relax state laws so that the people could access some of their shrines as was purported during the nomination. In addition, they also complained that there are too many state and international laws in the Matobo Hills that disregard traditional conservation practices and that the consideration of the practices in the management of the cultural landscape will never be a success unless they are fully incorporated into the existing state laws (Makuvaza and Makuvaza 2012). In response, the site management committee cited a lack of resources as the major reason for not being able to implement the Site Management Plan. The committee argued that the economic hardships that had gripped the country from the time when the Hills were proclaimed as a World Heritage Site prevented them from implementing the plan.

At the end of the meeting, it was suggested that in order to solve the problems, a new Site Management Committee should be selected since the existing one had failed to perform its duties. The local indigenous communities also suggested that the new committee should be autonomous and chaired by a retired judge, minister, or any distinguished individual. It was argued that an independent committee would perform its duties better and without bias. This idea was opposed by both the NMMZ and the ZPWMA arguing that one of their departments should retain the chair of the committee as the two organisations are responsible for the management of World Heritage Sites in the country. The existing committee also rejected the idea and complained that it was being judged unfairly for not performing its duties and should be given another chance to implement the Site Management Plan. It was also agreed that the existing committee should produce a review report of the Site Management Plan with recommendations on the way to move forward (Makuvaza and Makuvaza 2012).

Most informants that I interviewed regarding the conduct of the ZPWMA and the NMMZ over the management of the Matobo Hills felt that the two organisations reneged on their duties soon after the Hills were proclaimed as a World Heritage Site. They also said that the organisations have ignored the desires of the local indigenous communities of promoting traditional conservation practices in the Hills as was stated in the Site Management Plan. The informants further stated that, soon after the proclamation of the Hills as a World Heritage Site, the ZPWMA and the NMMZ began to pursue their own institutional interests and have, during the process, abandoned the local indigenous people and their traditional conservation practices. Consequently, the administration of the Matobo Hills has, in fact, remained almost the same as before the proclamation as a World Heritage Site.

SUMMARY

This chapter demonstrates that the perspectives of local indigenous people on the idea to reintroduce traditional conservation practices and involving them in the management of the Matobo Hills vary within the cultural landscape. While personal perspectives diverge, responses by the local indigenous people demonstrate that they are all concerned with the proper management of the Matobo Hills World Heritage Site from which they all depend for their continued existence. However, although their views differ, there is a general agreement that the fabric of the Matobo rural communities are undergoing rapid change, much of which is negatively affecting the idea of reintroducing traditional conservation practices and involving local indigenous people in the management of the World Heritage Site.

It would appear that, in this chapter, for the idea of reintroducing traditional conservation practices in the Matobo Hills to be successful, the local indigenous communities must be able to benefit from the collective management of the area which they consider to be their ancestral cultural landscape. The benefits cited by the local indigenous communities include employment, sharing of revenue, and involvement in practical tourism ventures. It would also appear that for the idea of reintroducing traditional conservation practices to actually work, the local indigenous communities must be empowered and motivated to make decisions and take responsibility of the decisions as primary guardians of the World Heritage Site. This way, the local indigenous communities would begin to feel that the ownership of the Matobo Hills has been returned to them. However, this is difficult to accomplish as the cultural heritage sites from which they would like to benefit do not, in practice, belong to them.

It has also been shown in this chapter that there are parallel hierarchies of traditional leadership in the Matobo Hills, the local government, and state organisations that are directly responsible for the management of the World Heritage Site. The informants made it clear that these parallel hierarchies have ambiguous and overlapping jurisdictions and mandates in the Matobo Hills such that they often cause institutional conflicts and struggle for power to manage the World Heritage Site. From the discussions, it would appear that the traditional leaders are in a better position to put the reintroduction of traditional conservation practices in the Matobo Hills into effect given their popularity with and more knowledge of the local indigenous communities. However, it would also appear that their authority is diminishing even though they are currently enjoying the support of the government.

This chapter also revealed that independent churches have dominated the Matobo Hills World Site. Like their traditional religious counterparts, independent churches have developed, expanded, and incorporated new beliefs and practices into the people of the cultural landscape. The focus of these churches is extensively based on their perception of social, economic, and material needs and not on the traditional conservation practices of the Matobo Hills. With the rising power of religious organisations in the Matobo Hills, the traditional conservation practices are gradually losing their legitimacy in the entire cultural landscape.

Lastly, the power struggle between the ZPWMA and the NMMZ over the management of the park and the entire Matobo Hills has and is continuously affecting the idea of reviving traditional conservation practices and involving local indigenous people in the management of the Matobo Hills. As shown in the chapter, the power struggle between the two organisations is grounded on conflicting economic agendas such that they are now being used to fulfil economic ends rather than the consideration of reintroducing traditional conservation practices and involving local indigenous communities in the management of the cultural landscape.

8. Discussion and Conclusion

INTRODUCTION

The underlying goal behind the idea of considering traditional conservation practices and involving local indigenous communities in the management of world heritage cultural landscapes is to ensure the prolonged existence of the sites. It is also to guarantee the permanence of the so-called authentic original values which are assumed to be embodied in world heritage cultural landscapes. As has been discussed, one way, among several approaches, to ensure the prolonged existence of world heritage cultural landscapes and their values is to consider the relevance of traditional conservation practices and to involve local indigenous communities in the management of these areas. The focus, therefore, in part, is to devolve the management of world heritage cultural landscapes from government organisations and other authorities to local indigenous communities.

Although researchers and conservation managers extensively agree on the relevance of traditional conservation practices and the involvement of local indigenous communities in the management of world heritage cultural landscapes, there are a range of challenges and constraints which make it difficult to put this initiative into actual practice.

This closing chapter discusses what I deem to be the salient challenges and constraints that deter the revival of traditional conservation practices and involvement of local indigenous communities in the management of world heritage cultural landscapes. As I discuss the challenges and constraints, I also draw upon experiences from the management of a number of world heritage cultural landscapes from across the globe. As a way of concluding this thesis, I then discuss what I judge to be important considerations when taking into account the use of traditional conservation practices and involvement of local descent communities in the management of world heritage cultural landscapes.

CHALLENGES AND CONSTRAINTS

One of the major challenges that affect the idea of considering the relevance of traditional conservation practices and involving local indigenous communities in the management of world heritage cultural landscapes, especially in southern Africa, is entrenched in its primary objective of protecting world heritage cultural landscapes instead of preserving the traditional conservation practices themselves. Suggestions by informants in the Matobo Hills that the idea of considering the importance of traditional conservation practices can only be possible in the communal areas and that only existing practices should be considered indicate that, while a number of practices still persist, others have or are in the process of diminishing in many parts of the cultural landscape.

This study has shown that social, economic, and political factors, to a very large extent, are contributing to the decline of traditional conservation practices in much of the Matobo Hills. This is because, as the local indigenous communities of the Matobo Hills are modernising, they are also discarding several of their old cultural practices while they embrace new ones. Although most of these factors are anthropogenic, natural causes such as recurring droughts which lead to habitat loss, among other things, are also gradually contributing to the decline of traditional conservation practices in the Matobo Hills.

Given this background, in order for the idea of considering traditional methods of conservation to work, the appropriate approach would be perhaps to begin by preserving the practices that are still existing and relevant such as the rain making ceremonies and stories that first helped to protect archaeological sites before they could be reintroduced for conservation. This approach would be in accordance with the objective of the Convention on Intangible Heritage which is to preserve intangible values in monuments and sites (see UNESCO 2003). The desire to have this issue addressed was expressed by some villagers who are concerned that, although tourism benefits from cultural practices, there are no major efforts by those who are in charge and in the tourism businesses to help preserve the cultural practices in the Matobo Hills. This is important because the local indigenous communities are aware that once some of their cultural practices have disappeared they cannot be easily resurrected.

Preserving traditional conservation practices, however, is not without its own challenges. One of the challenges is that there are some traditional conservation practices, shrines, and archaeological sites that local indigenous communities would not wish to disclose and share with the public. In southern Africa and perhaps in other parts of the continent and beyond, the use of shrines and the performance of cultural rituals are private and secretive affairs performed on selected ritual cultural landscapes. A study conducted by Zubieta (2006) to understand the link between the rain making ceremony and the Nyau ritual features of the Chewa people in the Chongoni Forest Area in central Malawi, for example, showed that these activities are performed in a secret ritual rock art site called Mwana wa Chentcherere II rock shelter which shapes their social actions and from which they derive their specific qualities.

Local indigenous communities with recent colonial experience, such as those of the Matobo Hills, may be averse to disclosing some of their cultural practices, shrines, and archaeological sites for fear that the sites could be appropriated as national monuments for economic reasons from which they will not benefit. As this study has shown, during the colonial period, local indigenous people in the Matobo Hills refused to disclose the location of several of their important cultural sites to the colonial authorities because they feared that their sacredness would be ruined and that the sites would be appropriated. Keeping their practices and cultural heritage sites a secret could be a way by local indigenous communities of safeguarding their cultural practices from being contaminated by modern values. It could also be a way of resisting the idea that they should be made public thereby being limited as a benefit for the concept of outstanding universal value which is assumed to be inherent in world heritage cultural landscapes. Additionally, it could be a way of preventing their shrines from being reduced to ordinary local attractions.

It would appear as though local indigenous communities can only make known to the public those practices, shrines, or archaeological sites that they deem to no longer be sacred and relevant. As further shown in this study, a Khami type site was kept a secret by the local indigenous people until recently when it was revealed to me during data collection for this thesis only because it is no longer important as a local community sacred shrine. Given the secretive nature of the local indigenous communities, it is quite likely that there are many cultural practices, shrines, and archaeological sites that are currently being kept as a secret in the Matobo Hills.

Another constraint that this research has shown is the European approaches of management that were converted into legal frameworks of conservation during the colonial period. As has been determined, these legal frameworks still function in the Matobo Hills today. However, as this study has shown, they continue to be an obstacle in the provision or respect of the interests and roles of local indigenous communities and their traditional conservation practices. Part of the reason is that, as observed by one informant, there are many of them in the Matobo Hills. Based on this observation, it can be argued that their multiplicity does not necessarily mean that the cultural landscape is adequately protected. Instead, they are a source of management problems as their applications overlap which, as in the case of the Matobo Hills, has led to the collision of interests between the ZPWMA and the NMMZ. As a further consequence of the clash of interests, the legal instruments have also persistently failed to address issues of poverty, employment, and land rights of local indigenous communities. The failure of legal frameworks to address issues of indigeninous people could also be attributed to the fact that many of the issues are now archaic and require reviewing. In Zimbabwe, for instance, in spite of numerous attempts to review the NMMZ Act, the process has not been concluded due to both lack of expertise in the subject area (Matenga 2011) and possibly funding. Until the review is completed, efforts to consider traditional conservation practices and involve local indigenous communities in the management of the Matobo Hills, for example, will continue to be hindered.

Failure to harmonise heritage legislations with other State legislations such as the Traditional Chiefs' and National Parks Acts, as in the case of Zimbabwe and with international conventions related to the management of World Heritage Sites, also further impedes efforts to revitalise traditional conservation practices and to involve local descent communities in the management of Matobo Hills. While this anomaly has since been realised (see Ndoro, Mumma and Abungu 2008), attempts to rescue the situation appear to have met limited success and, in some cases, slow progress. This has also affected the harmonisation of local heritage legislations with international conventions related to the management of World Heritage Sites. An evaluation by Deacon and Smeets (2013) to determine the extent to which community involvement in heritage management has been represented in the texts of the World Heritage Convention of 1972 and the Convention on Intangible Heritage of 2003 and their Operational Guidelines has shown that the communities concerned are given no specific status or roles even after their cultural heritage is inscribed on the Lists of these Conventions. Based on this review, Deacon and Smeets concluded that, even though the Conventions and their Operational Guidelines require greater community involvement in heritage identification and management, despite their good intentions, they have become an obstacle to creating opportunities for greater community involvement and recognition of traditional conservation practices.

Further to the observations made by Deacon and Smeets, there is evidence of non-compliance by several states parties, and UNESCO does not have actual power to ensure that they comply with the requirements of the Conventions and their Operational Guidelines. This is despite the fact that states parties are required to comply with the obligations of involving local indigenous communities and their cultural practices in the management of world heritage cultural landscapes as is spelled out in these documents (Keough 2011). At a workshop on the World Heritage Convention and Indigenous People in Copenhagen in September 2012, Professor Dalee Sambo Dorough argued that indigenous peoples have, in fact, been repeatedly pressured into surrendering their political, economic, social, and cultural pursuits when their lands are declared as World Heritage Sites while member states are never forced to give up their economic and political interests. She argued that this is guaranteed by the 1972 Convention itself which makes it clear that World Heritage Site designations are without prejudice to the sovereignty of the states on whose territory the respective sites are situated (Art. 6, para. 1). As a result of this situation, Professor Dorough concluded that it will require a major paradigm shift to effectively intersect the cultural, economic, social, and political context of indigenous people with the views of the World Heritage Convention (Disko and Tugendhat 2014, 9).

The renaissance of traditional conservation practices and the involvement of local indigenous communities in the management of world heritage cultural landscapes is further impeded by the fact that local indigenous people are not usually given a chance to occupy influential positions in local Site Management Committees or Site Management Steering Groups. This is not, however, suggesting that every proclaimed World Heritage Site has a steering group. There are some World Heritage Sites which do not have steering groups such as Khami in Zimbabwe. In cases where Site Steering Groups exist, they are typically composed of the so-called technocrats, professionals, and experts (Naeem 2013). Sometimes, as seen in the Matobo Hills, politicians are also included as part of the steering group or, as in the case of Britain, local government councillors often chair the committees (Belcher 2014). In this matrix, as demonstrated by experiences in the Matobo Hills, the representatives of the local indigenous communities are usually placed in insignificant roles of the steering groups and are co-opted only as committee members. This is because they are either considered as not having the capacity to implement Site Management Plans, or they are regarded as having no expertise in the field of world heritage management as well as in matters of related politics. As a result, the local indigenous communities are universally judged as having no influence to represent their countries in international committees such as the World Heritage Committee. Also during the workshop on the World Heritage Convention and Indigenous People in Copenhagen in September 2012, Mechtild Rössler disclosed that, although delegations to the World Heritage Committee are required to include both diplomats and experts, this is no longer the norm as diplomats have dominated because the World Heritage Convention has become more and more politicised (Disko and Tugendhat 2014). Willems (2014) has also observed that, for many years now, political representatives in national delegations to the World Heritage Committee have shown increasing disregard for expert advice. According to Willems, this disregard has led to the proclamation of sites which evidently would have managerial problems in the future such as the temple of Preah Vihear located at the border of Cambodia and Thailand. After it was initially rejected in 2007 because the Temple lies in a disputed border zone, the Committee decided to inscribe the site against the advice of the Thai government. This decision eventually led to an open military conflict between the two countries (cf. Silverman 2011). In the context of the implementation of the Convention, this becomes an issue as local indigenous communities are not afforded an opportunity to contribute their opinions in matters of traditional conservation practices of world heritage cultural landscapes.

As the Matobo Hills case further attests, the selection of the local World Management Committee could also thwart the consideration of traditional conservation practices and interests of local indigenous communities in the management of world heritage cultural landscapes. This is because the representatives may not represent the interests of the local indigenous communities. As seen in this study, the selection of a ZANU PF local politician to chair the Matobo Hills World Heritage Committee could have been encouraged by the belief that the accomplishment of certain objectives of the Site Management Plan would require political support. The problem with this approach is that the position could be used to further the personal political interests of the chairperson or of the political party rather than the advancement of traditional conservation practices or the involvement of local indigenous people in the administration of the cultural landscape. The other issue is that politicians may lack understanding of the management issues that are beyond political expertise. Moreover, the political party affiliated to the politicians may not be popular among the local descent people living around a World Heritage Site. In the case of the Matobo Hills, the choice of a chairperson who is affiliated to ZANU PF, a political party that is remembered for the persecution and death of people during the 1980s and the civil fighting in Matabeleland, could not have been fully welcomed by some of the local indigenous people currently surviving in the cultural landscape. In cases where there is political interference, the Site Management Steering Group is not likely to receive the support of the local indigenous communities to consider the return of traditional conservation practices or their involvement in the management of the site.

While arguments that the heritage legal frameworks discussed above should be reviewed to consider the interests of local indigenous communities and that they should also be cohesive with other local legislations and conventions related to world heritage management, fulfilling this objective is one thing and implementing it is another. The major challenge has been that, although a number of World Heritage Sites are located in indigenous territories, there are no mechanisms in place that enable implementation of the meaningful involvement of local indigenous communities and their traditional conservation practices. Quite often, as the Matobo Hills experience has demonstrated, lack of implementation of legal frameworks could be as a result of a number of issues: power struggles between government institutions or between locals and site authorities, lack of support of the Site Management Committees, lack of funding, or a mixture of all these and other factors. As this thesis has demonstrated, where two or more government organisations contest to profit from a world heritage cultural landscape, as in the case of the ZPWMA and the NMMZ, the implementation of the Conventions and of the Site Management Plans becomes a tangential issue. Consequently, the consideration of traditional conservation practices and the involvement of local indigenous communities in the management of the cultural landscape are both disregarded and impeded.

The desire of several local indigenous communities to benefit from world heritage cultural landscapes suggests that the idea to consider traditional conservation practices can only work if they have something to benefit from the conservation of the areas. The primary reason for this is that, with the decline of the national economy, local indigenous people of Matobo are becoming more and more money sensitive and more orientated towards material benefits. Their attempts to charge entrance fees at archaeological sites that are outside the park demonstrates that they also want to extend their revenue collection base in addition to selling thatching grass and souvenirs. It also means that they want to benefit from their ancestral shrines which they know are being exploited at their expense by government departments and private tour operators in the Matobo Hills especially in the national park.

While this is the case, the issue of local indigenous communities failing to benefit from the management of world heritage cultural landscapes is not unique to only the Matobo Hills. Across the African continent and in other parts of the world, many local indigenous communities are also failing to benefit from the management and protection of World Heritage Sites. In Mali, for instance, despite the great fame of Djenné as a World Heritage Site, the majority of local indigenous communities living in the town are still underprivileged as they are failing to benefit from its management. This is because of UNESCO's international vision of the town which is limited to archictecture and archaeology (Joy 2011). Near the Matobo Hills in Botswana, the proclamation of Tsodilo Hills as a World Heritage Site has not benefited the !Kung (San people) and the Hambukushu who are the local indigenous communities currently surviving in the cultural landscape (Thebe 2006). Elsewhere in Indonesia, there were expectations for the Borobudur Temple, which is situated in a rural area in central Java, to bring benefits to nearby local indigenous communities when it was proclaimed as a World Heritage Site in 1991. However, contrary to their hopes, since 1985, the focus for tourism has been the Recreational Park which was developed around the main temple. As a result of the developments, approximately two million visitors visit the park every year, 80% of which are domestic. However, despite the high numbers of tourists and development of the park, poverty has, in fact, remained a critical challenge in the neighbourhood of the Borobudur Temple (Kausar 2014).

Chirikure (2014) argued that one of the reasons why local indigenous communities fail to benefit from the management of world heritage sites is that, as non experts, they simply do not have the influence to negotiate the favourable terms necessary to create more gains for themselves. The other reason could be that the decline of tourism, as in the case of the Matobo Hills, also means that the local indigenous communities cannot benefit from the little revenue generated as it is controlled by powerful government departments and private players for survival in an economy that is struggling. This subsequently indicates that the idea of the CSOT suggested in this research cannot be accomplished as there is nowhere in the Indigenisation and Empowerment Act that compels companies to donate money to a CSOT (Chikuhwa 2013, 429). For these and other reasons, the idea to consider traditional conservation practices and to involve local indigenous communities in the management of world heritage cultural landscapes is further constrained as the communities do not perceive any benefits associated with supporting such conservation iniatives. In addition, as argued by Miura (2005), they continue to be disregarded and marginalised by various authorities in the name of conservation and tourism promotion.

A further challenge of considering traditional conservation practices and involving local indigenous communities in the management of several world heritage cultural landscapes emanates from the historical land appropriations which led to the eviction and the creation of new local indigenous communities. There are cases where ancestral lands have been returned to local indigenous communities when they have demanded them back, as in the case of Basarwa people in Botswana (Taylor 2007) or in the case of the Endorois people of Kenya whose ancestral lands were returned to them around Lake Bogoria, which is part of the Kenya Lake System World Heritage Site (Lynch 2011). However, in Africa, the majority have completely failed to reclaim their ancestral lands back.

The failure in recent years of some local indigenous people in the Matobo Hills to repossess some of their ancestral lands means that the idea to resurrect traditional conservation practices cannot succeed in a world heritage cultural landscape where the inhabitants are resentful that they are denied their ancestral lands and, therefore, a chance to put their traditional conservation practices into effect. As experiences of local indigenous communities in the Matobo Hills have shown, the idea also cannot be embraced if they continue to be told or to feel that world heritage cultural landscapes or parts of them as well as shrines and archaeological sites situated in them are owned and managed by the government or by other people and that the indigineous people do not have the ownership rights to use them.

However, the desire to reclaim ancestral lands could certainly have helped the renewal of traditional conservation practices and their involvement in the management of the World Heritage Site if, for example, they would have been involved in the planning of the early 1980s resettlement programme. This would have provided them an opportunity to start their own initiatives which would have incorporated traditional ways of conservation. Conservation initiatives that would have been started by the local indigenous communities are likely to have had more widespread support amongst the local indigenous people than those that are introduced to them or imposed by the government, international organisations, or private conservation societies. Local conservation initiatives are also likely to have been successful, especially if the government, local, and international organisations as well as private conservation societies are involved only as supporters and collaborators and not as imposers of such initiatives.

The last and perhaps the most important constraint is that other existing management and administrative state arrangements may make it difficult to put into practice the idea of traditional ways of conservation and involvement of local indigenous people in the management of world heritage cultural landscapes. As seen in this study, the rural adiminstrative arrangements of the area can actually usurp the powers of the traditional chiefs who are expected to promote the use of traditional conservation initiatives and involvement of local descent communities in the management of the world heritage cultural landscape. The legislations governing the adiministrative structures of the state are usually more powerful than those that govern the conduct of traditional chiefs. As seen in this research, this reduces the ability of traditional authorities to implement and enforce policies related to traditional ways of conservation. For this reason, traditional chiefs are often maginalised and are often avoided when matters regarding the management of cultural landscapes are discussed.

CONCLUSION:
IMPORTANT CONSIDERATIONS

One issue that has emerged from this study is that, even although it is generally agreed that traditional conservation practices and local indigenous communities are relevant in the management of world heritage cultural landscapes, it is not easy to address some of the challenges and constraints that are discussed above. Given this situation, there must be a way forward to deal with some of these issues. This section will present and discuss some considerations which I think are significant when taking into account the idea of using traditional ways of conservation and involvement of local descent communities in the management of world heritage cultural landscapes.

First, there is a need to have a clear understanding of the local indigenous communities themselves. This study shows that there could be different types of local indigenous communities located in rural and remote areas with far reaching networks. It is also demonstrated that there are other indigenous communities of identity and interest that are physically dispersed across different locations in the cultural landscape. Understanding these local indigenous communities is important because it is then clarified who to address as far as the use of traditional conservation practices and their involvement in the management of the world heritage cultural landscape is concerned. Therefore, it is very important to define the local indigenous people relevant to the management of the world heritage cultural landscape in question.

Secondly, it is also important to understand the issues that affect local indigenous communities in a world heritage cultural landscape. As seen in this study, these issues include, among others, the need of local indigenous communities to be employed, reclaim their ancestral lands, and to benefit from tourism ventures. Understanding issues that affect local indigenous people facilitates addressing them so that they can passionately support the idea of making use of traditional conservation practices and being involved in the management of world heritage cultural landscapes. Meeting the immediate needs of the local indigenous communities would also provide incentives that link conservation of the world heritage cultural landscape with their basic survival. Thirdly, there is need to have an indepth comprehension of the cultural landscape concerned and the traditional conservation practices which may be existing in the area if their use and involvement of local indigenous people in its administration can be a success. Understanding the cultural landscape is important because decisions can be made on which aspects and sections of the cultural landscape require traditional conservation practices and which traditional conservation practices can be applied. Understanding the cultural landscape itself can also help make decisions on whether or not traditional conservation practices can be effectively used for the conservation needs of the area. If not, other conservation measures can then be considered. It also helps to be aware of the limits of the boundary in which the traditional conservation practices are to be applied and the local indigenous people to involve. However, the latter consideration is often difficult to implement, as seen in this study, as the local indigenous communities often transcend the official margins of the world heritage site.

Fourthly, the underlying politics behind the management of world heritage cultural landscape must be understood before contemplating the idea of reviving traditional conservation practices and involving local indigenous communities in its management. As this study has shown, world heritage cultural landscapes such as the Matobo Hills are not exclusively cultural; they are also political landscapes. Understanding the politics of the world heritage cultural landscape may actually help determine whether or not the local indigenous communities would support the use of traditional conservation practices and their involvement in the management of the area. It may also help to make decisions on who to include in the local World Heritage Management Committee.

Last, but not least, there is need to consider the opinions of the local descent communities themselves if the idea of reviving traditional conservation practices and of involving them in the management of the world heritage cultural landscape is to be realised. Understanding the views of the local indigenous communities, as this study has established, is important because it becomes possible to know their conservation requirements and the ways they want them to be addressed. Based on their views, it also becomes possible to know the extent to which the local indigenous communities are involved in the management of the world heritage cultural landscape and if they would support the idea of using traditional conservation practices to guard their ancestral lands or not.

In conclusion, this study has shown that, although there are efforts to recognise traditional conservation practices and to involve local indigenous communities in the management of world heritage cultural landscapes, this consideration is inhibited by politics, diverse interests and values, as well as lack of recognition in state legislations and in international conventions related to the management of World Heritage Sites. This is because world heritage cultural landscapes are associated with different groups of people, individuals, and organisations which embrace different narratives to assert symbolic, cultural, political, and economic ownership over them.

References

Abrahams, G. 1989. A review of the South African heritage legislation 1987. In F. H. Cleere (ed.), *Archaeological Heritage Management in the Modern World* (One World Archaeology 9). 207-218. London: Unwin Hyman.

ACHPR. 2006. *Indigenous Peoples in Africa: The Forgotten Peoples?* (The African Commission's Work on Indigenous Peoples in Africa). Copenhagen: International Work Group for Indigenous Affairs.

ACHPR. 2007. *Advisory Opinion of the African Commission on Human and People's Rights on the United Nations Declaration on the Rights of Indigenous Peoples.* Banjul: African Union.

Adams, W. and Hulme, D. 2001. Conservation and community: Changing narratives, policies and practices in African conservation. In D. Hulme and M, Murphree (eds), *African Wildlife and Livelihoods: The Promise and Performance of Community Conservation.* 9-23. Oxford: James Curray.

Adams, W. M. 2004. *Against Extinction: The Story of Conservation.* London: Earthscan.

Ajayi, J. F. A. (ed). 1998. *General History of Africa VI: Africa in the Nineteenth Century until the 1880s.* California: University of California Press.

Alexander, J. 1991. The unsettled land: The politics of land redistribution in Matabeleland, 1980-1990. *Journal of Southern African Studies,* Vol. 17, No. 4: 581-610.

Allen, H. and Phillips, C. 2010. Maintaining the dialogue: Archaeology, cultural heritage and indigenous communities. In C. Phillips and H. Allen (eds), *Bridging the Divide: Indigenous Communities and Archaeology into the 21st Century* (One World Archaeology 60). 17-48. California: Left Coast Press.

Anaya, S. F. 1996. *Indigenous Peoples in International Law* (2nd Edn.). New York: Oxford University Press.

Andrews, T. D. and Buggey, S. 2008. Authenticity in Aboriginal cultural landscapes. *Journal of Preservation Technology* 39. (2-3): 63-71.

Armstrong, A. L. 1929. Rhodesian cave expedition 1929. *Prehistoric Society of East Anglia* 5: 144.

Armstrong, A. L. 1931. Rhodesian archaeological expedition (1929): Excavation in Bambata cave and researchers on prehistoric sites in Southern Rhodesia. *Journal of the Royal Anthropological Institute* 61: 239-276.

Arnold, G. and Jones, N. 1919. Notes on the Bushman cave at Bambata, Matopos. *Proceedings of the Rhodesian Association for the Advancement of Science* 17: 5-19.

Aschwanden, H. 1989. *Karanga Mythology*. Gweru: Mambo Press.

Ashton, E. H. 1981. *Report on the Socio-Historical Survey of Matopos.* Bulawayo: Natural History Museum.

Atalay, S. 2006a. Guest editor's remarks: Decolonising archaeology. *American Indian Quarterly 30* (3-4): 269-279.

Atalay, S. 2006b. Indigenous archaeology as decolonizing practice. *American Indian Quarterly 30* (3-4): 280-310.

Balint, P. J. and Mashinya, J. 2006. The decline of a model community-based conservation project: Governance, capacity and devolution in Mahenye, Zimbabwe. *Geoforum* 37: 805-815.

Banderin, F. 2009. Preface. In N. Mitchell, M. Rössler and P. Tricaud (eds), World Heritage Cultural Landscapes: *A Handbook for Conservation and Management.* 3-4. Paris: World Heritage Centre.

Banergee, S. B. 2000. Whose land is it anyway? national interest, indigenous stakeholders, and colonial discourses: The case of the Jabiluka uranium mine. *Organisation and Environment,* Vol. 13, No. 1: 3-38.

Barry, R. and Mundy, P. 1998. Population dynamics of two species of hyraxies in the Matobo National Park, Zimbabwe. *African Journal of Ecology,* Vol. 36, Issue, 3: 221-233.

Beach, D. N. 1980. The Shona and Zimbabwe 900-1850: *An Outline of Shona History*. Gweru: Mambo Press.

Beach, D. N. 1983. Oral history and archaeology in Zimbabwe. *Zimbabwean Prehistory 19*: 8-11.

Beach, D. N. 1986. *War and Politics in Zimbabwe 1840-1900.* Gweru: Mambo Press.

Becker, P. 1962. Path of Blood: *The Rise and Conquests of Mzilikazi, Founder of the Matabele Tribe of Southern Africa.* London: Longmans.

Belcher, G. 2014. Values in World Heritage Sites. In C. Sandis (ed.), *Cultural Heritage Ethics: Between Theory and Practice.* 181-196. Cambridge: Open Book Publishers.

Bender, B. 1999. Subverting the western gaze: Mapping alternative worlds. In P. J. Ucko and R. Layton (eds), *The Archaeology and Anthropology of Landscape: Shaping Your Landscape.* 31-43. London: Routledge.

Berkes, F., Colding, J. and Folke, C. 2000. Rediscovery of traditional ecological knowledge as adaptive management. *Ecological Applications, Vol. 10,* No. 5: 1251-1262.

Berkes, P. 1999. Sacred Ecology: *Traditional Ecological Knowledge and Resource Management.* Philadelphia: Taylor and Francis.

Bernard, P. S. 2003. Ecological implications of water spirit beliefs in southern Africa: *The need to protect knowledge, nature and resources rights.* USDA Forest Service Proceedings, RMRS-P-27.

Berniell-Lee, G., Calafell, F., Bosch, E., Heyer, E., Sica L., Mouquiama-Daouda, P., van der Veen L., Hombert, J. M., Quintana-Murci, L. and Comas, D. 2009. Genetic and demographic implications of the Bantu expansion: Insights from human paternal lineages. *Molecular Biology and Evolution 26* (7): 1581-1589.

Bhattacherjee, A. 2012. *Social Science Research: Principles, Methods and Practices* (2nd Edn). Zurich: Jacobs Foundation.

Bhebe, N. M. B. 1989. Benjamin Burombo: *African Politics in Zimbabwe 1947-1958.* Harare: The College Press.

Bhebe, N. M. B. 1979. *Traditional Religion in Western Zimbabwe, 1859-1923.* Britain: Longman.

Blaser, M., Feit, H. A. and McRae, G. (eds). 2004. *In the Way of Development: Indigenous Peoples, Life Projects and Globalization.* London: Zed Books.

Boaten, B. A. 1998. Traditional conservation practices: Ghana's example. *Research Review (NS)* Vol. 14, No. 1: 42-51.

Boswell, R. 2008. *Challenges to Identifying and Managing Intangible Cultural Heritage in Mauritius, Zanzibar and Seychelles.* Dakar: CODESRIA.

Bousman, C. B. 1998. The chronological evidence for the introduction of domestic stock into Southern Africa. *African Archaeological Review,* Vol. 15, No. 2: 133-150.

Bozongwana, W. 1983. *Ndebele Religion and Customs.* Gweru: Mambo Press.

Bradshaw, E., Bryant, K. and Cohen, T. 2012. Why *Cultural Heritage Matters: A Resource Guide for Integrating Cultural Heritage Management into Communities Work at Rio Tinto.* University of Queensland, Australia: Centre for Social Responsibility in Mining.

Breen, C. 2007. Advocacy, international development and World Heritage Sites in sub-saharan Africa. *World Archaeology* Vol. 39(3): 355-370.

Brooks, A. S., Gelburd, D. E. and Yellen, J. E. 1984. Food production and culture change among the !Kung San: Implications for prehistoric research. In J. D. Clark and S. A. Brandt (eds), *From Hunters to Farmers: The Causes and Consequences of Food Production in Africa.* 293-310. Berkely: University of California Press.

Bwasiri, E. J. 2008. The Management of Indigenous Living Heritage in Archaeological World Heritage Sites: A Case Study of Mongomi Wa Kolo Rock Painting Site, Central Tanzania. Master of Arts Dissertation Submitted to the Faculty of Humanities. Johannesburg: University of Witwatersrand.

Chakaipa, S. 2010. Local government institutions and elections. In J. de Visser, N. Steytler and N. Machingauta (eds), Local Government Reform in Zimbabwe: A Policy Dialogue. 31-68. University of the Western Cape: Community Law Centre.

Chatiza, K. 2010. Can local government steer socio-economic transformation in Zimbabwe: Analysing historical trends and gazing into the future. In J. de Visser, N. Steytler and N. Machingauta (eds), *Local Government Reform in Zimbabwe: A Policy Dialogue.* 1-25. University of the Western Cape: Community Law Centre.

Chenje, M. and Johnson, P. (eds). 1996. *Water in Southern Africa.* Maseru: SADC.

Chibi, T., Kandori, C. and Makone, B. F. 2005. *Mzingwane Catchment Outline Plan Report. Bulawayo*: Zimbabwe National Water Authority.

Chikuhwa, J. W. 2006. *Zimbabwe at the Crossroads.* Bloomington: Author House.

Chikuhwa, J. W. 2013. Zimbabwe: *The End of the First Republic*. Bloomington: Author House.

Child, H. 1968. *The History of amaNdebele.* Ministry of Internal Affairs. Rhodesia Government.

Chipunza, K. 2005. Protection of immovable cultural heritage in Zimbabwe: *An evaluation. In W. Ndoro and G. Pwiti (eds), Legal frameworks for the Protection of Immovable Cultural Heritage in Africa* (ICCROM Conservation Studies 5). 42-45. Rome: ICCROM.

Chirikure, S. 2014. Power imbalance and unequal benefit at UNESCO World Heritage Sites? *Africa Review of Books,* Vol. 10.

Chirikure, S., Manyanga, M., Pollard, A.M., Bandama, F., Mahachi, G., and Pikirayi, I. 2014. Zimbabwe culture before Mapungubwe: *New evidence from Mapela Hill south western Zimbabwe*. PLoS ONE, Vol. 9, Issue 9: 1-18.

Chitando, E. 2006. African Instituted Churches in Southern Africa: Paragons of Regional Integration. *African Journal of International Affairs,* Vol, 7, Nos. (1-2): 117-132.

Chiuta, T. M., Johnson, P. and Hirji, R. 2002. Water and the economy. In R. Hirji, P. Johnson, P. Maro and T. M. Chiuta (eds), *Defining and Mainstreaming Environmental Sustainability in Water Resources Management in Southern Africa.* 21-52. Maseru: SADC.

Chiwaura, H. 2005. The development of formal legislation and the recognition of traditional customary law in Zimbabwe's heritage management. In W. Ndoro and G. Pwiti (eds), *Legal Frameworks for the Protection of Immovable Cultural Heritage in Africa* (ICCROM Conservation Studies 5). 18-21. Rome: ICCROM.

Chiweshe, N. 2007. Black eagles and hyraxes- the two flagship species in the conservation of wildlife in the Matobo Hills, Zimbabwe. Ostrich, 78 (2): 381-386.

Clarke, M. F. 2010. *Lozikeyi Dlodlo Queen of the Ndebele.* Bulawayo: Amagugu Publishers.

Cobo, J. M. 1986. Study of the problem of discrimination against indigenous populations. UN Doc. E/CN.4/Sub.2/1986/7 and Add. 1-4. [online]. Available from http://www.un.org/esa/socdev/unpfii/en/second.html [Accessed January 2013].

Cockcroft, I. G. 1972. The Mlimo (Mwari) Cult. *Native Affairs Department Annual:* 10 (4).

Collett, D. P. 1992. *The Archaeological Heritage of Zimbabwe: A Masterplan for Resource Conservation and Development.* Harare: National Museums and Monuments of Zimbabwe.

Colwell-Chanthaphonh, C., Ferguson, T. J., Lippert, D., McGuire, R. H., Nicholas, G. P., Watkins, J. E. and Zimmerman, L. J. 2010. The premise and promise of indigenous archaeology. *American Antiquity,* Vol. 75, No. 2: 228-238.

Cooke, C. K. 1963. Report on excavations at Pomongwe and Tshangula caves, Matopo Hills, Southern Rhodesia. *South African Archaeological Bulletin* 18: 73-151.

Cooke, C. K. 1965. *The Matopo Hills and a View of the World.* Salisbury: Government Printer.

Cooke, C. K. 1986. *The Matopo Hills*. Harare: National Museums and Monuments of Zimbabwe.

Cooke, C. K. and Robinson, K. R. 1954. Excavations at Amadzimba cave, located in the Matopo Hills, Southern Rhodesia. *Occasional Papers of the National Museum of Southern Rhodesia* 2: 699-728.

Cooke, C. K., Summers, R. and Robinson, K. R. 1966. Rhodesian prehistory re-examined: Part I: the Stone Age. *Arnoldia*, No. 12, Vol. 2: 1-8.

Creamer, H. 1990. Aboriginal perceptions of the past: The implications for cultural resource management in Australia. In P. Gathercole and D. Lowenthal (eds), *The Politics of the Past* (One World Archaeology 12). 130-138. London: Routledge.

Da Silva, J. A. 1993. African Independent Churches Origin and Development. *Anthropos:* 393-402.

Daneel, M. L. 1970. *The God of Matopo Hills.* Hague: Mouton.

Danzinger Commission. 1949. Report of the commission appointed to enquire into the occupation of certain crown land known as Matopo National Park by certain Matabele natives. Salisbury: Institute of African Affairs.

Deacon, H. and Smeets, R. 2013. Authenticity, value and community involvement in heritage management under the World Heritage and Intangible Heritage Conventions. *Heritage and Society,* Vol. 6, No. 2: 129-143.

Deacon, J. 1993. Management guidelines for rock art sites in two wilderness areas in the Western Cape. Stellenbosch: Department of Environmental Affairs and Tourism.

Deacon, J. 2006. Sharing resources: Issues in regional archaeological conservation strategies in southern Africa. In N. Agnew and J. Bridgland (eds), *Of the Past, For the Future: Integrating Archaeology and Conservation*. 306-311. Los Angeles: Getty Conservation Institute.

Denbow, J. R. 2009. Prehistoric herders and foragers of the Kalahari: The evidence for 1, 500 years of interaction. In C Schrire (ed.), *Past and Present in Hunter-Gatherer Studies*. 175-94. Walnut Creek, California: Left Coast Press.

Disko, S. and Tugendhat, H. 2014. Report: *International Expert Workshop on the World Heritage Convention and Indigenous Peoples* (20-21 September 2012). Copenhagen: International Work Group for Indigenous Affairs.

Ekblom, A., Gillson,L., Risberg, J., Holmgren, K. and Chidoub, Z. 2012. Rainfall variability and vegetation dynamics of the lower Limpopo Valley, Southern Africa, 500 AD to present. *Palaeogeography,Palaeoclimatology,* Palaeoecology 363-634: 69-78.

Eldredge, E. A. 1992. Sources of conflict in Southern Africa, C. 1800-30: The 'Mfecane' reconsidered. *The Journal of African History,* Vol. 33, No. 1: 1-35.

Eldredge, N. (ed). 2002. Life on Earth: An *Encyclopedia of Biodiversity, Ecology and Evolution*. California: ABC-CLIO, Inc.

Ellert, H. 1993. *Rivers of Gold*. Gweru: Mambo Press.

Elliott, J., Kingsey, B. and Kwesha, D. 2006. Gathering evidence: The challenge of assessing sustainability after a resettlement programme in Zimbabwe. In J. Hill, A. Terry and W. Woodland (eds), *Sustainable Development: National Aspirations, Local Implementation*. 15-30. Hampshire: Ashgate Publishing Limited.

Eppel, S. 2004. "Gukurahundi" the need for truth and reparation. In B. Raftopoulos and T. Savage (eds), *Zimbabwe Injustice and Political Reconciliation*. 43-62. Harare: Weaver Press.

Fisher, J. L. 2010. Pioneers, Settlers, Aliens, Exiles: *The Decolonisation of White Identity in Zimbabwe*. Canberra: ANU E Press.

Flick, U. 2009. *An Introduction to Qualitative Research* (4th edition). London: SAGE Publications.

Folke, C. and Colding, J. 2001. Traditional conservation practices. *Encyclopedia of Biodiversity,* Vol. 5: 681-694.

Fothergill, R. J. 1953. *The Monuments of Southern Rhodesia. Bulawayo*: The Commission for the Preservation of Natural and Historical Monuments and Relics.

Fripp, C. E. and Hiller, V. W. (eds). 1949. *Gold and the Gospel in Mashonaland*. London: Chatto and Windus.

Frost, P. G. H. and Bond, I. 2007. The CAMPFIRE programme in Zimbabwe; payments for wildlife services. *Ecological Economics* 65: 776-787.

Gaffney, C., Hughes, G. and Gater, J. 2005. Geophysical surveys at king Lobengula's palace KoBulawayo, Zimbabwe. *Archaeological Prospection,* 12: 31–49.

Gandiwa, E., Heitkönig, I, M. A., Lokhorst, A.M., Prins, H. H. T. and Leeuwis, C. 2013. CAMPFIRE and human-wildlife conflicts in local communities bordering northern Gonarezhou National Park, Zimbabwe. *Ecology and Society* 18(4): 7. [online] URL: http://www.ecologyandsociety.org/vol18/iss4/art7/ [Accessed February 2016].

Gargett, V. 1990. *The Black Eagle*. Johannesburg: Acorn Books.

Garlake, P. 1987. *The Painted Caves: An Introduction to the PreHistoric Art of Zimbabwe*. Harare: Modus Publications.

Gelfand, M. (ed). 1968. *Gubulawayo and Beyond. Letters and Journals of the Early Jesuit Missionaries to Zambesia* 1879-1887. London: Geoffrey Chapman.

George, P. N. and Hollwell, J. J. 2007. Ethical challenges to a postcolonial archaeology. In Y. Hamilakas and P. Duke (eds), *Archaeology and Capitalism: From Ethics to Politics*. 59-82. Walnut Creek, California: Left Coast Press.

Geza, S. 1986. The role of resettlement in social development in Zimbabwe. *Journal of Social Development in Africa* 1: 35-42.

Gibbs, P., Phillips, H. and Russel, N. 2010. Blue and Old Gold: *The History of the British South Africa Police* 1889-1990. Pinetown: 30° South Publishers (PTY) Limited.

Gilbert, J. and Couillard, V. 2011. International law and land rights in Africa: The shift from states' territorial possessions to indigenous peoples' ownership rights. In R. Home (ed.), *Essays in African Land Law*. 47-68. Pretoria: Pretoria University Press.

Grobler, J. H. 1976. The Rhodes Matopo National Park: A case for survival. Letter to the Director of National Parks and Wildlife Management, Ref. 713/9/2/76. Bulawayo: National Parks and Wildlife Management.

Grobler, J. H. and Wilson, V. J. 1972. Food for the leopard *Panthera pardus* (Linn.) in the Rhodes Matopo National Park, Rhodesia. Arnoldia 5(35): 1-10.

Guvamatanga, G. 2014. Community share ownership pays dividends. *The Patriot-Celebrating Being Zimbabwean Newspaper* [online]. Available from <http://www.the patriot. co.zw/old-posts/community-share-scheme-pays-dividends/ [Accessed January 2015].

Hachipola, S. M. 1998. *A Survey of the Minority Languages of Zimbabwe.* Harare: University of Zimbabwe Publications.

Halaar, M. and Olthof, W. 1994. Rural local government and development planning with experiences from Buhera district, Zimbabwe (Working Paper Series No. 181). The Hague: Institute of Social Studies.

Hall, M. 1993. The archaeology of colonial settlement in southern Africa. *Annual Review of Anthropology*, Vol. 22: 177-200.

Hausman, A. J. 1984. Holocene human evolution in southern Africa. In J. D. Clark and S. A. Brandt (eds), *From Hunters to Farmers: The Causes and Consequences of Food Production in Africa.* 261-271. Berkeley: University of California Press.

Hedberg, I. and Staugard, F. 1989. *Traditional Medicine in Botswana.* Stockholm: Ipelegeng Publishers.

Heritage Foundation of Newfoundland and Labrador. 2008. I*ntangible Cultural Heritage Program.* Canada: St. John's NL.

Hubbard, P. and Mguni, S. 2007. Further reports of termites and formlings in the rock art of the Matopos, south western Zimbabwe. T*he Digging Stick,* Vol. 24 (2): 5-8.

Huffman, T. N. 1974. The linguistic affinities of the Iron Age in Rhodesia. *Arnoldia* No. 7, Vol. 7: 1-12.

Huffman, T. N. 1982. Archaeology and ethnohistory of the African iron Age. *Ann. Rev. Anthropol.* 11: 133-150.

Huffman, T. N. 1996a. Archaeological evidence for climatic change during the last 2000 years in southern Africa. *Quaternary International* 33: 55-60.

Huffman, T. N. 1996b. *Snakes and Crocodiles: Power and Symbolism in Ancient Zimbabwe.* Johannesburg: Witwatersrand University Press.

Huffman, T. N. 2000. Mapungubwe and the origins of the Zimbabwe culture. In M. Leslie and T. Maggs (eds), African Naissance: *The Limpopo Valley 1000 Years Ago.* 14-29. South African Archaeological Society, Goodwin Series 8.

Huffman, T. N. 2005. The stylistic origin of Bambata and the spread of mixed farming in southern Africa. *Southern African Humanities,* Vol. 17: 57-79.

Huffman, T. N. 2007. *Handbook to the Iron Age: The Archaeology of Pre-Colonial Farming* Societies in Southern Africa. Scottsville: University of KwaZulu-Natal Press.

Huffman, T. N. 2008. Climate change during the Iron Age in the Shashe-Limpopo basin, southern Africa. *Journal of Archaeological Science* 35, 2032–2047.

Hughes, G. 1995. An Archaeological Assessment and Research Proposal for Old-Bulawayo, Zimbabwe. Parts 2 and 3: Technical Report and Detailed Project Proposal. Bulawayo: Natural History Museum, Zimbabwe.

Hughes, G. 2000. KoBulawayo, Zimbabwe. Archaeological Excavation, April–May 2000: Interim Report, Birmingham University Field Archaeology Unit, Project No. 332.10. Bulawayo: Natural History Museum, Zimbabwe.

Hughes, G. and Muringaniza, J. S. 2003. Kings and Ancestors: Interpreting the Past at KoBulawayo, Zimbabwe. In P. Mitchell, A. Haour and J. Hobart (eds), Researching Africa's Past: *New Contributions from British Archaeologists.* 124–32: Monograph 57. Oxford: Oxford University School of Archaeology.

Igoe, J. 2006. Becoming indigenous peoples: Difference, inequality, and the globalization of East African identity politics. *African Affairs,* 105/420: 399-420.

ILO. 1957. Indigenous and Tribal Populations Convention, 1957 (No. 107), *Convention Concerning the Protection and Integration of Indigenous and Other Tribal and Semi-Tribal Populations in Independent Countries.* Geneva: International Labour Office.

ILO. 2003. ILO *Convention on Indigenous and Tribal Peoples,* 1989 [No. 169]: A Manual. Geneva: International Labour Office.

Inaba, N. 2005. The Ise shrine and the Gion festival: Case studies on the values and authenticity of Japanese intangible living religious heritage. In H. Stovel, N. Stanely-Price and R. Killick (eds), *Conservation of Living Religious Heritage* (ICCROM Conservation Studies 3). 44-57. Rome: ICCROM.

Irrigation Department. 1949. Matopo National Park: Native settlement. Salisbury: Irrigation Department.

Jimoh, S. O., Ikyaagba, E. T., Alarape, A. A., Abioha, E. E. and Adeyemi, A. A. 2012. The role of traditional laws and taboos in wildlife conservation in the Oban hill sector of Cross River National Park (CRNP), Nigeria. *J. Hum Ecol*, 39 (3): 209-219.

Joffroy, T. (ed). 2005. *Traditional Conservation Practices in Africa* (ICCROM Conservation Studies 2). Rome: Italy.

Jones, N. 1926. *The Stone Age in Rhodesia.* Oxford: Oxford University Press.

Jopela, A. P. 2010. Traditional Custodianship of Rock Art Sites in Southern Africa: A Case Study from Central Mozambique. Master of Arts Dissertation submitted to the Faculty of Humanities. Johannesburg: University of Witwatersrand.

Jopela, A. P. 2011. Traditional custodianship: A useful framework for heritage management in Southern Africa? *Conservation and Management of Archaeological Sites*, Vol. 13, No. 2-3: 103-122.

Joy, C. 2011. *The Politics of Heritage Management in Mali. From UNESCO to Djenné.* California: Left Coast Press.

Katsamudanga, S. 2003. The dilemma of preserving intangible heritage in Zimbabwe. Paper presented at the 14th ICOMOS General Assembly and Scientific Conference. Victoria Falls: Zimbabwe.

Kausar, D. R. 2014. Tracing the relevance of Barobudur for socio-economic development through tourism. In J. Kaminski, A. M. Benson and D. Arnold (eds), *Contemporary Issues in Cultural Heritage Tourism:* 200-2018.

Kayambazintu, D., Matose, F., Kajembe, G. and Nemarundwe, N. 2005. Institutional arrangement governing natural resources management of the Miombo woodland. In G. Kowero, B. M. Campbell and U.R. Sumaila (eds) *Policies and Governance Structures in Woodlands of Southern Africa.* 45-64. Jarkata: Center for International Forestry Research.

Keough, E. B. 2011. Heritage in peril: A critique of UNESCO's World Heritage Program. *Washington University Global Studies Law Review,* Vol. 10, Issue 3: 593-615.

Kiene, T. 2011. *The Legal Protection of Traditional Knowledge in the Pharmaceutical Field: An Intercultural Problem on the International Agenda*. Münster: Waxmann Verlag GmbH.

Kigongo, R. and Reid, A. 2007. Local communities, politics and the management of the Kasubi Tombs, Uganda. *World Archaeology,* Vol. 39, No. 3: 371-384.

Killick, D. 2009. Cairo-Cape: The spread of metallurgy through eastern and southern Africa. *Journal of World Prehistory,* Vol. 22, No. 4: 399-414.

King, L. 1948. A theory of bornhadits. The *Geographical Journal.* Vol. 112, No. 1/3: 83-87.

King, P. S. 1959. *Missions in Southern Rhodesia*. Cape Town: Citadel Press.

Kinsey, B. H. 1983. Forever gained: Resettlement and land policy in the context of national development in Zimbabwe. In J. D. Y. Peel and T.O. Ranger (eds), *Past and Present in Zimbabwe.* 92-113: Manchester: Manchester University Press.

Klein, R. G. 1983. The Stone Age prehistory of southern Africa. *Ann. Rev. Anthropol.* 12: 25-48.

Klein, R. G. 1984. The prehistory of Stone Age herders in South Africa. In J. D. Clark and S. A. Brandt (eds), *From Hunters to Farmers: The Causes and Consequences of Food Production in Africa*. 281-290. Berkely: University of California Press.

Kramer, E. 1998. A clash of economies: Early centralisation efforts in colonial Zimbabwe, 1929-1935. *Zambezia* XXV (i): 83-98.

Kreps, C. 2012. Intangible threads: Curating the living heritage of Dayak Ikat weaving. In M. L. Stefano, P. Davis and G. Corsane (eds), *Safeguarding Intangible Cultural Heritage*. 177-194. UK: Boydell Press.

Laher, R. 2014. The past is never just in the past: indigenous peoples and framework for confrontation and redress. In R. Laher and K. Sing'Oei (eds), Indigenous People in Africa: *Contestations, Empowerment and Group Rights.* 149-165. Pretoria: Africa Institute of South Africa.

Lane, P. 2014. Being "Indigenous" and beig "Colonised" in Africa: Contrasting experiences and their implications for a postcolonial archaeology. In N. Ferris, R. Harrison and M.V. Wilcox (eds), *Rethinking Colonial Pasts Through Archaeology.* 423-444. Oxford: Oxford University Press.

Layton, R. and Ucko, P. J. 1999. Introduction: Gazing on the landscape and encouraging the environment. In P. J. Ucko and R. Layton (eds), *Archaeology and Anthropology of Landscape: Shaping Your Landscape.* 1-30. London: Routledge.

Lee, R. B. and Hitchcock, R. K. 2001. African hunter-gatherers: Survival, history and the politics of identity. *African Study Monographs, Suppl.* 26: 257-280.

Lightfoot, C. J. (n.d). *The history and natural resources of the Matopo Hills.* Bulawayo: National Parks and Wildlife Management.

Lightfoot, C. J. 1980a. The ecology of the Matopo Hills under existing and potential systems of land use. Bulawayo: Natural History Museum.

Lightfoot, C. J. 1980b. The National Park in terms of Rhodes' Will and Estates. Bulawayo: Natural History Museum.

Lindgren, B. 2002. Power, education and identity in post-colonial Zimbabwe: The fate of King Lobengula of Matabeleland. *African Sociological Review* 6(1): 46-67.

Lloyd, M. (ed). 1979. *Journey to Gubulawayo. Letters of Frs. H. Depelchin and C. Croonenberghs,* S. J. 1879, 1880, 1881. Bulawayo: Books of Rhodesia.

Logan, B. I and Moseley, W. G. 2002. The political ecology of poverty alleviation in Zimbabwe's Communal Areas Management Programme for Indigenous Resources (CAMPFIRE). *Geoforum* 33: 1-14.

Logan, W. 2014. Heritage rights-avoidance and reinforcement. *Heritage and Soceity,* Vol. 7,No. 2: 156-167.

Lombard, M. 2013. Hunter-gatherers in southern Africa before 20, 000 years ago. In P. Mitchell and L. Paul (eds), *The Oxford Handbook of African Archaeology.* 367-386. Oxford: Oxford University Press.

Love, D., Uhlenbrook, S., Nyabeze, W., Owen, R. J. S., Twomlow, S., Savenije, H., Woltering, L. and van der Zaag, P. 2005. Analysis of hydrological change for IWRM planning: Case study of the Mzingwane River, Limpopo Basin, Zimbabwe. 6th Waternet-WARFSA Symposium. Ezulwini: Swaziland.

Lowry, D. 2004. The granite of the ancient north: Race, nation and empire at Cecil Rhodes' mountain mausoleum and Rhodes House, Oxford. In R. Wrigley and M. Craske (eds), Pantheons: *Transformations of a Monumental Idea.* 193-220. England: Ashgate Publishing Limited.

Lynch, G. 2011. Becoming indigenous in the pursuit of justice: The African commission on human and people's rights and the Endorois. *African Affairs,* Vol. 111, Issue 442: 24-45.

Machiridza, L. 2008. Developing the Rozvi archaeological identity in south western Zimbabwe. *Journal of the Prehistory Society of Zimbabwe*, No. 28: 21-31.

Mahachi, G. and Kamuhangire. E. 2008. Administrative arrangements for heritage resources management in sub-Saharan Africa. In W. Ndoro, A. Mumma and G. Abungu (eds), *Cultural Heritage and Law: Protecting Immovable Heritage in English-Speaking Countries of Sub-Saharan Africa* (ICCROM Conservation Studies 8). 45-51. Rome: ICCROM.

Mahachi, G. and Ndoro, W. 1997. The Socio-political context of southern African Iron Age studies with special reference to Great Zimbabwe, In G. Pwiti (ed.), *Caves, Monuments and Texts: Zimbabwean Archaeology Today* (Studies in African Archaeology 14). 89-104. Uppsala University: Department of Archaeology and Ancient History.

Makahamadze, T., Grand, N. and, N. and Tavuyanago, B. 2009. The role of traditional leaders in fostering democracy, justice and human rights in Zimbabwe. *The African Anthropologist,* Vol. 16, Nos. 1-2: 33-47.

Makumbe, J. 2010. Local authorities and traditional leadership. In J. de Visser, N. Steytler and N. Machingauta (eds), *Local Government Reform in Zimbabwe: A Policy Dialogue*, 87-99. University of the Western Cape: Community Law Centre.

Makuvaza, S. 2007. The colonial legacy in Zimbabwe: community involvement in heritage management and preservation, and some social and economic implications. *Journal of the Prehistory Society of Zimbabwe* 27: 59-68.

Makuvaza, S. 2008. Why Njelele, a rainmaking shrine in the Matobo world heritage area, Zimbabwe, has not been proclaimed a national monument. *Heritage Management,* Vol. 1, Issue 2: 163-180.

Makuvaza, S. 2010. Managing the Victoria Falls World Heritage Site: Problems, Stakeholders Views and Possible Solutions. Msc. dissertation, School of Biology and Environmental Science. Ireland: University College Dublin.

Makuvaza, S. 2012. Who owns the Special Area at Victoria Falls World Heritage Site? Political, organizational and governmental interests. *The Historic Environment,* Vol. 3, No. 1: 42-63.

Makuvaza, S. 2014. From colonialism to independence: the management of cultural heritage in Zimbabwe. In Smith, C. (ed.) *Encyclopedia of Global Archaeology.* 7965-7973. New York: Springer.

Makuvaza, S. and Burrett, R. 2011. Old Bulawayo (KoBulawayo)-the failure of heritage renewed: Public and state discourses. *Conservation and Management of Archaeological Sites,* Vol. 13, Nos. 2-3: 189-211.

Makuvaza, S. and Hubbard, P. 2012. Obtituary: Edward Sibindi. *Jour*nal of the Prehistory Society of Zimbabwe 30: 2-7.

Makuvaza, S. and Makuvaza, V. 2012. Empty promises and false hopes: The case of the Matobo Hills cultural world heritage landscape, south western Zimbabwe. *Heritage and Society,* Vol. 5, No. 1: 9-34.

Makuvaza, S. and Makuvaza, V. 2013. The challenges of managing an archaeological site in a declining economy: The case of Khami World Heritage Site in Zimbabwe. *Conservation and Management of Archaeological Sites,* Vol. 15, No. 3-4, 281-97.

Mangiza, M. N. D. 1986. Local government and planning in Zimbabwe: An examination of recent changes, with special reference to the provincial regional level. *Third World Planning Review* 8(2): 153-175.

Manhokwe, L. 2010. Top Down or Bottom Up? District Development Planning in Mudzi District, Zimbabwe. Masters of Arts in Development Studies Thesis. The Hague: International Institute of Social Studies.

Manyanga, M. 2007. *Resilient Landscapes: Socio-Environmental Dynamics in the Shashi-Limpopo Basin, Southern Zimbabwe C. AD 800 to the present* (Studies in African Archaeology 11). Uppsala: Department of Archaeology.

Mapara, J. 2009. Indigenous knowledge systems in Zimbabwe: Juxtaposing postcolonial theory. *Journal of Pan African Studies,* Vol. 3, No. 1: 139-155.

Mararike, C. G. 2001. A*frica's Heritage: Our Rallying Point: The Case of Zimbabwe's Land Issue.* Harare: Best Practices Books.

Marobela, M. N. 2010. The state, mining and the community: The case of Basarwa of the Central Kalahari Game Reserve in Botswana. *Labour, Capital and Soceity,* Vol. 43, No. 1: 137-154.

Marshall, Y. 2002. What is community archaeology? *World Archaeology*, 34(2): 211-219.

Masaka, D. and Chemhuru, M. 2011. Moral dimensions of some Shona taboos (zviera). *Journal of Sustainable Development in Africa,* Vol. 13, No. 3: 132-148.

Matenga, E. 2011. *The Soapstone Birds of Great Zimbabwe: Archaeological Heritage, Religion and Politics in Post Colonial Zimbabwe and the Return of Cultural Property* (Studies in Global Archaeology 16). Uppsala: Department of Archaeology and Ancient History, Uppsala University.

Matsa, M. and Masimbiti, T. 2014. The Community Share Ownership Trust initiative as a rural development solution in Zimbabwe: The Tongongara experience in Shurugwi district. *International Journal of Humanities and Social Science*, Vol. 4, No. 8(1): 151-163.

Maxwell, D. 1999. *Christians and Chiefs in Zimbabwe: A Social History of the Hwesa People c.1870s-1990s.* Edinburgh: Edinburgh University Press.

Maylam, P. 2005. *The Cult of Rhodes. Remembering an Imperialist in Africa*. Cape Town. David Philip Publishers.

McCartney, M., Butterworth, J., Moriarty, P. and Owen, R. 1998. Comparison of the hydrology of two contrasting headwater catchments in Zimbabwe. In K. Kovar, U. Tappeiner, N. E. Peters and R. G. Graig (eds), *Hydrology, Water Resources and Ecology in Headwaters* (Proceedings of the Headwater '98 Conference held at Meran/Merano, Italy). 515-522. IAHS Publi. No. 248.

McCaskill, D and Rutherford, J. 2005. Indigenous peoples of South-East Asia: Poverty, identity and resistance. In R. Eversole, J. McNeish and A. Cimadamore (eds), *Indigenous Peoples and Poverty: International Perspectives.* 126-157. London: Zed Books.

McGhee, R. 2008. Aboriginalism and the problems of indigenous archaeology. *American Antiquity* 7(4): 579-597.

McGregor, J. 2003. The Victoria Falls 1900-1940: Landscape tourism and the geographical imagination. *Journal of Southern African Studies* 29 (3): 717-737.

McNeish, J. A. and Eversole, R. 2005. Introduction: Indigenous peoples and poverty. In R. Eversole, J. A. McNeish and A. D. Cinamadore (eds), *Indigenous Peoples and Poverty: An International Perspective.* 1-26. London: Zed Books.

McNiven, I. J. and Russel, L. 2005. Appropriated Pasts: *Indigenous Peoples and the Colonial Culture of Archaeology.* California: AltaMira Press.

Meskell, L. 2010. Human rights and heritage ethics. *Anthropological Quarterly,* Vol, 83, No. 4: 839-860.

Meskell, L. 2012. T*he Nature of Heritage: The New South Africa.* Oxford: Blackwell Publishing Ltd.

Mitchell, N. J. 2008. Considering authenticity of cultural landscapes. *Journal of Preservation Technology* 39, 2-3: 25-31.

Mitchell, P. 1997. Book review: Late Pleistocene and Holocene Hunter-Gatherers of the Matopos: An Archaeological Study of Change and Continuity in Zimbabwe. *The African Archaeological Review,* Vol. 14, No. 4: 257-262.

Mitchell, P. 2002. *The Archaeology of Southern Africa.* Cambridge: Cambridge University Press.

Mitchell, P. 2013. Southern African hunter-gatherers of the last 25,000 years. In P. Mitchell and P. Lane (eds) *The Oxford Handbook of African Archaeology.* 473-488. Oxford: Oxford University Press.

Miura, K. 2005. Conservation of "living heritage site" a contradiction in terms? A case study of Angkor World Heritage Site. *Conservation and Management of Archaeological Sites,* Vol. 7: 3-8.

Moser S., Glazier, D., Phillips, J. E., el Nemr, L. N., Mousa, M. S., Aiesh, R. N., Richardson, S., Conner, A. and Seymour, M. 2002. Transforming archaeology through practice: Strategies for collaborative archaeology and the community archaeology project at Quseir, Egypt. *World Archaeology,* Vol. 34, No. 2: 220-248.

Mouiche, I. 2011. Democratisation and political participation of Mbororo in western Cameroon. *Africa Spectrum,* 46 (2): 71-97.

Moyo, S. 2013. Land reform and redistribution in Zimbabwe since 1980. In Moyo, S. and Chambati, W. (eds) *Land and Agrarian Reform in Zimbabwe. Beyond White-Settler Capitalism.* 29-78. Dakar: Senegal.

Moyo, S., O'Keefe, P. and Sill, M. 1993. *The Southern African Environment.* London: Earthscan Publications Ltd.

Msindo, E. 2010. Social and political responses to colonialism on the margins: Community, chieftaincy and ethnicity in Bulilima-Mangwe, Zimbabwe, 1890-1930. In P. Limb, N. A. Etherington and P. Midgley (eds), *Grappling With the Beast: Indigenous Southern African Responses to Colonialism,* 1840-1930. 115-156. Leiden: Koninklijke, Brill NV.

Msindo, E. 2012. Ethnicity in Zimbabwe: *Transformations in Kalanga and Ndebele Societies,* 1860-1990. New York: University of Rochester Press.

Mudege, N. N. 2008. Ethnography of Knowledge: *The Production of Knowledge in Mupfurudzi Resettlement Scheme*, Zimbabwe. Leiden: Koninklijke NV.

Mukamuri, B. B., Campbell, B. M. and Kowero, G. 2008. Local organisations and natural resource management in the face of economic hardships: A case study from Zimbabwe. In G. Kowero, B. M. Campbell and U. R. Sumaila (eds), *Policies and Governance Structures in Woodlands of Southern Africa.* 28-44. Jakarta: Center for International Forestry Research.

Mumma, A. 2003. Legal aspects of cultural landscape protection in Africa. *Cultural Landscapes: The Challenges of Conservation* (World Heritage Papers 7). 156-157. Paris: UNESCO World Heritage Centre.

Mumma, A. 2004. Community-based legal systems and the management of World Heritage Sites. In E. de Merode, R. Smeets and C. Westrik (eds), *Managing a Sustainable Future for the World Heritage* (World Heritage Papers 13). 43-44. Paris: Unesco World Heritage Center.

Munjeri, D. 2005. Legislation and practices: Implications and the way forward. In W. Ndoro and G. Pwiti (eds), *Legal Frameworks for the Protection of Immovable Cultural Heritage in Africa* (ICCROM Conservation Studies 5). 2-4. Rome: ICCROM.

Munjeri, D., Ndoro, W., Sibanda, C., Saouma-Ferero, G., Levi-Strauss, L. and Mbuyamba, L. (eds). 1995. *African Cultural Heritage and the World Heritage Convention* (First Global Strategy Meeting 11-13 October 1995). Harare: The National Museums and Monuments of Zimbabwe.

Mupira, P. 2013. Losing and repossessing land and ancestral landscapes: Archaeology and land reforms in the eastern highlands of Zimbabwe. In M. Relaki and D. Catapoli (eds) *An Archaeology of Land Ownership (Routledge Studies in Archaeology),* 192-217: New York: Routledge.

Murimbika, M. and Moyo, B. 2008. Archaeology and donor aid in the 'developing world': The case for local heritage in Zimbabwe. In F. P. McManamon, A. Stout and J. A. Barnes (eds), *Managing Archaeological Resources: Global Context, National Programs, Local Actions (One World Archaeology 58*). 87-106. California: Left Coast Press.

Murindagomo, F. 1990. CAMPFIRE Program (Dande Communal Lands)-Zimbabwe. In A. Kiss (ed.), *Living With Wildlife: Wildlife Resource Management with Local Participation in Africa* (World Bank Technical Paper Number 130). 123-139. Washington D.C: World Bank.

Muringaniza, J. S. 2002. Heritage that hurts: The case of the grave of Cecil John Rhodes in the Matopos National Park, Zimbabwe. In C. Ffodge, J. Hubert and P. Turnbull (eds), *The Dead and their Possessions: The Repatriation in Principle, Policy and Practice* (One World Archaeology 43). 317-328. London: Routledge.

Murray, C. A. 1946. Report on Survey of the Matopo National Park. Bulawayo: Natural History Museum.

Murray, P. 2013. *Zimbabwe* (2nd Edn). Guilford, USA: The Globe Pequot Press.

Musonda, S. 2005. Customary systems of heritage conservation: The Barotseland experience, Zambia. In W. Ndoro and G. Pwiti (eds), *Legal Frameworks for the Restoration of Immovable Cultural Heritage in Africa* (ICCROM Conservation Studies 5). 2-4. Rome: ICCROM.

Naeem, A. 2013. The conflict of ideologies and ambiguities in conservation policy: A legacy of shared built heritage in Pakistan. In K. D. Silva and N. Chapagain (eds), *Asian Heritage Management: Contexts, Concerns and Prospects.* 87-104. Oxford/New York: Routledge.

National Parks and Wildlife Management. 2000. *Rhodes Matopo National Park Management Plan.* Harare: Ministry of Environment and Tourism.

Ndagala, D. K. and Zengu, N. 1989. From the raw to the cooked. Hadzabe perceptions of their past. In R. Layton (ed.), *Who needs the Past? Indigenous Values and Archaeology* (One World Archaeology 5). 51-46. London: Routledge.

Ndahinda, F. M. 2011. Indigenousness in Africa: *A Contested Legal Framework for Empowerment of "Marginalised" Communities.* The Hague: T. M. C. Asser Press.

Ndlovu, N. 2005. Incorporating Indigenous Management in Rock Art Sites. Thesis submitted in fulfilment of the requirements for the Degree of Master of Arts. South Africa: Rhodes University.

Ndlovu-Gatsheni, S. J. 2009a. *The Ndebele Nation: Reflections on Hegemony, Memory and Historiography.* Amsterdam: Rozenburg Publishers.

Ndlovu-Gatsheni, S. J. 2009b. Mapping cultural and colonial encounters, 1880s-1930s. In B. Raftopoulos and A. Mlambo (eds), B*ecoming Zimbabwe: A History from the Pre-colonial Period to 2008.* 39-74. Harare: Weaver Press.

Ndoro, W. 2004. Traditional and customary heritage systems: Nostalgia or reality? The implications of managing heritage sites in Africa. In E. de Merode, R. Smeets and C. Westrik (eds), *Linking Universal and Local Values: Managing a Sustainable Future for World Heritage* (World Heritage Papers 13). 81-84. Paris: UNESCO World Heritage Centre.

Ndoro, W. 2005. *The Preservation of Great Zimbabwe: Your Monument Our Shrine* (ICCROM Conservation Studies 4). Rome: ICCROM.

Ndoro, W., Mumma, A. and Abungu, G. (eds). 2008. *Cultural Heritage and the Law: Protecting Immovable Heritage in English-Speaking Countries of Sub-Saharan Africa* (ICCROM Conservation Studies 8). Rome: ICCROM.

Ndzimu-unami, E. 2012. *The Rebirth of Bukalanga: A Manifesto for the Liberation of a Great People with a Proud History Part 1*. Plumtree: Mapungubwe Newscorporation.

Newitt, M. 1995. *A History of Mozambique.* London: Hurst and Company.

Ngara, T., Zhakata, W., Mugova, V., Makunike, B. and Musingarabwi, S. 1998. The Atmosphere. In M. Chenje, L. Sola and D. Paleczny (eds), *The State of Zimbabwe's Environment.* 101-137. Harare: Ministry of Mines, Environment and Tourism.

Nicholas, G. 2008. Native peoples and archaeology (indigenous archaeology). In D. Pearsall (ed.), *The Encyclopedia of Archaeology,* Vol. 3. 1660-1669. Oxford: Elsevier.

Niezen, R. 2003. *The Origins of Indigenism. Human Rights and the Politics of Identity.* California: University of California Press.

Night, P. 2003. *Conspiracy Theories in American History.* California: ABC-CLIO.

Nkomazana, F. 2006. Rural churches in Botswana: A case study of Jakalasi 2 village. Scriptura 93: 352-369.

Nobbs, E. 1920. Proposal report to establish a National Park in Matopos. Bulawayo: Natural History Museum.

Nobbs, E. A. 1924. *Guide to the Matopos*. Cape Town: T. Maskew Miller.

Northolt, S. A. 2008. *Fields of Fire: An Atlas of Ethnic Conflicts.* London: Stuart Nothold Communications Ltd.

Nthoi, L. S. 2006. *Contesting Sacred Space: A Pilgrimage Study of the Mwali Cult of Southern Africa.* Trenton, NJ: Africa World Press.

Nyamapfene, K. W. 1989. Adaptation to marginal land amongst peasant farmers of Zimbabwe. *Journal of Southern African Studies.* Vol. 15, No. 2: 384-389.

Nyathi, P. and Ndiweni, B. 2005. A living religious shrine under siege: The Njelele shrine/King Mzilikazi's grave and conflicting demands on the Matopo Hills area of Zimbabwe. In H. Stovel, N. Stanely-Price and R. Killick (eds), *Conservation of Living Religious Heritage* (ICCROM Conservation Studies 3). 58-66. Rome: ICCROM.

Oduro, T. 2006. Theological education and training: Challenges of African Instituted Church in Ghana. *Journal of African Instituted Church Theology*, Vol. 2, No. 1:1-15.

Ohmagari, K. and Berkes, F. 1997. Transmission of indigenous knowledge and bush skills among the Western James Bay Cree women of subarctic Canada. *Human Ecology* 25: 197-222.

Oliver, R. and Atmore, A. 2005. *Africa Since 1800* (5th Ed). Cambridge: Cambridge University Press.

Omer-Cooper, J. D. 1966. *The Zulu Aftermath: A Nineteenth-Century Revolution in Bantu Africa.* London: Longman.

Palgrave, K. C. 1977. *Trees of Southern Africa.* Cape Town: Struik Publishers.

Palmer, E. 1977. *A Field Guide to the Trees of Southern Africa* (2nd edn.). Johannesburg: William Collins Sons and Co. Ltd.

Palmer, E. and Pitman, N. 1972. *Trees of Southern Africa,* Vol. 3. Cape Town: Struik Publishers.

Pelican, M. 2008. *Mbororo claims to regional citizenship and minority status in north-west Cameroon.* Africa. Volume 78, Issue 4: 540-560.

Pelican, M. and Maruyana, J. 2015. The indigenous rights movement in Africa: Perspectives from Botswana and Cameroon. *African Study Monographs,* 36 (1): 49-74.

Phillipson, D. W. 1985. *African Archaeology.* Cambridge: Cambridge University Press.

Phillipson, D. W. 2005. *African Archaeology* (3rd edn). Cambridge: Cambridge University Press.

Pikirayi, I. 1993. *The Archaeological Identity of the Mutapa State: Towards an Historical Archaeology of Northern Zimbabwe* (Studies in African Archaeology 6). Uppsala: Societas Archaeologica Upsaliensis.

Pikirayi, I. 1997. The pottery of the historical Mutapa state. *Zimbabwea* 5. 30-47.

Pikirayi, I. 2001. *The Zimbabwe Culture: Origins and Decline of Southern Zambezia States.* California: AltaMira Press.

Pikirayi, I. 2006. The demise of Great Zimbabwe, AD 1420-1550: an environmental re-appraisal. In A. Green and R. Leech (eds), *Cities in the World, 1500-2000.* 31-47. Leeds: Maney Publishing.

Pikirayi, I. 2011. *Tradition, Archaeological Heritage Protection and Communities in the Limpopo Province of South Africa*. Addis Ababa: OSSREA.

Pikirayi, I. 2014. Theoretical directions in Zimbabwean archaeology. Paper presented at the 1st Annual Conference of Zimbabwe Association of Professional Archaeologists and Related Disciplines (ZAPARD), 12-14 December. Masvingo: Great Zimbabwe Conservation Center.

Pwiti, G and Ndoro, W. 1999. The legacy of colonialism: Perceptions of the cultural heritage in southern Africa, with special reference to Zimbabwe. *African Archaeological Review,* Vol. 16, No. 3: 143-153.

Pwiti, G. 1991. Trade and economies in southern Africa: The archaeological evidence. *Zimbabwea*, No. 3: 51-56.

Pwiti, G. 1996. C*ontinuity and Change: An Archaeological Study of Early Farming Communities in Northern Zimbabwe* (Studies in African Archaeology 13). Uppsala: Department of Archaeology.

Pwiti, G. 1997. Taking African cultural heritage management into the twenty-first century: Zimbabwe's master plan for cultural heritage management. *African Archaeological Review* 14: 81-3.

Pwiti, G. and Mvenge, G. 1996. Archaeologists, Tourists and Rainmakers: Problems in the Management of Rock Art sites in Zimbabwe. A case study of Domboshava National Monument. In G. Pwiti and R. Soper (eds), *Aspects of African Archaeology.* 817-24. Harare: University of Zimbabwe Publications.

Pwiti, G. and Ndoro, W. 2014. *The Archaeological Heritage of Africa*. Cambridge: Cambridge University Press.

Ranger, T. 1996. Great spaces washed with sun. The Matopos and Uluru compared. In K. Qarian-Smith, L. Ganner and S. Nuttal (eds), *Text, Theory, Space, Land, Literature and History in South Africa and Australia.* 157-172. London: Routledge.

Ranger, T. 1997. Taking hold of the land: Holy places and pilgrimages in twentieth-century Zimbabwe. *Past and Present,* No. 117: 158-194.

Ranger, T. 1999. *Voices from the Rocks: Nature Culture and History in the Matopos Hills of Zimbabwe.* Harare: Baobab.

Ranger, T. 2001. Priestesses and environment in Zimbabwe. In A. Low and S. Tremayne (eds), *Women as Sacred Custodians of the Earth? Women, Spirituality and the Environment.* 95-106. New York: Begergham Books.

Ranger, T. 2004. Nationalist historiography, patriotic history and the history of the nation: The struggle over the past in Zimbabwe. *Journal of Southern African Studies* 30. Number 2: 215-234.

Ranger, T. 2012. *Malindadzimu* (with contributions by Hubbard, P., Burret, R. and Chennels, A.). Bulawayo: Khami Press.

Ransford, O. 1968. *Bulawayo: Historical Battleground of Rhodesia.* Cape Town: Howard Timmins.

Rasmussen, K. R. 1978. *Migrant Kingdom: Mzilikazi's Ndebele in South Africa*. London: Rex Collings.

Reynolds, D. A. 1983. *An Introduction to Law.* Harare: The Government Printer.

Robinson, K. R. 1959. *Khami Ruins.* Cambridge: Cambridge University Press.

Robinson, K. R. 1961. *Archaeological report in Rhodesian Schoolboys' Exploration Society Expedition to Buffalo Bend.* Salisbury.

Robinson, K. R. 1966. Bambata ware: Its position in the Rhodesian Iron Age in the light of recent evidence. *The South African Archaeological Bulletin,* Vol. 21, No. 82: 81-85.

Robinson, K. R. and Cooke, C. K. 1950. Some unusual elements in the Wilton industry in the Matopos area of Southern Rhodesia. *The South African Archaeological Bulletin,* Vol. 5, No. 19: 108-114.

Rössler, M. 2003. Linking nature and culture: World heritage cultural landscapes. *Cultural Landscapes: The Challenges of Conservation.* 10-15. Paris: UNESCO.

Ruwitah, A. 1997 Lost tribe, lost language? The invention of the false Remba identity, *Zimbabwea*, No. 5: 53-71.

Sadr, K. 2005. Hunter-gatherers and herders of the Kalahari during the late Holecene. In P. Veth, M. Smith and P. Hiscock (eds), *Desert Peoples: Archaeological Perspectives.* 206-221. Malden, MA: Blackwell Publishing.

Saugestad, S. 2004. The indigenous peoples of southern Africa: An overview. In R. K. Hitchcock and D. Vinding (eds), *Indigenous Peoples' Rights in Southern Africa*. 22-43. Copenhagen: International Work Group for Indigenous Affairs.

Sawyer, S. and Gomez, T. 2012. Indigenous identity and a language of rights. In S. Sawyer and T. Gomez (eds), *The Politics of Resource Extraction: Indigenous Peoples, Multinational Corporations and the State.* 9-32. England: Palgrave MaCMillan.

Scarnecchia, T. 2011. Rationalizing "Gukurahundi": cold war and South African foreign relations with Zimbabwe, 1981-1983. Kronos No. 37, *Rethinking Cold War History in Southern Africa*: 87-103.

Schrire, C. 1980. An inquiry into the evolutionary status and apparent identity of San hunter-gatherers. *Human Ecology,* Vol. 8, No. 1: 9-32.

Segobye, A. K. 2005. Weaving fragments of the past for a united Africa: Reflections on the place of African archaeology in the development of the continent in the 21st century. South African *Archaeological Bulletin* 60 (182): 79-83.

Segobye, A. K. 2006. Divided commons: The political economy of southern Africa's cultural heritage landscapes-observations of the central Kalahari Game Reserve, Botswana. *Journal of the World Archaeological Congress*, Vol. 2, No. 1: 52-72.

Shephered, N. 2006. Local practice, global discipline. *Journal of the World Archaeological Congress,* Vol. 2, No. 1: 1-2.

Shutt, A. K. and King, T. 2005. Imperial Rhodesians: The 1953 Rhodes centenary exhibition in Southern Africa. *Journal of Southern African Studies,* 3(2): 357-379.

Silverman, H. 2011. Border wars: The ongoing temple dispute between Thailand and Cambodia and UNESCO's World Heritage List. *International Journal of Heritage Studies,* 17 (1): 1-21.

Silverman, H. and Ruggles, D. F. 2007. Cultural heritage and human rights. In H. Silverman and D. F. Ruggles (eds), *Cultural Heritage and Human Rights.* 3-20. New York: Springer.

Simons, H. A. B. 1968. A Late Stone Age occupation in the Hillside area of Bulawayo. *The South African Archaeological Bulletin,* Vol. 23, No. 90: 45-49.

Sinclair, P. J. J., Thurstan, S. and Bassey, A. 1983. Introduction. In S. Thurstan, P. Sinclair, A. Bassey and A. Okpoko (eds), *The Archaeology of Africa: Food Metals and Towns* (One World Archaeology 20). 1-42. London: Routledge.

Singleton, T. A. and Orser, C. E. (Jr). 2003. Descent communities: Linking people in the present to the past. In L. J. Zimmerman, K. D. Vitteli and J. Hollowell-Zimmer (eds), *Ethical Issues in Archaeology.* 143-152. California: AltaMira Press.

Smith, L. T. 1999. *Decolonizing Methodologies: Research and Indigenous Peoples*. London: ZedBooks Ltd.

Smith, R. M. 1977. Movement patterns and feeding behaviour of leopard in the Rhodes Matopos National Park, Rhodesia. *Arnoldia* 8(13): 1-16.

Sørensen, M. L. S. and Carman, J. (eds). 2009. *Heritage Studies: Methods and Approaches.* London: Routledge.

Special Committee. 1949. *Report of a survey of the carrying capacity of the Matopo National Park.* Bulawayo: Natural History Museum.

Stead, W. T. (ed). 1902. *The Last Will and Testament of Cecil John Rhodes with Elucidating Notes to which are Added Some Chapters Describing the Political and Religious Ideas of the Testator.* London: Norfolk Street, W.C.

Stocker, M. 1979. The Rudd Concession: A reappraisal of an intricate controversy. *Zimbabwean History* X: 219-220.

Stovel, H. 2005. Introduction. In H. Stovel, N. Stanely-Price and R. Killick (eds), *Conservation of Living Religious Heritage* (Papers from the ICCROM 2003 Forum on Living Religious Heritage: Conserving the Sacred) (ICCROM Conservation Studies 3). 1-11. Rome: ICCROM.

Sullivan, S. 2004. Local involvement and traditional practices in the world heritage system. In E. de Merode, R. Smeets and C. Westrik (eds), *Linking Universal and Local Values: Managing a Sustainable Future for World Heritage* (World Heritage Papers 13). 49-55. Paris: UNESCO World Heritage Centre.

Summers, R and Cooke, C. K. 1959. *An Archaeological Survey of Southern Rhodesia: Supplement to the Annual Report of the Commission for the Preservation of Natural and Historical Monuments and Relics. Bulawayo:* The Commission for the Preservation of Natural and Historical Monuments and Relics.

Summers, R. 1955. *Notes on a Tentative Correlation of Southern African Stone Age cultures.* London: Annual Report of the Institute of Archaeology.

Sylvain, R. 2002. Land, water, and truth: San identity and global indigenism. *American Anthropologist,* 104(4): 1,074–85.

Taylor, J. J. 2007. Celebrating San victory too soon? Reflections on the outcome of the Central Kalahari Game Reserve case. *Anthropology Today*, Vol 23, No. 5: 3-5.

Technical Committee. 2004. Management Plan for the Proposed Matobo Hills World Heritage Area. Harare: The National Museums and Monuments of Zimbabwe.

Thebe, P. C. 2006. Intangible heritage management, does the World Heritage listing help? In N. Agnew and J. Bridgland (eds), *Of the Past, for the Future: Integrating Archaeology and Conservation:* 312–321. Los Angeles: Getty Conservation Institute.

Timberlake, J., Fagg, C. and Barnes, R. 1999. *Field Guide to the Acacias of Zimbabwe*. Harare: CBC Publishing.

Tredgold, R. (ed). 1956. The Matopos: *A Revised edition of A Guide to the Matopos* (E.A Nobbs 1924). Lusaka: The Federal Department of Printing and Stationery.

Twidale, C. R. 1981. Granitic inselbergs: Domed, block-strewn and castellated. *The Geographical Journal,* Vol. 147, No 1: 54-71.

Twidale, C. R. 1982. The evolution of bornhardits: The nature of these dramatic landforms that rise abruptly from flat plains is now beginning to be more fully understood. *American Scientist,* Vol. 70, No. 3: 268-276.

Twidale, C. R. 1986. Granite platforms and low domes: Newly exposed compartments or degraded remnants? *Geografiska Annaler. Series A, Physical Geography*, Vol. 68, No. 4: 399-411.

Tyson, P. D. and Lindsay, J. A. 1992. The climate of the last 2000 years in Southern Africa. *Holecene* 2(3): 271-278.

Tyson, P. D., Karlen, W. Holmgren, K. and Heiss, G. A. 2000. The Little Ice Age and medieval warming in South Africa. *South African Journal of Science* 96: 121-126.

UNESCO. 2003. *Convention for the Safeguarding of Intangible Cultural Heritage.* Paris: UNESCO World Heritage Centre.

UNESCO. 2008. *Operational Guidelines for the Implementation of the World Heritage Convention:* Paris: UNESCO World Heritage Centre.

United Nations. 2009. S*tate of the World's Indigenous Peoples: Economic and Social Affairs.* New York: United Nations Publications.

Urbina, S. 2002. *Legal Method and the Rule of Law.* The Hague: Kluwer Law International.

Vansina, J. 1995. New linguistic evidence and the Bantu expansion. *Journal of African History* 36 (2): 173-195.

van Doornum, B. 2008. Sheltered from change: hunter-gatherer occupation of Balerno Main Shelter, Shashe-Limpopo confluence area, South Africa. *Southern African Humanities,* Vol. 20: 249-284.

Vincent, V. and Thomas, R. G. 1961. *An Agricultural Survey of Southern Rhodesia: Part I: Agro-Ecological Survey*. Salisbury: Government Printer.

Vinnicombe, P. 1966. *The early recording and presentation of rock paintings in South Africa. Studies in Speleology* 1 (4): 153-162.

Wachira, G. M. 2012. Rights of indigenous peoples in Africa. In M. Ssenyonjo (ed.), *The African Regional Human Rights System: 30 years After the African Charter on Human and Peoples' Rights.* 195-212. Leiden: Martnus Nijhoff Publishers.

Wadley, L. 1993. Late Pleistocene Later Stone Age south of the Limpopo River. *Journal of the World Prehistory,* Vol. 7, No. 3: 243-296.

Wadley, L. 2015. Those marvellous: the Middle Stone Age of Southern Africa. *Azania*, Vol. 50, No. 2: 155-226.

Walker, N. 1980. Later Stone Age research in the Matopos. *The South African Archaeological Bulletin,* Vol. 35, No. 131: 19-24.

Walker, N. 1983. The significance of an early date for pottery and sheep in Zimbabwe. *The South African Archaeological Bulletin,* Vol. 38, No. 138: 88-92.

Walker, N. 1991. Excavations and re-examination of some Stone Age sites in the Matopos. *Zimbabwe* No. 3: 5-22.

Walker, N. 1995. *Late Pleistocene and Holocene Hunter-Gatherers of the Matopos. An Archaeological Study of Change and Continuity in Zimbabwe.* Uppsala: Soceitas Archaeologica Upsaliensis.

Walker, N. 1996. *The Painted Hills: Rock Art of the Matopos* (A Guidebook). Gweru: Mambo Press.

Walker, N. and Thorp, C. 1997. Stone Age archaeology in Zimbabwe. In G. Pwiti (ed.), *Caves, Monuments and Text: Zimbabwean Archaeology Today* (Studies in African archaeology 14). 9-32. Uppsala: Uppsala University.

Ward, V. 1997. A century of change: Rock art deterioration in the Natal Drakensberg, South Africa. *Natal Museum Journal of Humanities,* Vol. 9: 75-97.

Watkins, J. 2000. *Indigenous Archaeology: American Indian Values and Scientific Practice.* Walnut Creek, California: AltaMira Press.

Weinrich, A. K. H. 1973. *Black and White Elites in Rural Rhodesia.* Manchester: Manchester University Press.

Weitzer, R. 1990. *Transforming Settler States: Community Conflict and Internal Security in Northern Ireland and Zimbabwe.* Berkeley: University of California Press.

Wels, H. 2003. *Private Wildlife Conservation in Zimbabwe: Joint Ventures and Reprocity.* Leiden: Koninklijke Brill NV.

Welz, M. 2013. *Integrating Africa: Decolonization's Legacies, Sovereignty and the African Union.* Oxfordshire: Routledge.

Werbner, R. P. 1989. *Ritual Passage, Sacred Journey: The Form, Process and Organisation of Religious Movement.* Washington: Smithsonian Institution Press.

Willems, J. H. W. 2014. The future of world heritage and the emergency of transnational heritage regimes. *Heritage and Society,* Vol. 7, No. 2: 105-120.

Willems, J. H. W. and Comer, D. 2011. Africa, archaeology and world heritage. *Conservation and Management of Archaeological Sites,* Vol. 13, Nos. 2-1: 160-73.

Woodhouse, H. C. 1969. Rock paintings of southern Africa. *African Arts,* Vol. 2, No. 3: 44-49.

Zubieta, L. F. 2006. *The Rock Art of Mwana waChentcherere II Rock Shelter, Malawi: A Site Specific Study of Girls' Initiation Rock Art.* Leiden: African Studies Center.

Zvobgo, C. J. M. 1996. *A History of Christian Missions in Zimbabwe* 1890-1939. Gweru: Mambo Press.

NEWSPAPERS

The Chronicle, Zimbabwe

1995. Departments to share park proceeds. 11 November. Bulawayo: Zimbabwe.

1995. Fewer locals now visit Matopo Park. 30 October. Bulawayo: Zimbabwe.

1995. High fees at park cause concern. 22 August. Bulawayo: Zimbabwe.

1995. Review park fees. 31 October. Bulawayo: Zimbabwe.

1995. Support for single entry fee to Matopos. 21 October. Bulawayo: Zimbabwe.

1998. Settlers agree to vacate estate. 15 September. Bulawayo: Zimbabwe.

1999. Rock art paintings threatened. 6 September. Bulawayo: Zimbabwe.

THE SUNDAY NEWS, ZIMBABWE

1998. Rhodes-a constant thorn in the side of the locals. 6 September. Bulawayo: Zimbabwe.

1998. Settlers occupy Matopos estate. 18 July. Bulawayo: Zimbabwe.

1998. Call to plough back Rhodes Estate profits. 13 September. Bulawayo: Zimbabwe.

1998. "Warlord" lobbies to remove Rhodes' grave. 13 December. Bulawayo: Zimbabwe.

INTERVIEWS AND DISCUSSIONS

Chief Malaki Masuku, Personal Interview, Mtwakazi, March 7, 2015.

Chief Mathe, Personal Interview, Silobi Townhsip, August 16, 2014.

Dube Livingstone, Group Discussion, Fumugwe Township, April 8, 2014.

Dube Sipho, Personal Interview, Tshapo Business Center, April 7, 2014.

Headman Ncube, Personal Interview, Ntunjambili Township, August 15, 2014.

Headman Zibuyeni Ncube, Personal Interview, Empandeni, August 20, 2014.

Hubbard Paul, Email Interview, January 26, 2014.

Khumalo Muzi, Personal Interview, Kezi, August 15, 2014.

Lunga Tha, Personal Interview, Amagagu International Heritage Center, April 7, 2014.

Mahlangu Timothy, Group Discussion, Fumugwe Township, April 8, 2014.

Malinga Cecilia, Personal Interview, Lucydale Farm, April 8, 2014.

Masuku Witness, Personal Interview, Ebunyonyeni Village, August 15, 2014.

Misheck Dube, Personal Interview, Amagugu International Heritage Center, April 8, 2014.

Moyo Micah, Personal Interview, Dewe Village, June 26, 2014.

Moyo Mukhululi, Personal Interview, Gulati Township, August 15, 2014.

Moyo Themba, Personal Interview, Lushumbe Primary School, June 21, 2014.

Moyo Widy, Group Discussion, Fumugwe Township, 8 April 2014.

Mpofu Cleopas, Personal Interview, Ntunjambili Township, August 15, 2014.

Mundy Peter, Personal Interview, National University of Science and Technology, June 6, 2014.

Mthunzi Zweli, Personal Interview, Dula Village, August 16, 2014.

Ncube Charles, Personal Interview, Natisa Township, April 14, 2014.

Ncube Mark, Personal Interview, Bulawayo, March 13, 2014.

Ncube Tsimba Fili, Personal Interview, Amagugu International Heritage Center, April 7, 2014.

Ndlovu Jeffrey, Personal Inteview, Empandeni Mission, August 20, 2014.

Ndlovu Somandla, Personal Interview, Silozwe Townhsip, June 26, 2014.

Ngwenya Onenia, Group Interview, Fumugwe Township, April 8, 2014.

Nyathi Pathisa, Amagugu International Heritage Center, March 10, 2014.

Pwiti Gilbert, Discussions and Email Interview, University of Zimbabwe, August 6, 2014.

Sibanda Mabuthelela, Personal Interview, Ezinyangeni Village, August 15, 2014.

Sibanda Ndawana, Personal Interview, Ezinyangeni Village, August 15, 2014.

Sibanda Nkululeko, Group Discussion, Fumugwe Township, April 8, 2014.

Sibanda Singobile, Personal Interview, Ntunjambili Township, August 15, 2014.

Stephens Gavin, Personal Interview, Bulawayo, August 8, 2014.

Jabulani Moyo, Group Discussion, Fumugwe Township, April 8, 2014.

Curriculum Vitae

Simon Makuvaza was born on 29 April 1972 at Gutu Mission hospital in Zimbabwe. Makuvaza is currently employed as a Research Fellow at the National University of Science and Technology in Bulawayo, Zimbabwe. He previously worked as a lecturer of archaeology (January-September 2011) at the Catholic University of Malawi in Limbe. From 1997 to 2010, he also had worked as an archaeologist for the National Museums and Monuments of Zimbabwe.

Makuvaza holds an Msc in World Heritage Management (2010) from the University College Dublin in Ireland and a General Masters in Business Adminstration (2006) from the National University of Science and Technology in Bulawayo. Makuvaza further hold a Bachelor of Arts Special Honours Degree in Archaeology and a Bachelor of Arts General Degree that he both attained from the University of Zimbabwe in 2001 and in 1996 respectively.

Makuvaza has published widely in Zimbabwean and international journals on archaeology and heritage management. He is also the editor of The Managament of Cultural World Heritage Sites and Development in Africa: History, Nomination Processes and Representation on the World Heritage List, Springer (2014). His research interests are archaeological heritage management, world heritage management and heritage and local indigenous communities.